The Tyranny of the Ideal

The Tyranny of the Ideal

JUSTICE IN A DIVERSE SOCIETY

Gerald Gaus

PRINCETON UNIVERSITY PRESS

Princeton and Oxford

Copyright © 2016 by Princeton University Press
Published by Princeton University Press, 41 William Street,
Princeton, New Jersey 08540
In the United Kingdom: Princeton University Press, 6 Oxford Street, Woodstock,
Oxfordshire OX20 1TR

press.princeton.edu

Cover image: *The Wanderer above the Sea of Fog*, 1818 (oil on canvas), by Caspar
David Friedrich (1774–1840). Courtesy of Hamburger Kunsthalle, Hamburg,
Germany / Bridgeman Images

First paperback printing, 2019

Paper ISBN 978-0-691-18342-8

Cloth ISBN 978-0-691-15880-8

Library of Congress Control Number: 2016930321

British Library Cataloging-in-Publication Data is available

This book has been composed in Linux Libertine

For my graduate students, with thanks for
all they have taught me

For those who have eaten from the tree
of knowledge, paradise is lost.

—KARL POPPER, *The Open Society and Its Enemies*

Summary of Contents

Contents

Preface

POLITICAL PHILOSOPHY IS AMBIVALENT ABOUT THE USE OF MODELS. FOR almost fifty years one model—the original position—has been a mainstay of political philosophy. From their nearly half-century obsession with the veil of ignorance and maximin, one might think that political philosophers love nothing more than an apparently interminable modeling dispute. The original position, however, is the grand exception: for the most part political philosophers have been wary of formal models.[1] To be sure, some models have become part of the canon—the social contract, the Prisoners' Dilemma, Arrow's theorem—but for the most part, advances in modeling the problems of social and political philosophy have been made by political scientists and, especially, economists. To name just some of the towering figures, Kenneth Arrow, Ken Binmore, James Buchanan, Herbert Gintis, Russell Hardin, John Harsanyi, William Riker, Amartya Sen, and Robert Sugden have done remarkable work formalizing key problems in social and political philosophy. Happily we political philosophers can claim Cristina Bicchieri, Fred D'Agostino, David Gauthier, Jean Hampton, Gregory Kavka, Brian Skyrms, and Peter Vanderschraaf. Some younger political theorists—such as Hélène Landemore, Michael Moehler, Ryan Muldoon, and David Wiens—have developed innovative and insightful formal models, helping us to better understand the relation between disagreement, consensus, and pursuit of ideals in political life. Yet, overwhelmingly, the insights of all these thinkers have been resisted by mainstream contemporary political philosophy.[2]

It is not that political philosophers do not employ models—they simply prefer narrative to more formal models. The use of metaphors, for example, pervades political philosophy, especially in recent writ-

---

[1] As one famous philosopher once remarked to me, "if it has figures in it, it isn't ethics."

[2] See Landemore's helpful reply to critics of "model thinking": "Yes, We Can (Make It Up on Volume)," pp. 197–202.

ings on ideal theory. We find important analyses depicting ideal theorizing in terms of voyages of discovery, tunneling from the present to
the ideal, filling in maps of social worlds, and, crucially, mountain
climbing.[3] Rather than being (as Hobbes claimed) simple abuses of
speech[4] or substitutes for good arguments (which they can indeed be),
when they are useful, metaphors present informal models of problems
in political theorizing. Think of G. A. Cohen's camping trip, which
without a doubt models a certain type of social world for us, and which
political philosophers seem to have little reluctance to discuss.[5] As
Ariel Rubinstein has powerfully argued, we constantly employ narra-
tives that model some important feature of the social world; they abstract from some variables and tell tales of simplified social worlds that
bring out fundamental social and normative considerations, or social
dynamics, that are easily overlooked, and they help make intelligible
what seems unclear or mysterious—or show what seemed so clear is
really deeply problematic.[6] When we construct a more formal model
we are not really doing something fundamentally different than in our
informal ones: we are doing much the same thing in a more rigorous
way, trying to better understand just what assumptions our narrative
model was making, and where our narrative actually leads. We are still
telling tales of possible worlds, but we can better see just how our tales
work—why they work the way they do. In this book I analyze various
formal models of how we might orient our understanding of justice by
aiming at the ideal, how the ideal might orient our attempts to bring
about a more just social world, and how we might understand the
Open Society that forsakes a collective ideal of justice. These models
are developments of familiar narrative models, such as I examine in
chapter I. Although the basic ideas are continuous with familiar narra-
tives, in chapters II–IV of this book I am more explicit in stating the
assumptions of the various models, and where I think those assump-

[3] See Robeyns, "Ideal Theory in Theory and Practice"; Brennan, "Feasibility in Optimizing Ethics"; Schmidtz, "Nonideal Theory."
[4] Hobbes, *Leviathan*, p. 17 (chap. 4, ¶4); Hobbes's entire argument in ¶¶22–34 of
chap. 47, comparing the Roman Church to the realm of fairies, is itself thoroughly
metaphorical.
[5] Cohen, *Why Not Socialism?*
[6] Rubinstein, *Economic Fables*, esp. chap. 1.

tions take us. And, yes, the models will abstract and idealize (§I.3.3), as all theory must; when we formalize our models we are aware of where, and in what way, we have idealized or abstracted.

"Those who are suspicious of formal (and in particular, of mathematical) models of reasoning," observes Amartya Sen in his Nobel Prize Lecture, "are often skeptical of the usefulness of discussing real-world problems in this way."[7] As Sen goes on to point out, however, often our informal analyses of our problems do not fully appreciate their complexities: features of the problem that are almost invisible on an informal treatment can be brought clearly into the foreground when we think in more disciplined terms. This is especially the case with ideal theory, which, we shall see, makes complex claims about how the ideal seeks to orient our quest for justice. Chapters II and III show that once we get clearer about what way ideal theory is a distinctive alternative (say, to Sen's resolutely nonideal approach), we shall uncover some rather surprising features of ideal theorizing, features that in my opinion show it to border on incoherence. Only a society that disagrees about the ideal can effectively seek it, but such a society will never achieve it. This is a strong claim; I will work up to it in small, and I hope, clear and careful steps. And more specifically in relation to Sen, chapter IV will show how his formal work in social choice aggregation reveals a path through some of the most perplexing tangles concerning social morality in a diverse society.

Political philosophers opposed to a formal model often point out that some relevant variable has been omitted, some possible strategy not included. Now by their nature all models are incomplete: they build possible worlds that we understand by reducing complexity. The aim is to gain understanding of our complex world through understanding a simpler one that captures key elements, which are obscured when we consider the problem in all its complexity. Good modeling has two features: it is aware of when and where it has simplified and, having explored the insights of simpler models, moves on to look at how things change when we add a bit more complexity.[8] I shall pro-

---

[7] Sen, "The Possibility of Social Choice," p. 73.

[8] The work of Robert Boyd and Peter J. Richerson is an exemplar of developing simple models, appreciating their insights, and then moving on to more complicated

ceed in small steps, trying to capture more and more complications as the analysis proceeds. So a plea for patience on the part of the reader— the analysis of chapter II commences with a fairly simple model, the inadequacies of which will be the focus of later discussions. Of course, even at the end, the analysis will capture only some things, not everything. The fundamental question for philosophic modeling, as it is for all philosophy, is whether we have gained insight through constructing a clear analysis.

One reason that political philosophers often recoil at more formal approaches is that we (and I do mean "we") are not typically math whizzes. As in my *On Philosophy, Politics, and Economics*, I seek as far as possible to present these formal models (as a game theorist friend of mine puts it) "in words." When words fail me, I employ graphical representations; only in one or two places do I employ (simple) algebraic equations. I have also used extensive examples—both contrived and actual—to clarify the various points; and I have built in some redundancy regarding statements of the core ideas. Any political philosopher should be able to work through the presentation; no doubt some pausing and rereading will help, but I have tried to minimize the need for it. When readers disagree with me, they should know precisely on what point and why. I take this to be an advantage, not a liability.

While my method is considerably more formal than the standard in political philosophy (although informal in the context of other disciplines), my aims are not simply analytic, but normative (at least on my understanding of normative). As Karl Popper stressed in his great, frequently disparaged *The Open Society and Its Enemies*, political philosophy has often been under the spell of a Platonic conviction that there is an ideally just social arrangement, that wise people would eventually concur on it, and that our actual political practice should orient itself by this ideal. We may not be able to achieve it down to the last detail, but it should be an aspiration that guides, and gives meaning to, our political existence. Popper wrote when Marxism, the great twentieth-century ideology of the ideal, was a powerful political pro-

---

models that build on the simpler ones. See the progression of their models in *The Origin and Evolution of Cultures*.

gram, threatening the very existence of the Open Society. I count my-self as immensely fortunate that this particular pursuit of the ideal is no longer a practical political worry. It no longer threatens political tyranny over us. But within the academy, and especially current Anglo-American political philosophy, the allure of the ideal is as pow-erful as ever. The sophisticated work of G. A. Cohen, of David Estlund, and even that of John Rawls (who, we will see, has a much more am-biguous place in ideal theorizing) inspires political philosophy to imagine perfectly just, morally homogeneous, "well-ordered" societies where we all agree on the correct principles, our institutions conform to them, and we all are committed to them. In comparison to this ideal of final justice and moral homogeneity, our actual diverse societies, with diverse religious, moral, and political perspectives, look like life in the chaotic cave. If only we could make some progress on a collec-tive quest to the ultimate end of the homogeneity of the perfectly just well-ordered society.

In this book my criticism of this posture is largely internal: I try to show that under the conditions of human existence, we cannot know what such an ideal would be—unless we disagree about it. Only those in a morally heterogeneous society have a reasonable hope of actually understanding what an ideal society would be like, but in such a soci-ety we will never be collectively devoted to any single ideal. The ideal of the realistic utopia of the well-ordered society tyrannizes over our thinking, preventing us from discovering more just social conditions. And, as Sen rightly observed, we will see that ideal theory forces a morally unattractive choice on us: fix local justice or pursue the ideal.

But, then, what is the moral status of an open, diverse society that is constantly disagreeing about justice? Chapter IV sketches a defense of the moral bases of the Open Society; I try to show how different moral perspectives can converge on a practice of moral responsibility and, importantly, how they can share each other's insights to work toward improvements in the basic moral framework of the Open Soci-ety. I also indicate how societies that disagree about the ideal are mor-ally more secure than those that have traveled significantly toward "well-orderedness." The Open Society is not a chaotic cave; we should refuse to follow the philosopher who promises a path to a final end of moral agreement, the ideally just society. The Open Society is a moral achievement of the first order, allowing highly diverse perspectives to share a public world of moral responsibility, sometimes clashing, but often interacting in ways that make the world better for all, and allows us to better understand our different moral truths. Or so I shall argue.

I have been extremely fortunate in having been able to refine these ideas before a number of diverse audiences. Some material from chapter IV was delivered as the Brian Barry Lecture at the London School of Economics. Other parts of the project were presented at the Copenhagen Conference on the Epistemology of Liberal Democracy, the Workshop in Philosophy, Politics, and Economics at George Mason University, the Kings College (London) Political Economy seminar, the 2011 Dubrovnik Conference organized by the Ohio State University Philosophy Department, the workshop on Fairness and Norms at the University of Tilburg, the University of Rijeka Scientific Colloquium, the Groupe de Recherche Interuniversitaire en Philosophie Politique workshop at McGill University, the Center for Human Values at Princeton University, the University of Pennsylvania PPE workshop, the workshop on public reason at Darmstadt Technical University, the "Whither American Conservatism?" conference held at the University of Texas-Austin Law School, the Workshop on New Directions in Public Reason at the University of Birmingham, and meetings of the Central Division of the American Philosophical Association and the American Political Science Association. My thanks to all the organizers and participants, whose objections and questions really have been critical in helping refine these ideas.

It was a treat and honor to discuss with Professor Sen the relation of these ideas to his own approach at the Rutgers Law School Symposium "The Idea of Justice." Along the way, Christian Coons, Dave Estlund, Javier Guillot, Alan Hamlin, Mike Munger, and Shaun Nichols have offered valuable advice. I am particularly grateful to have had the opportunity to work away on these problems while visiting the Public Choice Research Center at Turku University and the Philosophy Department at the National University of Singapore; again presentations to those groups were most helpful in thinking these issues through. Keith Hankins and I coauthored a paper exploring some parts of this project, which we presented to the University of North Carolina–Chapel Hill PPE workshop and the Workshop on Political Utopias organized by the Bowling Green State University Philosophy Department. Important material in chapter IV is drawn from my work with Shaun Nichols. My thanks to Keith and Shaun for letting me draw on this joint work.

The University of Arizona Philosophy Department is a truly wonderful place to think about a variety of issues in unorthodox ways; I am still astounded by the depth and breadth of our political philosophy group. Early on in this project Tom Christiano, Keith Lehrer, and I read Scott Page's *The Difference*; the reader will be able to discern how important that was for my thinking. Later, Dave Schmidtz and I taught a graduate seminar on ideal theory and diversity; Dave and the graduate students constantly forced me to think of things in different ways, as any diverse group should. One of the wonderful things about great graduate students is that, no matter what the subject, they raise cool points that get you to think about your work in new ways. Consequently, my graduate seminars on Rawls, moral and social evolution, Hobbesian political thought, and norms and conventions, as well as the Social Choice Group, all made important contributions to this book. I am especially grateful to members of the Social Choice Group for reading a version of the manuscript—and finding problems. I hesitate to single out specific graduate students, for fear I will overlook someone who offered important advice. But he who hesitates is lost. My very special thanks, then, to Sameer Bajaj, Jacob Barrett, Piper Bringhurst, Joel Chow, Kelly Gaus, Adam Gjesdal, Keith Hankins, Brian Kogelmann, Attila Mráz, Julian Müller, Jeremy Reid, Greg Robson, Stephen G. Stich, John Thrasher, Kevin Vallier, and Chad Van Schoelandt.

Throughout this project, my longtime friend Fred D'Agostino has, time and time again, given me helpful advice and encouragement. His paper "From the Organization to the Division of Cognitive Labor" in many ways spurred the entire project. The other critical influence was the work of Ryan Muldoon. When I read Ryan's dissertation, "Diversity and the Social Contract" (University of Pennsylvania) I was awestruck at its originality and thoughtfulness. The reader will see that I have some important disagreements with Ryan, and he would object to much of the analysis, but these, I think, pale in comparison to our agreement as to what a political philosophy for a diverse society must accomplish. My deep thanks, then, to Fred and Ryan. I am also very grateful to Rob Tempio of Princeton University Press for his early interest in this somewhat unorthodox project. I have greatly benefitted from the comments and suggestions of Princeton's readers; the final draft is considerably better thanks to their ideas. Lastly, I would like to thank Paul Dragos Aligica, not only for encouraging my work, but for helping me see its relation to that of the Ostroms and institutional analysis. Paul's work, coming from economics and political science, confirmed to me that diverse perspectives really can converge on the benefits of diversity and a defense of the Open Society.

The Tyranny of the Ideal

The Allure of the Ideal

Orienting the Quest for Justice

> A map of the world that does not include Utopia is not
> even worth glancing at.
>
> —OSCAR WILDE

1 ORIENTING TO UTOPIA

1.1 Beyond the Contemporary Debate and Its Categories

THERE ARE NUMEROUS UNDERSTANDINGS OF SO-CALLED IDEAL POLITI-
cal theory—so many that the literature has now reached the stage in
which taxonomies of the ideal/nonideal distinction are being presented. Laura Valentini identifies three different ways in which the
contrast is employed—"(*i*) full compliance *vs.* partial compliance theory; (*ii*) utopian *vs.* realistic theory; (*iii*) end-state *vs.* transitional
theory"[1]—while Alan Hamlin and Zofia Stemplowska identify other
"dimensions": (*i*) full *v.* partial compliance; (*ii*) idealization *v.* abstraction; (*iii*) fact sensitivity *v.* insensitivity; and (*iv*), perfect justice *v.*
local improvements.[2] Although such "conceptual cartography"[3] is
helpful in organizing the now-large literature, it has important limitations. If we become too focused on classifications and distinctions, we
are apt to miss how these different dimensions can be integrated (in
various ways) into an overall, coherent, and compelling articulation of
an ideal political philosophy. To be sure, when an idea is "messy"[4]
because of its many dimensions the resulting debate may be confused;

---

[1] Valentini, "Ideal vs. Non-ideal Theory," p. 654.
[2] Hamlin and Stemplowska, "Theory, Ideal Theory and the Theory of Ideals," pp.
48–49.
[3] Valentini, "Ideal vs. Non-ideal Theory," p. 655.
[4] Ibid.

philosophers are apt to talk past each other. Here drawing sharp distinctions between different questions will be valuable. However, often philosophy is messy because the elements of the mess are intertwined in complex ways in a coherent view of the problem. We will see that almost all these different dimensions will come up in this book, as I explore a compelling, but somewhat complex, view of what a theory of an ideal may be, and when and why it is attractive.

Moreover, if we focus too much on the current debate, its categories and concerns, we are apt to fall into the all-too-common error of supposing that somehow these issues "have all originated in response to the methodological paradigm set by John Rawls."[5] No doubt the current round of literature has been spurred by themes in Rawls's work, but many of these issues have arisen, and been investigated, throughout the history of political thought, both recent and distant. In 1982 Barbara Goodwin and Keith Taylor presented a sophisticated answer to whether "utopian" thought must be realistic,[6] employing possible world analysis, inquiring whether an ideal world must be realistically achievable in one move, or could be reached in several moves as one navigates through intermediate possible worlds (an idea that I shall develop in detail in chapter II).[7] And other scholars have shown that the two millennia of utopian thought was often concerned with articulating *ideals* that provided the goals of progressive thought and practice.[8] Indeed, Karl Kautsky famously praised More's *Utopia* as articulating a socialist ideal, which satisfied important "realization" constraints. "More conceived of the realization of his ideals: he was the father of Utopian Socialism, which was rightly named after his *Utopia*. The latter is Utopian less on account of the inadequacy of its aims than on account of the inadequacy of the means at its disposal for their achievement."[9] I certainly do not wish to deny that the recent debate has stressed some new and important issues and has achieved new

---

[5] Ibid.

[6] Thus "utopian vs. realistic theory" is an overly simple rendering of the complexity within utopian theory; the current literature often wrongly supposes that utopian theories were resolutely antirealistic. See, e.g., Jubb, "Tragedies of Non-ideal Theory," p. 230.

[7] Goodwin and Taylor, *The Politics of Utopia*, pp. 210–14.

[8] Kenyon, "Utopia in Reality."

[9] Kautsky, *Thomas More and His Utopia*, p. 249.

insights, but contemporary philosophers too often see their concerns as new and unique when, in fact, they are echoes, as well as developments, of a long line of political thinking.

We thus need to be cognizant of the current debates, while stepping back and keeping in mind that we are exploring a larger and more enduring theme in political thinking. My aim in this chapter, then, is not to analyze or enter into the current debate, though I too shall engage in a bit of classification and line drawing (I am, after all, a philosopher). I shall identify several different enduring models of utopian-ideal thought, arguing that one stands out as meriting closer investigation. I argue that this is an attractive understanding of utopian-ideal theory, that it makes sense of the theory's appeal, and why those such as Oscar Wilde (in our epigraph) thought ideals are a necessary part of any "map" of political reform. I believe this understanding is broad enough to include a wide range of traditional utopian theory, as well as many current ideal theories. It also makes sense—if I may say so, much better sense—of many of the current facets of the ideal theory debate among contemporary philosophers, such as that between Amartya Sen and Rawls on the importance of ideals in pursuing justice. After I articulate this theory and its appeal in this chapter, the next two chapters analyze it in considerable depth. I certainly do not claim that all who would deem themselves "ideal theorists" or "utopians" are involved in this long-standing project, though I do think many more are committed to it than they realize. And it is a project that demands the attention of those of us who are skeptical that our diverse societies should be arranged around any conception of utopia.

1.2 Of Paradise

Right from the beginning political philosophy has sought to describe the ideal state, which, even if not fully achievable, gives us guidance in constructing a more just social world. As Plato, the first of the ideal theorists, acknowledged, it is in "the nature of things that action should come less close to truth than thought," and so our ideal constructions will not be "reproduced in fact down to the least detail."[10]

---

[10] Plato, *The Republic*, p. 178 [v. 473]. For discussions of Plato as an instance of uto-

On this view, as Ingrid Robeyns has put it, the ideal functions as "a mythical Paradise Island" that tells us where "the *endpoint* of our journey lies." Although the ideal does not "necessarily tell us anything about the route to take to Paradise Island," it orients our journey.[11] Only after identifying the ideal can we take up the task of figuring out how to get there (or, if we cannot quite get to the ideal, to come as close to it as possible). As Rawls says, "By showing how the social world may realize the features of a realistic Utopia, political philosophy provides a long-term goal of political endeavor, and in working toward it gives meaning to what we can do today."[12] To this he adds, "[the] idea of realistic Utopia is importantly institutional."[13] We wish to identify the institutional structures and patterns of interaction of an achievable ideally just social world, for it is this that ultimately provides the guidance we need to reform our own social world's institutions. Of course, we may never arrive at the ideal social world, but with an ideal guiding us the hope is that we can rest assured that our efforts to secure justice have at least moved us in the right direction.

If the goal of the ideal is to orient our navigation through less-than-ideal social worlds, we need to understand where we are now in relation to it. The ideal can orient us only if we have some idea of where it is, and where we presently are. Consequently, this *orienting function* of ideal political philosophy seeks not only to inform us about the long-term goal of creating a perfectly just society, but also to ground at least some significant class of judgments as to whether a move from, say, our present social world to a near social state moves us closer to, or further from, the ideal.[14] Rawls believed that ideal justice provided

---

pian thought, see Berneri, *Journey through Utopia*, chap. 1; Kumar, *Utopia and Anti-Utopia in Modern Times*, chap. 1; Kenyon, "Utopia in Reality."

[11] Robeyns, "Ideal Theory in Theory and Practice," p. 345. Emphasis was in original. The motif of the voyage is a feature of classical utopian writing. In Bacon's *New Atlantis* a ship arrives at a marvelous island. In *Utopia* More reports the life in a far-off island, that has distinct similarities to the features of England—a far off version (reached by a long journey) of the current world. See also Goodwin and Taylor, *The Politics of Utopia*, chap. 2.

[12] Rawls, *The Law of Peoples*, p. 138.

[13] Ibid., p. 16. This is also stressed by Hamlin, "Feasibility Four Ways." Traditional utopian writing concurred. See Kenyon, "Utopia in Reality," p. 154.

[14] See Robeyns, "Ideal Theory in Theory and Practice," pp. 346–47; Stemplowska and Swift, "Ideal and Nonideal Theory," p. 379. By "significant class of judgments" I mean

guidance for thinking about justice in our nonideal societies, assisting to "clarify difficult cases of how to deal with existing injustices" and to orient the "goal of reform," helping us to see "which wrongs are more grievous and hence more urgent to correct."[15] Existing institutions are thus to be judged in light of ideal justice, and ideal theory thus provides a goal for societies that pursue justice.[16] Famously, the back cover of *Justice as Fairness* (2001) informs us that "Rawls is well aware that since the publication of *A Theory of Justice* in 1971 American society has moved *further away* from the idea of justice as fairness."[17] Rawlsians thus not only seek to depict a perfectly just society but can employ this knowledge to orient their comparative judgments about, say, the justice of American society in 1971 and 2001.

1.3 Climbing

We shall discover in chapter II that this orienting function of the ideal turns out to be surprisingly complicated. It seeks to combine two tasks—(*i*) identification of the ideally, optimally, or perfectly just society, and (*ii*) comparative justice judgments of less-than-ideal societies. Our all-things-considered judgments about what changes are recommended by justice (§I.1.5) critically depend on judgments about where the ideal is, and how far from it (in a sense that needs to be explained) we are. As Amartya Sen observes, this implies that to make an all-things-considered judgment as to whether justice recommends a move from our current world to nonideal world *a*, or nonideal world *b*, we must know which is closer to the ideal, utopian point u.[18] We may have

---

to imply that the ordering of less-than-ideal social worlds need not be complete, but neither is it so incomplete that the theory approaches what I shall call "dreaming" (§I.1.4).

[15] Rawls, *Justice as Fairness*, p. 13.

[16] Rawls, *A Theory of Justice*, p. 216. (Unless explicitly noted, all references are to the 1999 revised edition.)

[17] Rawls, *Justice as Fairness*, back cover. Emphasis added.

[18] Sen, *The Idea of Justice*, pp. 98–99. I consider Sen's own proposal in §IV.1.2. In Valentini's terms, the ideal is functioning here as an "end-state." "Ideal vs. Non-ideal Theory," pp. 660–62. Wiens refers to this as a "target" function of the ideal, an idea that he challenges in "Prescribing Institutions without Ideal Theory." Hamlin and Stemplowska are also critical: "Theory, Ideal Theory and the Theory of Ideals," pp. 51ff.

firm grounds for concluding that *a* is more just than *b*, but unless we also know where *a* and *b* are in relation to *u*, we do not know whether moving to *a* or *b* would be recommended by justice. Given these complexities, Sen argues that we should simply focus on what we are really concerned about, the relative justice of *a* and *b*, and forget about comparing them to *u*, which is not only difficult but, happily, unnecessary. He writes:

> The possibility of having an identifiably perfect alternative does not indicate that it is necessary, or indeed useful, to refer to it in judging the relative merits of two alternatives; for example, we may be willing to accept, with great certainty, that Mount Everest is the tallest mountain in the world, completely unbeatable in terms of stature by any other peak, but that understanding is neither needed, nor particularly helpful, in comparing the peak heights of, say, Mount Kilimanjaro and Mount McKinley. There would be something off in the general belief that a comparison of any two alternatives cannot be sensibly made without a prior identification of a supreme alternative.[19]

This passage is crucial for understanding the contrast between ideal theories and Sen's comparative approach. An ideal theory begins with identifying an ideal within a set of possible worlds—or, using a somewhat more formal language, a "global optimum" in the domain {X}— and evaluates all options in relation to it, whereas Sen's analysis does not concern itself with an ideal but only "whether a particular social change would enhance justice."[20] The latter, Sen frequently tells us, is a comparative, essentially pairwise, exercise. What we need to know is whether *a* is more just than *b* (whether Mount McKinley is higher than Mount Kilimanjaro); we need not know anything about *u* (or Mount Everest) to make this decision. We seek a theory that allows us to make comparisons about "the advancement or retreat of justice."[21]

A. John Simmons offers a counteranalysis:

---

[19] Sen, *The Idea of Justice*, p. 102.
[20] Ibid., p. ix.
[21] Ibid., p. 8.

While Sen's point about Everest and determining the heights of smaller mountains is obviously true, its use in Sen's analogy is, I think, potentially misleading.... Which of two smaller "peaks" of justice is the higher (or more just) is a judgment that matters conclusively only if they are both on equally feasible paths to the highest peak of perfect justice. And in order to endorse a route to that highest peak, we certainly do need to know which one that highest peak is. Perhaps for a while we can just aim ourselves in the general direction of the Himalayas, adjusting our paths more finely—between Everest and K2, say—only when we arrive in India. But we need to know a great deal about where to find the serious candidates for the highest peak before we can endorse any path to them from here.[22]

If we focus on the metaphor of a mountain range, our aim may be to reach the highest peak; if that is the goal of our journey it will not help much to know which of two local peaks is higher (a or b). Even if a is higher than b, we want to know whether climbing a takes *us closer or further from highest peak in the range*. We do not only want to know whether the elevation a is greater than b (whether Mount McKinley is higher than Mount Kilimanjaro); we want to know something about the longitude and latitude—whether moving our society to a or b moves us closer to u.[23]

The dispute between Sen and Simmons turns on the relevant dimensions involved in deciding whether justice recommends a move to a or b. Here we must introduce more rigor to get beyond instructive, but loose, metaphors and really grasp what the debate is about. As is well known, Sen has made fundamental contributions to axiomatic social theory, which concerns the properties of preference orderings and methods of aggregating two or more such orderings into a social

[22] Simmons, "Ideal and Nonideal Theory," p. 35. Geographic metaphors are commonplace in the literature; see Stemplowska, "What's Ideal about Ideal Theory?," p. 336; Robeyns, "Ideal Theory in Theory and Practice," p. 345; Schmidtz, "Nonideal Theory."

[23] This debate is not only between Simmons and Sen. For an analysis supporting the necessity of ideals, see Valentini, "On the Apparent Paradox of Ideal Theory." For a criticism, see Lawford-Smith, "Ideal Theory—a Reply to Valentini."

preference ordering. Now individual i's complete transitive preference ordering O_i is an ordering of options of some option set, such that for any two elements $\{a, b\}$ in that set, either a is preferred to b, b is preferred to a, or a and b are indifferent.[24] What is important about any single O_i is that it is, *in the end*, unidimensional, in the sense that no matter how many dimensions of evaluation may have been involved in i's deliberations in coming to her ranking, once she has a well-formed ordering, all the options can be arrayed along a single dimension from best to worst.[25] Given this social choice presupposition, Sen is absolutely correct to suppose that the height of the mountains (a metaphor for how highly ranked in terms of justice an option is) exhausts the relevant dimensions, for there *is* only one dimension in an individual's ordering and, as we shall see, for Sen, judgments of justice are about the orderings of impartial spectators over social worlds (§IV.1.2).[26]

We can give two interpretations—one substantive and one formal—of Sen's claim that only pairwise judgments are necessary; that is, that in determining the justice of $\{a, b\}$, we need not worry about how a and b compare to the best, or optimal, social world, u. On what we might call the *inherent binariness of judgments of justice* interpretation, Sen is advancing a substantive thesis about justice, according to which a judgment of the relative justice of any two social worlds $\{a, b\}$ never depends on information about a third alternative, the optimum social world, u. (Or, more strongly, the $\{a, b\}$ judgment never depends on any third option c, whether or not $c = u$.)[27] This is a substantive thesis as it

[24] The assumptions of completeness and transitivity can be weakened; investigating incomplete preferences over rankings of states of affairs in terms of justice is a central concern of Sen's in *The Idea of Justice*. See my "Social Contract and Social Choice."

[25] Trivially, the person's ordering will be single-peaked with the best at the top, declining down to the least preferred, showing that it is unidimensional. See my *On Philosophy, Politics, and Economics*, pp. 162–64.

[26] If we aggregate different individual orderings into an overall social ordering, this aggregation may reveal multiple dimensions. In his work on justice, Sen is careful to employ only the most modest forms of aggregation, in which the pathologies associated with such aggregative multiple dimensionality (e.g., cycles) do not appear (§IV.1.2).

[27] On binariness and its relation to such independence, see Sen, *Collective Choice and Social Welfare*, pp. 7ff., 16ff. For a deeper analysis, see his "Choice Functions and Revealed Preference."

implies that, in evaluating the justice of social worlds a and b, information about the proximity of a and b to u (or any c) is irrelevant. The justice of a and the justice of b depend solely on the features of the states of affairs that constitute them, and this does not include their relation (say in terms of proximity) to other alternative, c. This is perhaps the most natural interpretation of Sen's advocacy of his pairwise approach, and of many of his criticisms of Rawls's insistence on the importance of knowing the ideal when making judgments about less-than-ideal social worlds. However, his pairwise approach by no means necessarily assumes it. Another, more formal, interpretation might be called the all-things-considered *ordering view.* Suppose that person i's preference ordering of the relative justice of a set of options $\{a, b, c\}$ depends not only on how well a and b do when evaluated in terms of the relevant standards of justice, but also on the relative distance of, respectively, a and b, to a third, superior option c (which may or may not be the ideal state, u). That is, in thinking through the issue of whether a was more or less just than b, a person considers both the inherent justice of worlds a and b, as well as how "far away" (again, leaving aside for now what that might mean) a and b are from c. If our person i nevertheless arrived at a complete transitive ordering of $\{a, b, c\}$ in terms of each element's justice on both these dimensions, the "distance from c" information would already be accounted for in i's preference ordering, and the place of a and b in it. Given this, it would still be strictly true that *given* this ranking, to say whether a or b is more just, does not require knowing what social world is at the top of the ordering; knowing the top of the ordering is not relevant to a pairwise choice. Yet, unlike on the *inherent binariness* interpretation, to arrive at the ordering, distance information would be required, and so knowledge of the ideal would be presupposed in developing the ranking.

Given that Sen is deeply skeptical that knowledge of the ideal is really of much use at all, we should definitely reject this second interpretation of his social choice approach. However, neither should we saddle him with a pure version of the *inherent binariness* interpretation. Sen need not be absolutely committed to ignoring all "distance" or "directional" information (again, for now let us use these vague ideas drawn from Simmons). For example, suppose that though a's features were more just than b's, small modifications of b would lead to a far more just world, c, while this is not the case with a. Nothing Sen says indicates that he could not take this into account, and so judge that all things considered b is more just than a, because of its "proximity" to c. Nevertheless, it seems safe to read Sen as saying that such judgments are not fundamental to a theory of justice, and for the most part we should focus on the fundamental inherent features of a social world when determining its justice. Thus, basically, in determining the justice ranking of $\{a, b, c\}$ we should focus on the justice of the inherent (not relational vis-à-vis other worlds) features of each world and how people fare in it. Consequently, knowledge of the ideal is of little or no use when making pairwise comparisons about nonideal worlds. In seeking more justice, we basically wish to climb up the ordering of more inherently just social worlds. To do that we do not need to see the top of the ordering, or make many "distance" judgments. It is essential to realize that Sen's climbing-up-the-order approach in no way implies that improvements must be incremental or conservative; if we are now at the social world judged fortieth and our option set includes the thirty-ninth and tenth options in our ordering, Sen certainly does not hold that we first move to the thirty-ninth. It is fundamental to distinguish Sen's claim that judgments of justice are basically binary, and so do not rely on their relation to an ideal point, from the common misunderstanding that they are therefore incremental.[28]

Simmons's counterpoint to Sen is best interpreted as insisting that the social choice ordering model is inappropriate because we should keep distinct at least two dimensions of evaluation in comparing the justice of a and b. Fundamental to thinking about justice is not simply the inherent justice of a's and b's social structures, but "how close" in terms of, say, similarity or feasibility,[29] a and b are to the ideal point (or global optimum) u. Thus because there are now two dimensions of evaluation being kept separate,[30] it is perfectly possible for a to be

---

[28] Cf. Gilabert, "Comparative Assessments of Justice, Political Feasibility, and Ideal Theory."

[29] I shall distinguish these in some detail in chapter II.

[30] Recall that one possibility for a social choice analysis was the all-things-considered *ordering view*, which aggregates both dimensions into an overall social ordering; thus the importance of keeping them distinct.

closer to u on one dimension (say, the justice of its institutional structure), but further away on the distance dimension (in some proximity sense it is further from u than is b).

On this multidimensional analysis, then, it matters a great deal where the ideal is, because some metric of distance to the ideal is a fundamental element of the overall comparative judgments of whether justice recommends a move to a or b. And the multidimensional analysis allows us to see why the ideal would be necessary in orienting our judgments about justice; we wish to make not only evaluations of the binary inherent justice of two states, but also determinations as to whether one or the other brings us closer in the proximal sense to the ideally just condition. We can now see a way to more rigorously thinking about how the ideal can orient our judgments of justice, a task to which I turn in the next two chapters. In this book, then, I shall explore multidimensional ways of thinking about justice, for they provide the most compelling response to Sen's elegant unidimensional analysis— an analysis that makes the ideal otiose.

1.4 Dreaming

As I have stressed—and as we will see in upcoming chapters—this multidimensional, orienting-through-the-ideal approach to political philosophy is complicated. We need to know the justice of various social states as well as their proximity to the ideal (where these are different, not well correlated, dimensions of justice). One way to avoid the inevitable complications is Sen's: unleash comparative judgments from reliance on an ideal, and so render the ideal unnecessary.[31] Then we need to know only the relative justice of social states. Something like the opposite simplifying strategy is to depict only the ideally just state or condition, and make no claims about the justice of less-than-ideal situations. There is nothing incoherent about this; it could be that all less-than-ideal states are incommensurable or equal (everyone but the winner is equally a loser), and so cannot be ranked in terms of strictly better or worse than one another. It is too strong to say that such a

---

[31] Or, alternatively, develop a single ordering where "more just" always implies "closer to the ideal" as in what I called the all-things-considered interpretation of the social choice approach (§I.1.3).

theory is entirely useless,[32] but a political philosophy that is unable to describe any but the top, ideal social state, is of little use in helping us sort through the options for justice that confront us.[33] It is as if we have developed a clear conception of the ideal square, but are unable to say which of three drawings, a square, a rectangle, or a circle, is closest to it.

One might contend that a political philosophy that presents a vision only of the fully just society can have value. This contention would seem supported by the historical importance of Martin Luther King's "I Have a Dream" speech. Recall, however, that his litany of dreams of justice and harmony in America was offered as a source of hope and faith to help overcome the alienation and bitterness of his audience, arising from the fact that their actual, here-and-now demands for justice were met with contempt and hatred. The speech commenced not with mere dreams, but an assertion that the American founders issued "a promissory note to which every American was to fall heir. This note was a promise that all men would be guaranteed the inalienable rights of life, liberty, and the pursuit of happiness." So, King proclaims to the marchers, "we have come to cash this check—a check that will give us upon demand the riches of freedom and the security of justice."[34] A world where the requirements of complete justice—or perhaps even a world where the commitments of the American founders—are fully met is perhaps an unattainable ideal. I do not claim that a useful ideal theory must posit attainable ideals. But King nevertheless insisted that the ideal orients current political demands. Even if the check that King demanded be cashed was one that fell far short of the promised value, the critical point is that the ideal orients political demands in our manifestly nonideal world. King's "dream" is not one from which we awake—a dream of a perfect world—that is unrelated to the pursuit of justice in nonideal social worlds. By "dreaming" I mean to isolate a different view of ideal justice that not only proposes an unattainable

[32] See Stemplowska and Swift, "Ideal and Nonideal Theory," pp. 377–80.

[33] Swift argues in favor of this ordering function of philosophical analysis. "The Value of Philosophy in Nonideal Circumstances."

[34] King, "I Have a Dream...."

ideal, but is willing to admit that this ideal may be, and often is, entirely irrelevant to improvements in justice in nonideal conditions.

Divorced from judgments of justice about the social world in which we find ourselves, and those to which we might move, mere dreams of ideal justice may inspire or give hope, though they may also lead to hopelessness, despair, and cynicism. To wake from a dream of a world of perfect justice and confront the realities of our social world, without any way to connect the dream to the problems and questions arising in our social world, is all too likely to disorient thinking about justice.[35] We might think of it as surrealist justice, seeking to depict in our world a vision of a dream world that does not really translate.[36] What one "knows" about justice is discontinuous with the questions of justice arising from life in one's actual and near social worlds. David Miller is quite right: on such a view "there is nothing left for political philosophy but lamentation over the size of the gap that unavoidably exists between the ideals it defends and the actual conditions of human life."[37]

David Estlund upholds such a "hopeless" view of justice:

Consider a theory that held individuals and institutions to standards that it is within their ability to meet, but which there is no reason to believe they will ever meet.... It would be morally utopian if the standards were impossible to meet, but, again, by hypothesis, they are not. Many possible things will never happen. The imagined theory simply constructs a vision of how things should and could be, even while acknowledging that they won't be.... So far, there is no discernable defect in the theory, I believe. For all we have said, the standards to which it holds people and institutions

---

[35] In Bacon's *New Atlantis* (p. 23), a very few of those sailors who have happened on utopia have elected to return to the less-than-ideal world. "What those few that returned may have reported [about our utopia] abroad I know not. But you must thinke, Whatsoever they have said, could bee taken where they came, but for a Dreame."

[36] On the other hand, writing of the Bolshevik avant-garde, Buck-Morss maintains that "By not closing the gap between dream and reality, the artwork of the avant-garde left both dream and reality free to criticize each other."*Dreamworld and Catastrophe*, p. 65.

[37] Miller, *Justice for Earthlings: Essays in Political Philosophy*, p. 231.

may be sound and true. The fact that people will not live up to them even though they could is a defect of people, not of the theory. For lack of a better term, let us call this kind of theory a version of *hopeless realism*.[38]

I have claimed that such a theory is of little use. Estlund admits it may well be: "The value of unrealistic theory is not my point.... The point is that a hopeless normative theory might be the true theory. Admittedly, not all truths are of great value. The telephone book contains many relatively unimportant truths. We are talking about the truth about justice, however, and I am inclined to think that there is more importance here, but perhaps this is only because we would have thought that it would be of practical value."[39] There may well be no realistic prospect that we will do as justice "requires," and thus it may also be that given this, such justice "might have no practical value at all" once we ask what, given our imperfections, we ought now to do.[40] Estlund seems to rather relish this possibility. He makes a great deal of cases where "it ought to be the case that Alf Xs" even though it would be deeply inadvisable for Alf to seek to X, because he is likely to fail, and in trying to X he is apt to bring about worse results than if he had pursued a more "realistic" alternative.[41] But Estlund's thesis is even more radical: it stresses that knowing that X ought to be the case might not be of relevance to practice in the sense of giving some reasons to look for ways to secure X, if not now, then in the future. Thus knowledge that X ought to be the case may have "no practical value at all."

Like others, Estlund draws on Lipsey and Lancaster's "theory of the second best," according to which if u is the Pareto-efficient state, it does not follow that a state of affairs that is almost identical to u will be almost Pareto efficient.[42] Thus, at first blush, it would seem that the

[38] Estlund, *Democratic Authority*, p. 264. For extended analyses, see Estlund's "Utopophobia" and "Human Nature and the Limits (If Any) of Political Philosophy."

[39] Estlund, "Utopophobia," p. 133.

[40] Ibid., pp. 132–33.

[41] See Estlund, "Prime Justice." This sort of concern has led political philosophers to elevate the role of deontic logic, and analyses of "ought implies can." "Can it be the case that 'you ought to X' if you are unlikely to X even if you 'try'?" (Or sometimes even if you "keep trying"?) See Estlund, "Prime Justice," and "Human Nature and the Limits (If Any) of Political Philosophy"; Lawford-Smith, "Non-ideal Accessibility."

[42] Lipsey and Lancaster, "The General Theory of Second Best." See Estlund, "Utopo-

goal of approximating the ideal might be ill founded: if we cannot reach it, getting close may be of no use at all in securing justice.[43] Knowing ideal justice thus could be more like knowing rather abstruse theorems in mathematics than a guide to action.[44]

Estlund's point is, broadly speaking, a conceptual one: a theory of justice may be the true theory, even if it has no practical value. Others have denied this—it is certainly a live issue.[45] It is not, however, my concern to adjudicate this dispute; for the most part, I set it aside. My chief concern is analyzing a class of ideal theories according to which the specification of an ideal *is* of critical importance in making relative judgments of justice and, in some way, of orienting practice. Still, while not seeking to jump into this particular fray, I am supposing that throughout its long history, political thinkers so often have been drawn to utopian ideals because they have been convinced that they *do* help orient our less-than-ideal judgments, and *do* provide recommendations about how to think about social and political change, even when this change seems infeasible now, or even in the near future. This is not a conceptual truth, but a truth about the utopian tradition in political philosophy. As I have stressed, it is simply a misreading of utopian thought to equate it with hopeless, unrealizable ideals: it sim-

---

phobia," p. 121; Wiens, "Against Ideal Guidance," p. 441; Wiens, "Political Ideals and the Feasibility Frontier," p. 22.

[43] Appeals to Lipsey and Lancaster's work on the second best in economics is suggestive, but political theorists have been rather too quick to assume that analyses of efficiency carry over into theories of the ideal. Chapter II of this volume presents a model that explains when, in a theory of the ideal, approximations to the structure of the ideal state also approximate its justice, and when they do not. Illuminating this, we shall see, is a distinct advantage of this model.

[44] Others have likened moral inquiry to physics. See Enoch, "The Disorder of Public Reason." Yet another model of inquiry into justice has been "epistemology"—the theory of knowledge (see Swift, "The Value of Philosophy in Nonideal Circumstances," pp. 366ff.). Even this manifestly more appropriate (because it is also a normative inquiry) comparison does not seem quite apt. The epistemologist might give us an account of the conditions for justified belief, but while a person such as Betty, who continues to use a Ouija board, violates the norms of rationality, she does not fail to give anyone else what is owed them, nor do others have a right to demand that she cease and desist using her Ouija board. Martin Luther King was neither merely dreaming of perfect justice, nor was he merely imparting to white Americans important theoretical knowledge about the norms of justified racial relations.

[45] See Farrelly, "Justice in Ideal Theory: A Refutation."

ply does not follow that one who resists a "hopeless utopia" is a "uto-pophobe." It is hard not to be worried about a trend in academic philosophy that searches for "true justice" and "utopia" by turning its back on so much of this tradition, resolutely defending the possibility that its subject is utterly useless.

1.5 Recommending—Rescuing Justice from Uselessness

In the remainder of this book, then, I set aside ideal theory as mere dreaming; whether or not achieving the ideal is itself *hopeless*, my concern is the type of political theorizing in which the ideal is not *useless*—in which the ideal serves as a criterion that assists in regulating, directing, or facilitating less-than-ideal judgments of comparative justice. On these views knowledge of the ideal is informative in making less-than-ideal judgments. But even such a theory of the ideal, which is not mere dreaming—in which knowledge of the ideal informs evaluative judgments about the relative superiority of nonideal conditions—could still be a sort of purely academic enterprise, conveying theoretical knowledge of comparative evaluations that never provides anyone with guidance. From the point of view of working toward justice, such a theory would be useless all the way down: the whole enterprise would result in, perhaps, a beautiful theory of justice that yields evaluations of a wide variety of imperfect social states oriented by the ideal, but never manages to yield recommendations about what actual agents ought to do or strive for. The theory would be thoroughly useless.

I am not so naive as to suppose that this is not an attractive goal for many philosophers, but it does make rather puzzling the paraphernalia of the practice of justice: demanding, complaining, blaming, claiming, agitating, "the justice system," punishments, editorials, social movements, consciousness-raising, and revolutions. Estlund's theory, while allowing that "prime justice" may be hopeless, admits the category of "concessive" justice—the justice that applies to Alf when he knows that he will not conform to prime or ideal justice. A theory that is hopeless all the way down is truly a truncated theory of justice.[46] Such a theory fails to make sense of the way justice enters into our form of life.

---

[46] Estlund, "Prime Justice."

Again, this is not to say that ideal justice itself must be implementable; even in a nondreaming account, ideal justice still can be a hopeless (but not a useless) vision that orients, inspires, and guides us. Nor is it to say that for every well-formed judgment that one social state is more just than another, a theory of justice must yield a practical recommendation to move to the more just condition. Note the range of practical activities listed in the previous paragraph; claims and demands can be quite specific, but social movements and consciousness-raising guide action in much vaguer ways. The point is merely that, as I shall consider it here, ideal theory is not simply about theoretical evaluative judgments of social states. The orientation of *judgments* of justice cannot be the entire story; there must arrive a point at which a political philosophy concerned with justice yields recommendations about moving to more just social states. An ideal might be simply aspirational, but not the entire field of justice.

When a political philosophy focused on justice moves from judgments of justice to recommendations, it must move away from the sphere of pure moral philosophy, understood simply as the justification of normative judgments.[47] At this point, political philosophy must draw on social and economic theory, political science, and psychology in seeking to formulate policies, recommendations, and demands.[48] Depending on the context, this will require employing different social science toolkits and predictive models. A political theorist advocating a constitutional structure, one advocating a tax policy, and one advocating a change in particular laws (say, about school segregation), will obviously draw on different data, toolkits, and models, but it will be rare indeed that no significant social science will be drawn on. Even at the judicial stage, where it may seem that "recommendations" are simply derivations from legal requirements, courts regularly invoke social theory and science. Thus, for example, in the landmark *Brown v. Board of Education of Topeka*, which was without doubt about basic claims of justice, the Supreme Court noted the psychological harms of school segregation.[49] Because the recommendation task of a theory of justice

[47] This is not to say that it ever must have occupied such a sphere.

[48] See Wiens, "Demands of Justice, Feasible Alternatives, and the Need for Causal Analysis."

[49] *Brown v. the Board of Education of Topeka*, 347 U.S. 483; 74 S. Ct. 686; 98 L. Ed. 873

or political philosophy requires a set of tools, data, and models, analyzing this aspect of a theory of justice requires understanding the ways that political philosophy draws on social science.

2 Social Realizations and the Ideal

2.1 Perfect Principle Conformity and Ideal Societies

I have thus far dealt with "the ideal" as an unspecified variable for optimal or perfect justice. Although I wish the analysis to remain reasonably general—it certainly should not turn on a precise understanding of the ideal—it is important to identify the constraints on characterizing an ideal as I will examine it. My aim is a sufficiently broad characterization such that it captures the essentials of an interestingly large group of theories while, at the same time, lending itself to a coherent and fruitful analysis.

G. A. Cohen's account of justice is often depicted as a sort of "ideal theory," indeed often as an instance of the most extreme type.[50] Cohen—and in this respect he shares much with Estlund[51]—is adamant that a claim that some fundamental principle of justice J is the correct principle cannot be defeated by a demonstration that J is outside the bounds of what humans plausibly can be expected to do. That is, on his view J's claim to be a fundamental principle cannot be defeated by the finding that, given psychology and other social sciences, it is highly improbable that people will conform to it. The fundamental truths of justice, it is said, do not depend on such practicality considerations, nor do they derive from any set of facts about a group's current beliefs and convictions.[52] This suggests a characterization of the ideal, the

> *Principle-Defined Ideal*: Supposing that we have identified principles of justice J that do not depend on feasibility constraints or sociological facts (such as current beliefs about justice), for any

---

(1954). The court specifically cited a social science study on doll choice by children: white dolls were chosen consistently over black dolls.

[50] Farrelly, "Justice in Ideal Theory: A Refutation," pp. 846–47.

[51] For their differences, see Estlund, "Utopophobia," pp. 129–30.

[52] Cohen, *Rescuing Justice and Equality*, pp. 20–21, chaps. 6 and 7.

social state, S, it is an ideal social state if and only if in S everyone affirms J and perfectly conforms to J. All other social states are nonideal.

Cohen's text actually does not support this interpretation of the ideal. "Ideal theory," he says, is "what transpires in the ideal society, and nonideal theory ... applies to settings in which, *among other things,* citizens do not affirm and act upon the correct principles of justice."[53] The implication of the italicized phrase is that nonideal states are not merely defined by lack of endorsement and conformity to the relevant principles. In contrasting the ideal liberal and socialist societies, Cohen tells us that "in the ideal socialist society, equal respect and concern are not projected out of society and restricted to the ambit of an alien superstructural power, the state. If the right principles are, as Marx thought, the ones that are right for everyday, material life, and if they are practices in everyday life, as the socialist ideal utopianly envisages they will be, then the state can wither away."[54]

We see here that the ideal is characterized by not only conformity to the relevant principles, but a specification of the aspects of the social world to which the principles apply ("the practices"); the socialist and liberal dispute about the ideal does not involve a dispute simply about principles, but about the parts of the world that are to be regulated by the principles. Whereas, Cohen suggests, the liberal sees ideal justice as regulating the state (and, we might add, more generally, the basic structure of social cooperation), the socialist holds that the principles apply to various practices of everyday life. This, though, means that the identification of the ideal society must involve specification of various types of institutions, practices, or spheres of life;[55] if there is no state or no basic structure, for example, Cohen indicates that there simply *cannot* be liberal justice. But then a liberal ideal must provide

[53] Ibid., p. 221. Emphasis added.
[54] Ibid., p. 1. Note Cohen's rather interesting reading of Marx as a utopian socialist. Certainly Cohen seems to qualify as one. Recall Engels's characterization of the utopian socialists: "To all these socialism is the expression of absolute truth, reason, and justice.... And ... absolute truth is independent of time, space, and of the historical development of man." Engels was not a great fan of such views. "Socialism: Utopian and Scientific," p. 693.
[55] See here Habermas, "Reconciliation through Public Reason," p. 129.

an account of what constitutes state structures, or what institutions are part of the basic structure. In Rawls's liberal ideal, for example, the family sits (somewhat uncomfortably) in the basic structure.[56] Rawls's liberal ideal thus differs from that of a liberal who would exclude the family, yet both may endorse Rawls's two principles of justice.[57] And conceptually, the liberal and socialist might agree on the same principles, yet their visions of the "ideal society" could still radically differ with regard to the parts of social life to which they apply.

Although, then, we might start off thinking of "ideal justice" as simply universal endorsement of, and action in accordance with, the correct, true, or best principles of justice, to make sense of ideal justice we need to suppose a set of institutions, practices, or spheres, and the agents that act in them—and all this requires some account of how institutions or agents (could possibly, are apt to, can without excessive strain) operate, and how various spheres are demarcated.[58] As Henry Sidgwick observed, "even an extreme Intuitionist would have to admit that the details of Justice and other duties will vary with social institutions."[59] Even the idea of agency itself needs specification. For example, it needs to be determined whether groups are agents subject to principles of justice and, if so, what *are* group agents, and for what can they possibly be held accountable.[60] At the very minimum, our vision of Paradise must specify features of the social world to which the

---

[56] Rawls, "The Idea of Public Reason Revisited," pp. 595ff.

[57] "(I) Each person is to have an equal right to the most extensive total system of equal basic liberties compatible with a similar system for all. (II) Social and economic inequalities are to be arranged so that they are both: (a) to the greatest benefit of the least advantaged, consistent with a just savings principle [the difference principle], and (b) attached to offices and positions open to all under conditions of fair equality of opportunity." Rawls, *A Theory of Justice*, p. 266.

[58] See §V.3 on the charge that this confuses justice with "rules of regulation." The point here is that even if one seeks to sharply distinguish principles of justice from some of their institutional embodiments, an ideal cannot be simply equated with maximal fulfillment of principles of justice.

[59] Sidgwick, *The Methods of Ethics*, p. 20.

[60] See, for example, List and Pettit, *Group Agency*. For worries that there may be much more diversity within group agency than List and Pettit's model accommodates, especially concerning moral responsibility, see my "Constructivist and Ecological Modeling of Group Rationality."

principles apply, and some suppositions about the workings of the agents regulated.[61]

2.2 Justice and Its Social Realization

I have been stressing that even theories that, prima facie, identify the ideal in terms of perfect conformity to principles also include reference to social institutions and the way they function. More fundamentally, though, any plausible notion of the ideally just society must take seriously the way such a society would actually work out. Recall Sen's charge that Rawls succumbs to "institutional fundamentalism." Although he focuses on institutionalism and rules, the general category Sen is attacking is rather broader, encompassing much of what is called "deontology," whether that be focused on institutions, rules, or fidelity to principles.[62] Sen rejects such "fundamentalism" because "justice is not just a matter of judging institutions and rules, but of judging societies themselves."[63] I believe that Sen is correct that there is something extraordinarily severe and unattractive about a conception of justice that is entirely blind to the social realization of conformity to its principles, as if the only thing relevant to justice is that a certain set of principles be obeyed, come what may. Sen is right that such a view would be implausible. What is wrong, however, is his charge that Rawls or other plausible versions of principle-based justice are blind in this way.[64] It is certainly true that Rawls sought to include "an *important element* of pure proceduralism" in the design of institutions: to a significant extent he aims to discover a set of institutions whose outcomes, whatever they might be, would be just.[65] But these

[61] Estlund, for example, writes that "requirements of social justice morally require things of societies as such." As he recognizes, this means that collective responsibility is a matter for ideal justice. "Human Nature and the Limits (If Any) of Political Philosophy," p. 210.

[62] Sen, *The Idea of Justice*, pp. 21, 210. Drawing on the philosophic tradition of India, Sen associates these ideas with *niti*—a severe, rule- or principle-based approach to justice. See §IV.1.2.3.

[63] Ibid., p. 20. Emphasis added.

[64] But see Sen, "A Reply," pp. 327–28.

[65] Rawls, *A Theory of Justice*, pp. 57–58. Emphasis added.

institutions are designed in light of their known and predicted effects: the aim is a "fair, efficient, and productive system of social cooperation" that is "maintained over time."[66] Recall Rawls's characterization of teleology and deontology: "Utilitarianism is a teleological theory whereas justice as fairness is not. By definition, then, the latter theory is deontological, one that does not specify the good independently from the right, or does not interpret the right as maximizing the good. (It should be noted that deontological theories are defined as nonteleological ones, not as views that characterize the rightness of institutions and acts independently from their consequences. All ethical doctrines worth our attention take consequences into account in judging rightness. One that did not would simply be irrational, crazy)."[67]

A sharp distinction between an ideal theory focused on principles and one focused on social structures is, ultimately, untenable. All principle-based theories "worth our attention" are sensitive to their social realizations.[68] And this includes Kantian principled theories as well. We can better appreciate how this is so by looking at Rawls's interpretation of Kant's universal law formulation of the categorical imperative, which he models in terms of a four-step "CI procedure." The first three steps of the CI procedure are fairly straightforward:

(1) I am to do X in circumstances C in order to bring about Y. (Here X is an action and Y a state of affairs).

The second step generalizes the maxim at the first to get:

(2) Everyone is to do X in circumstances C in order to bring about Y.

At a third step we are to transform the general precept at (2) into a law of nature to obtain:

(3) Everyone always does X in circumstances C in order to bring about Y (as if by a law of nature).[69]

In the fourth step we are to consider the "perturbed social world" that would result from the addition of this new law of nature; we seek to

---

[66] Rawls, *Justice as Fairness*, p. 50.
[67] Ibid., p. 26.
[68] Ibid.
[69] Rawls, "Themes in Kant's Moral Philosophy," p. 499.

understand the new "equilibrium state" on which this perturbed social world would settle. We are then to ask ourselves whether, when we regard ourselves as a member of this new social world, we can "will this perturbed social world itself and affirm it should we belong to it."[70]

Thus on Rawls's analysis of Kant's "deontology," our endorsement of a moral imperative takes place against the background of a model of the social world and the effects of introducing a maxim. To characterize an ideally just condition is not simply to posit that certain principles are in fact followed; we must consider the social realization of conformity and consider whether we can maintain our judgment that the realized world would be ideally just. Consider a case that worried Rawls: we come to the conclusion that a particular principle is the best principle of justice, and we reflect on the social world where everyone conforms to it. Assume additionally, however, that when we consider the social realization of this perfect compliance individuals become deeply alienated from their sense of justice.[71] Perhaps they curse their very sense of justice, and bemoan the day they discovered true justice, which sets them at odds with their deepest convictions about their place in the universe. Cynicism and alienation are rife. We might wonder: is this a just world, in which those devoted to justice so suffer for their devotion? If we think not, we have at least two options: either conclude that under these social realizations, perfect compliance with this principle is not ideally just, or posit a social world where the social realization of universal justice is not so dire and identify *that* as the ideal.[72] Either option acknowledges that the social realization of universal compliance with our proposed principle is relevant to a claim that it regulates the ideal social world.

In an important series of papers, David Wiens has also cast doubt on whether a plausible ideal theory can be cast entirely in terms of a set of substantive principles, with comparative justice determined simply by comparative satisfaction of the correct principles.[73] Wiens

[70] Ibid., p. 500.

[71] Rawls, *A Theory of Justice*, p. 295. See also Weithman, *Why Political Liberalism?*, p. 53, and my "The Turn to a Political Liberalism."

[72] This second route is taken by Barry and Valentini, "Egalitarian Challenges to Global Egalitarianism," p. 509.

[73] Wiens, "Against Ideal Guidance"; "Will The Real Principles of Justice Please Stand Up?"; "Prescribing Institutions without Ideal Theory."

distinguishes *evaluative criteria* from *directive principles*. On his interpretation, for example, "Rawls's principles are meant to characterize an ideal balance of certain basic values, that is, the balance of basic values realized by a fully just institutional scheme."[74] The original position is thus understood as a way in which a complex set of criteria—liberty, equality, reciprocity, fairness, and so on—can be employed to yield directive principles for a set of institutions. "These moral conditions modeled by the original position operationalize certain 'commonly shared' basic values and, thus, represent basic evaluative criteria (as I understand that concept)."[75] Wiens argues that there are social worlds where the set of values that lie behind Rawls's two principles of justice would not be best satisfied by recommending worlds whose institutions most closely satisfy the two principles. Consider, for example, social worlds *a* and *b*. In social world *a* the difference principle is best satisfied; in social world *b* it is not quite as well satisfied, but *b*'s institutions guarantee much more equality than in world *a*. Wiens posits the relations in figure 1-1.

Let us stipulate that there are no effects on the satisfaction of the first principle of justice or fair equality of opportunity: they are equally well met in *a* and *b*. Wiens's insight here is that the values that the original position seeks to model would plausibly favor world *b* over *a* even if, *ex hypothesi*, the two principles are better met in *a*. The two principles of justice, we might say, only adequately model Rawls's underlying evaluative standards in a (proper) subset of the social worlds to be evaluated. This reading is confirmed by Rawls, who argued that the "General Conception of Justice," not his famous two principles, is the best articulation of the underlying values modeled in the original position in some empirical circumstances (essentially those of pressing scarcity).[76] Thus Rawls explicitly acknowledged the inadequacy of evaluating the justice of all social worlds in terms of the two principles

[74] Wiens, "Against Ideal Guidance," p. 436.

[75] Ibid. The quoted phrase is from Rawls, *A Theory of Justice*, p. 16.

[76] "All social values—liberty and opportunity, income and wealth, and the social basis of self-respect—are to be distributed equally unless an unequal distribution of any, or all, of these values is to everyone's advantage." Rawls, *A Theory of Justice*, p. 54. The general conception has a diminished place in the revised (1999) edition of *Theory*; note that it appears in the 1971 edition under the final statement of his principles (1971, p. 302), but is omitted from the relevant passage (p. 267) in the 1999 edition.

	Principle	Least advantaged	Most advantaged
World a	Difference principle	x	$130x$
World b	Stricter equality	$9/10x$	$45x$

Figure 1-1. Distributive shares under two principles (modified from Wiens, "Against Ideal Guidance," p. 443)

(which he called the "Special Conception" of justice). It must follow, then, that if he advances a coherent theory, which sometimes employs the two principles to evaluate social institutions and in other cases the General Conception, there must be deeper underlying evaluative standards than the Special Conception.

One might dispute the importance of the case of Rawls. One might grant that both his "four step CI-procedure" and his recognition that the two principles are inappropriate in some circumstances do indeed indicate that Rawls tests principles in terms of the acceptability of their social realizations given fundamental values or evaluative standards. But one might argue that Rawls is driven to this because of his conviction that justice is the preeminent virtue of social institutions: if, as for Rawls, the overall acceptability of institutions essentially turns on their justice, then the requirements of justice must converge with our judgments of the overall acceptability of a social world and its institutions. Because Rawls holds justice to be such a central virtue of social life and institutions, a social world's overall evaluation must closely track its justice. Others, however, insist that justice is simply one of many virtues:[77] even from the perspective of political philosophy, they claim, our overall evaluation of a social world depends on many values, of which justice is but one. Think again of Wiens's worlds a and b, and suppose we agree with him that b is morally superior to a, even though a better satisfies Rawls's difference principle. But if justice is simply one of many virtues of social institutions, one might say that, while b is better, it is not "through-and-through just"[78]—it fails to meet the principles of justice as well as does a.

[77] Compare Rawls, A Theory of Justice, p. 3; Cohen, Rescuing Justice and Equality, pp. 302ff.

[78] Cohen, Rescuing Justice and Equality, p. 7; see also generally chap. 2.

This is a conceivable view. However, to the extent that justice is one of many virtues of the morally relevant social world, "truths" about justice do not tell us a great deal about the acceptability of our social world. Just as one might say, "Yes, yes, this social world is pretty inefficient, but inefficiency isn't that important" one could then say, "Yes, yes, this social world is pretty unjust, but justice isn't that important." Ideal justice is simply about everyone conforming to some principle come what may, but it may not be especially praiseworthy that such an ideal is achieved. In this case, while the ideal may still orient our thinking about justice, justice no longer orients our evaluation of social and political worlds. Justice is insulated from its social realizations by diminishing its significance.[79] Of course between these radical extremes—of justice being preeminent and it being just one of many virtues of social worlds—justice may be very important, but not quite the first virtue of social institutions. But the more important justice is to our overall evaluation, the more important becomes its social realization, for the closer we expect our evaluations of justice to track our overall evaluations.

2.3 How Well Justified Are Our Principles of Justice?

We might press a more fundamental worry: can we really be so confident of any derivation of principles of justice that we are warranted in insisting that a society that is miserable or deeply dysfunctional, but yet perfectly conforms to them, is the ideally just social world?[80] When we search for a plausible basis for such a radical insulation of the justification of our judgments of justice from their social realizations, we seem to be led to something like a strongly foundationalist account of justification. Roughly, on a strongly foundationalist account, some belief β_1 (i) is the basis of the justification of other beliefs $\{\beta_2 \ldots \beta_n\}$ such as beliefs about just institutions; (ii) β_1 is not justified by any other

---

[79] We might say that although Cohen seeks to save justice from Rawls, he seeks to do so by diminishing it.

[80] Cf. Gilabert and Lawford-Smith: "It is ways of implementing principles in the world that are feasible or infeasible, not principles themselves." "Political Feasibility," p. 811. See also Barry and Valentini, "Egalitarian Challenges to Global Egalitarianism," pp. 507–11.

beliefs; and (*iii*) given the degree of self-evident justification of β_1, there is no other belief β^* that could possibly defeat (i.e., undermine) the justification of β_1. In terms more familiar to moral and political philosophy, β_1 may be among our "deep intuitions"[81] that simply cannot be defeated by pointing out other conflicting values, including those associated with "facts" about the social realizations of the principles expressing β_1.[82] So on this view, if people who conform perfectly to the correct principle of justice, which expresses β_1 in social world S, are deeply alienated and cynical, or lead impoverished lives, this might lead us to think that people in S simply are not up to justice, but it couldn't lead us to seriously question whether we are correct about the principles of justice. The correct principle is so near self-evident that no mere facts about the disaster of implementing it, or that reflective and goodwilled people do not will such a world, could defeat its justification.[83]

Strongly foundationalist accounts of justified belief have a number of intractable problems, the most important of which is their central claim that "deep intuitions" have very high (approaching unity) levels of credence; it is this that insulates them from defeat by other values, including values that are realized in facts concerning social realizations. Although on some accounts perceptual beliefs may approach this (*some* are tempted to say: "If I believe I perceive red, I cannot be wrong, and this could not be defeated by other beliefs"),[84] it is very

---

[81] Cohen, *Rescuing Justice and Equality*, p. 22. See also §V.3.

[82] I consider the idea of defeat at some length in *Justificatory Liberalism*, chaps. 5–7. On foundationalism, see pp. 91ff. What I say in the following paragraphs is not directly applicable to (nor is it entirely irrelevant to) Cohen's "fact insensitivity of principles" thesis, which involves a number of claims about the structure of justification and the role of "principles" per se. A detailed discussion of this much-discussed thesis would take us too far afield here; my concern is simply whether (*i*) a claim that some principles are the correct account of justice can be defeated by facts about their social realizations, not whether (*ii*) the justification of those principles depends on social facts. The relation of claims (*i*) and (*ii*) is too complex to explore here.

[83] Cf. Estlund, who seems to grant that only facts about impossibility could defeat a claim of justice. "Human Nature and the Limits (If Any) of Political Philosophy," e.g., p. 210. It is not clear, however, whether Estlund is arguing that a principle of justice immune to facts about dire social realizations is plausible, or simply not incoherent.

[84] And even this is implausible: a person's percepts may be undefeatable, but not that person's perceptual beliefs. That the stick *looks* crooked to me when half im-

hard to accept that intuitions about social justice could possibly have this status. On any plausible view, the level of self-justification of beliefs about justice should be set low enough to admit defeat. Note that this does not mean that basic beliefs about justice cannot be self-justified and foundational (and so in *this sense* they still can have "fact independent" justification), but simply that whatever its degree of self-justification, it is sufficiently less than unity such that its (self-) justification can be defeated by other considerations.[85] Once we allow that regardless of how deep it is, an intuition about justice can be defeated, we can press that the dastardly character of the social world that best realizes our intuitive principles could, at least in principle, defeat the claim that a world that meets these principles is just (in Kantian terms, we could not will that these principles be a law of nature in that social world).

I am not claiming that our moral judgments must be "coherentist" in any formal sense, nor must we embrace "reflective equilibrium." I do, however, believe that we have very good grounds for (*i*) denying that any intuition that a substantive principle of justice is correct has such a high credence that it could not be defeated by other considerations; (*ii*) that when specifying a just social world, the realizations of universal or widespread acting on a principle are relevant defeaters for the claim that it is the most just principle in this social world. And (*iii*) so too for the ideally just society: to say that universal conformity to a principle is an aspect of the ideally just society can be defeated by the social realizations of acting on it in the ideal social world. None of this is to say that any and all adverse social realizations defeat the claim that a principle correctly identifies justice (if, say, we have a social world of evil agents, it may still be the correct principle), but only that social realizations are always of potential relevance, and so cannot be simply "bracketed" on the grounds that since "we know the truth about justice, no mere facts could ever change this."

I believe that this is an important point about the justification of principles of justice and their social realizations. It is the deep reason

---

mersed in water seems privileged, and I cannot be wrong; that it is a crooked stick is often erroneous.

[85] I go into these matters in some depth in *Justificatory Liberalism*, chap. 7.

why we should reject what Sen might call "principle fundamentalism": that is to say, so long as the principles are satisfied, justice doesn't concern itself with the way people's lives go. However, the core analysis of this and the following chapters does not depend on accepting this point. All that is strictly required is that, for whatever reason, the ideal theorist acknowledges that determining the comparative justice of social worlds partly depends on the worlds' institutional structures and their dynamics, given the population operating, and subject to, them.

3 MODELING THE IDEAL (AND NONIDEAL)

3.1 Setting the Constraints Regulating Coherent Social Worlds (One Sense of Feasibility)

We now can see that our initial distinction between the orienting role of ideal theory and political philosophy as recommending was too stark (§I.1.5). While we might have initially viewed the mere orientation function of ideal theory as one of "pure moral philosophy," which is unconcerned about recommending moves to new social structures, and thus also unconcerned with predictive models of social worlds, we now see that even the most ideal of theories of justice must engage in modeling the ideal social world, as we need to make some effort to inquire about the social realizations of our ideal principles. Plato's *Republic* is a good example of ideal theorizing, for it seeks to model the ideal state based on true justice: if we accept Plato's account, we have some idea as to how ideal justice would pan out, at least under ideal circumstances. Notice that Plato does not say: ideally, acting on the principles of ideal justice must work out well—after all, they are ideal! Rather, he specifies some conditions (the nature of economic life, human psychology, international relations, and so on), and then engages in a long modeling exercise to show that under these conditions the social realizations of his understanding of justice are acceptable.

This is of even more importance for Rawls, who stresses not only that the ideal of justice must suppose a certain background social world, but that the postulated basic features of the social world must not stretch credulity:

Some philosophers have thought that ethical first principles should be independent of all contingent assumptions, that they should take for granted no truths except those of logic and others that follow from these by an analysis of concepts. Moral conceptions should hold for all possible worlds. Now this view makes moral philosophy the study of the ethics of creation: an examination of the reflections an omnipotent deity might entertain in determining which is the best of all worlds. Even the general facts of nature are to be chosen. Certainly we have a natural religious interest in the ethics of creation. But it would appear to outrun human comprehension.[86]

Rawls abjures the ethics of creation, where just about all parameters of possible social worlds, including the laws of nature, are open to specification; instead, he seeks to develop "the conception of a perfectly just basic structure... under the fixed conditions of human life," assuming that given these fixed conditions the social world is characterized by "reasonably ideal" circumstances.[87]

The last decade has witnessed intense debate among political philosophers whether a theory of "ideal distributive justice" should, as does Rawls's, postulate social facts as, for instance, that without incentives people will not voluntarily work at the most socially useful job, or that they will not voluntarily pay taxes without any coercive threats.[88] This is often understood as a debate about feasibility, in one of the many senses of this complex concept: what constitutes a "feasible ideal" in the sense of one that identifies an ideal social world that is fixed by credible parameters of the socially, economically, and politically possible.[89] For our present purposes, the important point is not

---

[86] Rawls, *A Theory of Justice*, pp. 137–38.

[87] Ibid., pp. 216, 211.

[88] "Thus even under reasonably ideal conditions, it is hard to imagine, for example, a successful income tax scheme on a voluntary basis." Ibid., p. 211. Cf. Cohen, *Rescuing Justice and Equality*, chap. 1.

[89] We can distinguish numerous applications of the notion of feasibility as applied to worlds *u*, the ideal, and some other world, *a* (such as our own), including: (*i*) in *u*, are the "oughts" generated by its governing principles feasible for humans (can/will they comply?); (*ii*) in our present world *a*, are the oughts that characterize *u* still true/valid though not feasible?; (*iii*) is it feasible to move from world *a* to *u*?; (*iv*) is the way that an ideal theory depicts the functioning of world *u* (and, we can add, *a*) feasible? The recent literature has tended to focus on versions of (*i*) and (*ii*). Importantly (*i*) is

whether Rawls has correctly identified the parameters, but that any account of the ideal must settle on some parameters or constraints in modeling the social realization of the principles of justice if its ideal is not to "outrun human comprehension." What Rawls calls the "ethics of creation" allows, as it were, social philosophers to treat almost every parameter as open to setting at any value they see fit: manna falls at will from heaven so all resources are available in infinite quantities, genders can change at will, one can be a critical critic *and* fisherman at the same moment since time-space variables allow simultaneous activity by the same person in any number of time-space coordinates, one lives forever, we have worlds where actions have no opportunity costs, or perhaps one is reincarnated in various lives such that by the end of time all bad luck will be equalized, or whatever. If the principles of justice hold in all possible worlds, they hold in all these creations, for the idea of "possibility" is inherently one that is set against a set of constraints. There is no such thing as "absolutely impossible": every claim of possibility is of the form "X is possible (is not precluded by) the set of constraints (including laws) L."[90]

Of course no theory of ideal justice allows *that* many variables to remain open. A plausible current proposal is to distinguish "hard" constraints, such as the laws of nature and the natural sciences, and "soft" constraints, such as those concerning present human motivations.[91] The idea is that the hard constraints entirely rule out some sorts of

---

not equivalent to (*iv*): everyone may obey the "ought" in world *u* (and so it is feasible to expect them to), yet the upshot may not be as the ideal theorist postulates—the social realizations might not be what the theorist anticipates (my point in §I.2.2). My present concern here is (*iv*); I consider (*iii*) in chapter II, §1.3. I have very little to add to the extensive debate about (*i*) or (*ii*), which, to my mind, seems more about moral than political philosophy. Feasibility (*iv*) is much more important than (*i*); it largely encompasses the interests of political philosophy in (*i*). Even within, say, (*iii*) or (*iv*) there are numerous dimensions of feasibility. Majone characterizes feasibility as a "cluster concept" in "On the Notion of Political Feasibility," p. 261. See Hamlin's excellent analysis in "Feasibility Four Ways."

[90] This is a reason why the current fascination with "ought implies can" seems unlikely to yield much insight. What one "can do" does not crucially depend on whether a theory defines "can" in terms of possibility or a conditional probability, but rather on the constraints a theory has set. It is this that is critical.

[91] See Gilabert and Lawford-Smith, "Political Feasibility," pp. 812ff.; Carey, "Towards a 'Non-ideal' Non-ideal Theory," pp. 149ff.; Räikkä, "The Feasibility Condition in Political Theory," p. 32; Wiens, "Political Ideals and the Feasibility Frontier," p. 7.

social realizations as infeasible, while the soft constraints can be seen in more probabilistic terms, yielding judgments of more-or-less feasible. It is also supposed that hard constraints cannot be removed by humans, while soft constraints describe "that some particular fact could be changed, now or at some point in the future."[92] While no doubt there is something to this, when we begin to model social worlds and predict social realizations, the distinction pretty much evaporates for at least three reasons.

(*i*) In determining whether a social world, *u*, is feasible, we need to know not only that constraint *C* cannot be violated, but what social states *C* rules out. Once we add technological innovations, for example, whether *C* is or is not a constraint on whether social state *u* can be realized can radically vary and, indeed, be manipulated, often more easily than "soft" constraints, such as the degree to which humans are public-spirited. Consider Thomas Malthus's two "hard" constraints in his *Essay on Population*:

First, That food is necessary to the existence of man.

Secondly, That the passion between the sexes is necessary and will remain nearly in its present state.[93]

For Malthus these "laws, ever since we have had any knowledge of mankind, appear to have been fixed laws of our nature; and, as we have not hitherto seen any alteration in them, we have no right to conclude that they will ever cease to be what they now are, without an immediate act of power in that Being who first arranged the system of the universe; and for the advantage of his creatures, still executes, according to fixed laws, all its various operations."[94] In contrast, William Godwin's utopian anarchism (to which Malthus was partly replying) saw the second as a "soft" constraint, which could be overcome by intellectual progress.[95] Godwin accepted that his anarchist-socialist ideal, which resisted the struggle for existence, needed some way to

---

[92] Carey, "Towards a 'Non-ideal' Non-ideal Theory," p. 150.
[93] Malthus, *Malthus—Population*, p. 4.
[94] Ibid.
[95] Godwin, *An Enquiry concerning Political Justice*, vol. 2, pp. 850ff.

control population.[96] So what is hard and what is soft is by no means uncontroversial. Leaving aside this dispute, suppose one does accept that enjoyment of, and consequently the having of, sex is a hard constraint. To cope with this constraint a "socialist" utopia such as Thomas More's included institutions such as colonization to control population.[97] However, as John Stuart Mill recognized, one could accept Malthus's "hard constraint" (that people will continue to enjoy sex), but deny that it precluded a more socialist ideal by technological change—the diaphragm.[98] Thus under some technologies the hard constraint that people will continue to enjoy sex does not constrain utopian social worlds.

(*ii*) Because technological variables are difficult to determine, the ideal theorist seldom is in the position to assert with anything like a probability of 1 that some hard constraint definitely rules out desired social states. Moreover, it is often difficult to determine whether some hard constraint is "redundant" in the sense that, while it is a constraint on possible social realizations, it in fact does not constrain the set of relevant options in an ideal theory. Assuming that it is a hard constraint that we cannot go faster than the speed of light, this may well not impact any utopian scheme and so is to be ignored. But, perhaps, it *could* affect social realization, if instantaneous communications was part of paradise. As Giandomenico Majone concludes, because "it is often difficult to determine a priori which limitations are binding... feasibility statements must then be interpreted in probabilistic terms."[99] This, then, means that, as far as theoretical understanding of the ways a utopia might function, the distinction between probabilistic "soft constraints" that may be overcome, and "hard" constraints that definitely rule out possibilities, is not of great import.

[96] On his rejection of Malthus's "struggle," see Godwin, *Of Population*, pp. 619ff.

[97] More, *Utopia*, "Of Their Traffic." As late as the nineteenth century colonization was seen as a method of population control, which could assist the laboring classes. See Mill, *Principles of Political Economy*, pp. 194–95, 748–49, 958ff.

[98] Mill was arrested as a young man for handing out instructions for constructing such devices. See Schwartz, *The New Political Economy of J. S. Mill*, appendix 2, "The Diabolical Handbills."

[99] Majone, "On the Notion of Political Feasibility," p. 261. See also Hamlin, "Feasibility Four Ways."

(*iii*) Lastly, because social realizations depend on the interaction of a number of variables, what appears as a number of soft constraints can set into a much harder one. For example, suppose that a theory posits five soft constraints each of which yields a 20 percent chance that the utopia will arise, and all come to bear. Given the joint probabilities, there is only about a .00032 chance utopia will come about.

In modeling whether some social world is feasible given a set of constraints (*C*) that govern its behavior, then, pretty much all constraints should be understood probabilistically. Given this, for any set *C* of constraints there is a probability distribution of possible social worlds that might emerge on a given model. Let us call this probability distribution *the ideal theory's predictive modeling of the social realizations of meeting C.* It is fundamental that we should not fall into the trap of thinking that for every set of constraints *C* an ideal theory could predict a unique social world arising out of it. Every ideal involves specifying constraints or parameters (I shall not distinguish these here), taking some as very likely to affect social outcomes, and others as less apt to.

3.2 The Aim of Ideal Theory

On a naive view—which, alas, seems widely embraced in political philosophy—the aim of an ideal political theory is uncovering "the truth," as if, in making decisions between rival theories, we decide on the basis of a clear and unidimensional goal—truth. Not even natural science is well understood as having a monistic goal of "the truth." As Thomas Kuhn has shown, a true scientific theory aims at maximizing a set of values: accuracy of fit with the data (and of course that requires a decision about what the relevant data are), simplicity (this can mean different things, such as ease of computation or axiomatic parsimony), consistency (not simply internal, but also with related theories), scope (is the theory a comprehensive explanation of a range of phenomena?), and fecundity (does the theory open up fruitful lines of research?).[100] And in some fields, perhaps social utility is a desidera-

---

[100] Kuhn, *The Essential Tension*, p. 322.

tum.[101] Some think accuracy is all that is necessary, but as Kuhn stresses, on accuracy grounds alone, Copernicus's system was not, until revised by Kepler, more accurate than Ptolemy's, yet Kepler had already made a theory choice in favor of Copernicus's system before he began to work on revising it.[102] In some cases a theory may rank higher on all these criteria, and so dominate competitors, but often one theory will rank high on some, another theory on others. And as Kuhn effectively argued, there simply is no algorithm for combining these values into a single value to be maximized.[103] Different scientists will trade off these values in different ways, sometimes leading to different theory choice, even among those who share the same values and agree on the data.

Theory choice in political philosophy too has multiple desiderata. According to Rawls, a political philosophy should aim (*i*) "to focus on deeply disputed questions and to see whether, despite appearances, some underlying basis of philosophical and moral agreement can be found";[104] (*ii*) "to orient us in the (conceptual) space, say, of all possible ends, individual and associational, political and social";[105] (*iii*) at "reconciliation… to calm our frustration and rage against society and history," leading us "to accept and affirm our social world positively, not merely be resigned to it";[106] and (*iv*), as a variation of reconciliation, to propose a realistic utopia, "probing the limits of practical possibility.[107] Our hope for the future of our society rests on the belief that the social world allows at least a decent political order, so that a reasonably just, though not perfect, democratic regime is possible."[108] Without claim-

[101] Kuhn notes that this has entered into theory choice in chemistry. Ibid., p. 335. Of course it is obviously relevant to the social sciences.

[102] Ibid., p. 323.

[103] Ibid., pp. 328ff. See also D'Agostino, *Naturalizing Epistemology*, esp. chaps. 3, 5, and 6.

[104] Rawls, *Justice as Fairness*, p. 2.

[105] Ibid., p. 3.

[106] Ibid.

[107] This is especially clear in Rawls, *The Law of Peoples*, §1.

[108] Rawls, *Justice as Fairness*, p. 4. Rawls, I think, does not mean mere possibility qua not impossible, but a realistic possibility. On the importance of Rawls's quest to identify a reasonably just social world that is within our grasp, see Weithman, *Why Political Liberalism?*, pp. 8ff.

ing that these are canonical desiderata, we can readily see that, depending on how they are weighted, different theorists will endorse different theories, and so model the ideal in different ways. Importantly, a political philosopher who gives significant weight to the third and fourth aims is unlikely to decide that a political philosophy of hopeless realism is the way to go (§I.1.4). Estlund's theory of the hopeless ideal is hardly apt to "calm our frustration and rage against society and history," by inducing us "to accept and affirm our social world positively, not merely be resigned to it." Given Rawls's understanding of the aims of political philosophy, he is committed to an ideal that fixes parameters within, but at the limits of, some plausible range. In contrast, a theory that stresses orienting, or one that focuses on the importance of conformity with strong intuitions about justice, is apt to fix less of the parameters in the modeled social worlds, allowing for possible but hopeless ideals.[109] What must be stressed is that to invoke "possibility" as a constraint is itself to fix *some* parameters; it is the area (conceptual, empirical, etc.) defined by the fixed parameters that define the space of possibility or, as I shall say, the option space of an ideal theory. So it is not as if Rawls fixed parameters in his ideal social world whereas Estlund's utopia does not: the difference is in the parameters that are identified, and the range of variance that is allowed in others, and that in turn will depend on the criteria employed in theory choice.

3.3 Abstraction and Idealization

Onora O'Neill has insisted on the "fundamental, and frequently overlooked" distinction between abstraction and idealization, the latter of which many take as the heart of ideal theory.[110] In the strict sense, she argues, abstraction is a form of "*bracketing*, but not of *denying*, predi-

---

[109] Estlund makes much of the possibility constraint in "Human Nature and the Limits (If Any) of Political Philosophy."

[110] See O'Neill, *Towards Justice and Virtue*, p. 40. See also O'Neill, "Abstraction, Idealization and Ideology in Ethics"; and O'Neill, "Justice, Gender and International Boundaries." For discussions focusing on ideal theory, see Valentini, "On the Apparent Paradox of Ideal Theory"; Lawford-Smith, "Ideal Theory—a Reply to Valentini"; Jubb, "Tragedies of Non-ideal Theory"; Estlund, "Utopophobia."

cates that are true of the matter under discussion."[111] Reasoning from an abstraction, O'Neill maintains, claims neither that the predicates hold *nor* do not hold, and so reasoning from an abstract premise does not lead validly from a truth to a falsehood. "Idealization is another matter: it can easily lead to falsehood. An assumption, and derivatively a theory, idealizes while it ascribes predicates—often seen as enhanced 'ideal' predicates—that are false of the case in hand, and so denies predicates that are true of that case."[112] In her view Rawls's account of justice is based on (suspicious) idealization assumptions. "For example, in *A Theory of Justice* the veil of ignorance, that constitutes the original position and forms part of the procedure for identifying justice, is defined by reference to an *ideal* that requires mutual independence between the preferences of distinct agents, and assumes that there is a restricted set of primary goods of which agents always prefer more to less."[113]

Whatever the merits of this distinction in some contexts, when we apply to it modeling choice situations and social worlds, it is extraordinarily difficult to grasp.[114] In modeling terms, we can define "abstraction" as leaving some variable out of our model (we bracket it and put it aside) whereas "idealization" employs a variable but assigns it a value that departs from the best estimation, thus "denying... predicates that are true of the matter under discussion." Suppose, then, we are modeling the realization of a principle of justice in a social world, and in one case (*i*) we simply do not include some variable, such as the fact that people are gendered, and in another (*ii*) we suppose falsely that all persons remain a single gender for their entire lives. Now it seems clear that the abstraction in (*i*) may lead us much further away from a sound understanding than the idealization in (*ii*), in trying to grasp the social realizations of our principles. Abstracting away from some factors can lead to fundamental errors, while positing false values for some variables may actually improve the model. For example, to suppose that everyone prefers more primary goods over less from a

---

[111] O'Neill, *Towards Justice and Virtue*, p. 40.

[112] Ibid., p. 41.

[113] Ibid., p. 45.

[114] See here Hamlin and Stemplowska, "Theory, Ideal Theory and the Theory of Ideals," pp. 50–51.

restricted list is strictly false, but trying to model an entire population's distribution of preferences over all possible primary goods could lead us into such complexities that we end up throwing up our hands in despair because it's all so complicated. This is not, of course, to say that all abstractions are objectionable while all idealizations are helpful; it is to say, however, that all theoretical understanding supposes that we set some issues aside, and that all models require that we posit values that we know, say, are overly uniform, too optimistic, or too simple, but they can be part of the best understanding of a social world, either ideal or real.[115] It thus seems misguided to identify "ideal" theory with one that employs "idealizations."[116]

In economics "ideal" sometimes refers to a model that makes radical idealizing assumptions, such as perfect information or zero transaction costs. Such an "ideal model" creates a radically simplified and quite impossible world (there are no worlds of zero transaction costs) as a way to understand important dynamics in real-world economies. Here it is not simply the case that the model makes false (idealized) assumptions, but that the world it describes is, strictly speaking, impossible. We should not confuse this sense of an "idealized" world with an ideally just social world that we seek to analyze with a model that makes counterfactual, simplifying assumptions. In modeling the ideal world we seek to capture how it will function as well as we can, and to do this requires some abstraction and idealization. But the world so described is our best estimate of what a real, ideal world would actually look like, not an impossible world that we use to judge our own. Very few think that the ideally just social world is strictly impossible, even though many seem to allow that it might be, for now, deeply infeasible. As almost all insist, "ought implies can," so if the ideally just social world is to ground any sort of "ought judgment," then the "ought" must not be strictly impossible.[117]

---

[115] The classic defense of "idealization" in economics is, of course, Milton Friedman's "The Methodology of Positive Economics."

[116] "In spite of its popularity the notion of ideal theory tends to be employed somewhat loosely, to indicate any theory constructed under false, that is, idealized assumptions, which make social reality appear significantly 'simpler and better' than it actually is." Valentini, "On the Apparent Paradox of Ideal Theory," p. 332.

[117] See Estlund, "Human Nature and the Limits (If Any) of Political Philosophy."

4 Two Conditions for Ideal Theory

In this chapter I have set out what I believe to be the most powerful case for a political philosophy that seeks to identify the most just, or—more broadly—the best social world from the perspective of the political.[118] Such a political theory would orient our thinking about the justice in our own society; the ideal might be beyond our ability to fully implement, but it would still serve as our "mythical Paradise Island," which provides the goal of our quest for greater justice in the worlds that we can bring about. So, as I have said, in a useful political theory, the ideal cannot be mere *dreaming* of a utopia that is disconnected from our evaluations of less exalted social worlds (§I.I.4). I am not claiming that such dreaming has no value, but it has precious little value for answering the question that confronts the political theorist: how are we to rank the alternatives that, at least potentially, are open to us, and what moves (reforms) does our political philosophy recommend? Moreover, I have argued that if orientation via the ideal is truly necessary, then the task confronting political theory must be more complex than Sen's proposal of simply climbing up the ranking of social worlds (§I.1.3). What I shall call the "optimization" problem must include more than simple pairwise judgments (is social world *a* more just than *b*?); it must be important to also ask "is *a* or *b* closer to the ideal?" Unless this second question is distinguished from the first, and is important in its own right, Sen would be quite correct that "there would be something off in the general belief that a comparison of any two alternatives cannot be sensibly made without a prior identification of a supreme alternative" (§I.1.3). Thus if a theory of the ideal is not to collapse into a version of Sen's climbing model, it must identify, in addition to a dimension comparing the justice of different social states in the theory's option space, a dimension that, in some way, relates the present world to the ideal in a different way. Ideal theory, if it is to be a distinct enterprise, must have at least two dimensions of evaluation that must be kept distinct. Under this condition the judg-

---

[118] To simplify, I shall simply speak of the "most just" social world, but the analysis of this book generalizes to most understandings of "the politically best," where this includes the realization of values that go beyond justice.

ments of ideal theory cannot be reduced to Sen's unidimensional model.

I have also stressed that pursuit of the ideal cannot be insensitive to the social realizations of our principles of justice (or, more broadly, our standards of evaluation). It is, as Rawls said, "by showing how the social world may realize the features of a realistic Utopia . . . [that] political philosophy provides a long-term goal of political endeavor, and in working toward it gives meaning to what we can do today" (§I.1.2).[119] But for this hope of greater meaning to be achieved, we must understand the social world we have designated as the realistic utopia, and we must understand how, in our long-term endeavor, the less-than-ideal social worlds we create along the way approximate it. Understood thus, ideal theory is a complicated endeavor: we need to be clear about the option space—the parameters that are assumed in our specifications of social worlds (aspects of human nature, the laws of economics, ecology, the laws of biology, the nature of agency), and how they can vary. Having identified the ideal social world, we must be able to compare it to our own, and understand its relation to intermediate social worlds. If we can do all that, we can orient our quest for greater justice, knowing where we are, where we would like to go, and the social worlds that lie in the direction of the best.

We can formalize these requirements in terms of two conditions that any acceptable theory of the ideal (T) must meet:

> *Social Realizations Condition*: T must evaluate a set (or domain) of social worlds $\{X\}$. For all social worlds i, which are members of $\{X\}$, T evaluates i in terms of its realization of justice (or, more broadly, relevant evaluative standards). This must yield a consistent comparative ranking of the members of $\{X\}$, which must include the present social world and the ideal, in terms of their overall justice.

> *Orientation Condition*: T's overall evaluation of nonideal members of $\{X\}$ must necessarily refer to their "proximity" to the ideal social world, u, which is a member of $\{X\}$. This proximity measure cannot be simply reduced to an ordering of the members of

---

[119] Rawls, *The Law of Peoples*, p. 128.

{X} in terms of their inherent justice as in the Social Realizations Condition.

I have stressed that ideal theory does not require that all the worlds in {X} need be achievable (for example, *u*, the ideal, might not be on some views). We could also accept that whatever the criteria of "realistic" or "feasible" are (see §II.1.3) *T* need not hold that movements to all social worlds in {X} (given where we are) must be feasible for us. But unless *T* holds that many of the social worlds in {X} are more than mere hopeless possibilities, but in some sense real options for us, *T* will not be able to serve the function of orienting our quest for justice. Unless some of the worlds in {X} are realistic alternatives, *T* will not be able to issue any recommendations for reform, which, again, would show that *T* fails to orient our quest for justice. I assume that these addendums are part of the Orientation Condition.

The Social Realizations Condition expresses the requirement that the theory of the ideal aims to evaluate the justice of various social worlds, which realize to different extents, and in different ways, the relevant principles or standards of justice. This is an implication of our social realization thesis (§I.2), and our antidreaming conclusion (§I.1.4). The Orientation Condition expresses the idea that, while a simple ranking (à la Sen) of the inherent justice of each social world can satisfy the Social Realizations Condition, an overall judgment of the relative attraction of any two members of {X}, *a* and *b*, must necessarily depend (though not decisively) on *a*'s and *b*'s relative distance and direction in relation to *u*. This, of course, means that *T* must provide some coherent concept of social world proximity (or, more generally, location) that does not collapse into an ordering in terms of inherent justice (recall again Sen's argument and Simmons's reply, §I.1.3). The addendum that we must have a realistic chance of achieving some worlds in {X} interprets the thought that a theory of the ideal seeks to orient our quest for, not simply our judgments about, justice.

The question for ideal theory, then, is whether the Social Realizations and Orientation Conditions both can be met or, more usefully: under what assumptions can they be met, and are these assumptions plausible? I now turn to these matters.

CHAPTER II

The Elusive Ideal

Searching under a Single Perspective

> "Would you tell me, please, which way I ought to go
>   from here?"
> "That depends a good deal on where you want to get to,"
>   said the Cat.
>
> —Lewis Carroll

1 Perspectives on Justice

1.1 Evaluative Perspectives and the Social Realizations Condition

IN HIS *Lectures on the History of Political Philosophy*, RAWLS TELLS US that "a normalization of interests attributed to the parties" is "common to social contract doctrines."[1] This remark is made in the context of discussing Rousseau's notion of the general will, which is also said to require a shared "point of view."[2] On Rawls's reading of Rousseau, private individuals are characterized by a variety of different interests that are magnified by self-bias and selfishness. Such individuals can live together under freely endorsed common laws only if they "share a conception of the common good."[3] This shared conception, in turn, is generated from individuals' shared fundamental interests and capacities, which derive from their shared human nature. As Rawls sees it, these common fundamental interests allow individuals to abstract from their differences and occupy a *shared legislative point of view*, based on a shared conception of the common good.[4] Furthermore, when occupying this common view the parties all have the same basis

---

[1] Rawls, *Lectures on the History of Political Philosophy*, p. 226.
[2] Ibid., pp. 229ff.
[3] Ibid., p. 224.
[4] Ibid.

for their deliberations, and so everyone wills the same laws, and this is what allows them to live together under freely endorsed common laws.

Rawls is informally articulating the concept of a perspective—or, as I shall say, *an evaluative perspective*—which has been more thoroughly explored and formally modeled in the last decade.[5] The rest of this book develops and analyzes the idea of an evaluative perspective on ideal justice. Although we shall see that evaluative perspectives are implicit in much political theory—especially in thinking about ideal justice—they are unfamiliar to most political philosophers. I try to render some formal ideas intuitive as far as is possible, without sacrificing too much rigor. More formal issues are dealt with in appendixes. Nevertheless, it is a bit of work to understand the idea of a perspective and how it enters into political philosophy, but it will pay off: features of theories of justice that are not obvious come to the forefront once we focus on perspectives.

As I shall understand it, an evaluative perspective, Σ, includes three fundamental elements (we shall see in §II.1.2 that two additional elements are required for ideal theory):

(ES) A set of *evaluative standards* or criteria by which alternative social worlds in a domain $\{X\}$ are to be evaluated.

(WF) For all worlds i in the domain $\{X\}$, a specification of the *world features* of i that are relevant to evaluation according to ES, the evaluative standards. Specifying the relevant world features (WF) requires a set of categorizations that constitute the justice-relevant description of world i on perspective Σ. A description of a social world includes its institutions, social and economic dynamics, and relevant background conditions, including relevant economic and psychological facts (§§I.2.1–2, I.3.1). The domain $\{X\}$ includes the current social world and the ideal, as well as other nonideal worlds in the option space.

(MP) A *mapping* function takes the evaluative standards (ES) and applies them to a social world, i, as specified by WF, yielding what I shall call a *justice score* for world i, the social world de-

---

[5] See Page, *The Difference*, pp. 30ff.; Muldoon, *Diversity and the Social Contract*.

scribed by world features WF_i. The mapping function has two roles. (*i*) The mapping function must employ a model or models that predict how the justice-relevant features of a social world (WF_i) will interact to produce a social realization. This is the *modeling task* of the mapping function (§I.3.1). (*ii*) The mapping function must take the set of evaluative standards (ES) and determine their relative importance in such a way that they provide a single evaluation of this social realization. This might be called the *overall evaluation task* of the mapping function. Given (*i*) and (*ii*), a mapping function takes ES and maps it on to a realization based on WF and in so doing generates a justice score for a social world.

Rawls's description of the normalized interests supposed by all social contracts seems to refer only to the set of evaluative standards (ES)—the parties' shared interests. But without specifying the world's features to be evaluated (WF) and a mapping function (MP), a shared set of evaluative standards will not suffice for a shared evaluation of a social world's justice. If individuals are going to adopt a *shared point of view* they must also agree about precisely what they are evaluating (the basic structure? the family? churches?),[6] their ultimate social realizations, and how to apply their shared standards to that which is being evaluated. It is important to stress that these elements of a perspective are not arbitrary, nor simply an artifact of our model: together they satisfy requirements for an ideal theory that we uncovered in chapter I. A theory of ideal justice, *T*, that includes ES, WF, and MP satisfies the Social Realizations Condition (§I.4), namely:

> *T* must evaluate a set (or domain) of social worlds {*X*}. For each social world *i*, that is a member of {*X*}, *T* evaluates *i* in terms of its realization of justice (or, more broadly, relevant evaluative standards). This must yield a consistent comparative ranking of the members of {*X*}, which must include the present social world and the ideal, in terms of their justice.

A theory meeting ES, WF, and MP evaluates a set (or domain) of social worlds {*X*} in terms of their realization of justice. The cardinal justice

6 See §I.2.1.

score guarantees a comparative (noncyclical) ranking of the members of $\{X\}$, which includes the present social world and the ideal.

Some explanatory comments about these elements of an evaluative perspective are in order. Consider first the world features (WF). I suppose that in perspective Σ, no two social worlds share the exact same justice-relevant features. Social world a may have justice-relevant features $\{f, g, h\}$, while b has some, but not all of these features (e.g., f and g, but not h), and c, a still different set of features (e.g., f and h, but not g). Social worlds are thus individuated by their justice-relevant features. Note that condition WF refers only to the justice-relevant features of a social world and their realization, since only these are strictly necessary to generate the evaluations required by ideal theory.[7] We should not think, though, that our model implies that an ideal theorist starts out by knowing which features of the world are relevant to justice. In the development of its perspective, Σ would no doubt start by identifying a large set of features, and then, given its evaluative standards (ES), would determine which are relevant to justice. Indeed, later on (§§III.2.4–5), I shall stress how the evaluative standards and world features are interconnected within a perspective—a perspective's evaluative standards affects its view of what features of the world are relevant to evaluation and vice versa. Certainly no assumption is made here that these features of a perspective are independent of each other—indeed we shall see quite the opposite obtains. All the model requires is that before a final judgment of the justice of any social world i can be generated, perspective Σ must have settled on the criteria of evaluation (ES) and the features to be evaluated (WF).

To begin to clarify the crucial, but typically overlooked, mapping relation (MP) between the evaluative standards and the justice-relevant features of the social worlds, consider three different procedures that might be employed. The first we might call "categorical" and is probably the most common type of evaluation in philosophy. Categorical judgments are concerned with whether or not a social world is just; employing this procedure would yield a series of yes/no judgments.[8]

---

[7] On specifying possible worlds in a theory of justice, see Wiens, "Against Ideal Guidance," pp. 437ff.; Lawford-Smith, "Non-ideal Accessibility"; Goodwin and Taylor, *The Politics of Utopia*, pp. 210–14; Elster, *Logic and Society*.

[8] They thus give rise to deontic judgments, partitioning acts into the permissible,

Whatever their attractions in other contexts, such judgments are of little use for an ideal theory that seeks to orient our quest for justice by guiding us to better (i.e., more just) worlds, short of the ideal. According to the Social Realizations Condition, we need an evaluative function capable of generating a range of justice judgments. John Broome contrasts the philosopher's use of "categorical" judgments with the economist's focus on "comparative" judgments. Whereas the philosopher asks "Is *a* just or unjust?" the economist asks "Is *a* more or less just than *b*?"[9]

The idea of a comparative judgment, however, is itself ambiguous between *strictly comparative* and *scalar* interpretations. On the strictly comparative interpretation one can form a judgment about a given social world, *a*, only by comparing it to another social world, *b*. On this reading, judgments of justice have the same logical structure as preferences: they are primitive binary relations. Although philosophers often conceive of preferences, at their most basic level, as unitary states such as desires, so that one can have simply "a preference for *x*," in decision theory they are inherently binary: one can only have a preference for *x* over something else, say *y*. Thus in decision theory a preference for *x* over *y* is not a comparison of, say, the strength of one's preference for *x* and of one's preference for *y* (concepts that do not enter into decision theory); "*x* is preferred to *y*" is the most primitive preference judgment. Similarly, then, a comparative notion of justice might say that the most primitive justice judgment is binary: "*a* is more just than *b*." Such a comparative judgment would be primitive as it is not a comparison of two judgments—of *a*'s and *b*'s justice. Furthermore, on this understanding of the comparative nature of justice, because all judgments of justice share this primitive binary comparative structure with preference, just as we could have intransitive pref-

required, and impermissible. On the contrast between deontic and optimizing evaluations, see Wiens, "Against Ideal Guidance," pp. 437ff. Such deontic judgments are crucial to Estlund's and others' evaluations of ideal justice. See, for example, Estlund's "Human Nature and the Limits (If Any) of Political Philosophy" and Lawford-Smith, "Non-ideal Accessibility." It is important to stress that such deontic judgments may well be a part of the principles and rules that partially constitute a social world and its evaluation; the point is that the overall evaluation of the justice of the world, required by the Social Realizations Condition, employs a richer classification system.

[9] Broome, *Ethics Out of Economics*, p. 164.

erences (x is preferred to y, y is preferred to z, yet z is preferred to x), we could also have intransitive judgments of justice (a is more just than b, b is more just than c, yet c is more just than a).[10] As is well known, unless we impose some sort of transitivity axiom (as does Sen's social choice theory approach; §I.1.3) pairwise judgments made on the basis of N-dimensional underlying considerations can lead to a host of such pathologies.[11]

Because of this, without modification (such as imposing consistency conditions) such a strictly comparative approach is inappropriate as a model of ideal theorizing: the Social Realizations Condition may well not be met. Very roughly, unless we impose some sort of transitivity on the set of binary judgments in $\{X\}$ (thereby creating an ordering of $\{X\}$) we cannot be assured that there will be a best element in the set—an ideal. A set with cycles at the top of the ordering of $\{X\}$ would leave us without an ideal, and cycles involving many elements in the middle could lead us around in circles in our quest for greater justice.[12] To avoid these problems, I model the evaluation of the justice of social worlds as based on a scalar function jointly defined by the evaluative standards, the world features and the mapping function, which is not inherently comparative (though, importantly, neither is it categorical). On this model, an evaluative perspective Σ has a set of evaluative standards (ES) and a consistent way of applying them to social worlds (MP), which generate for any social world a score of its justice, which is about the justice of *its* world without comparison to others. Comparing the justice of two social worlds is thus not a primitive binary relation, but a comparison of two different justice evaluations. Some understanding of comparative justice along these lines is necessary if we are to model the Social Realizations Condition: our ideal theory requires an optimal element (the ideal) in

[10] For an argument that our moral thinking is characterized by such cycles, see Temkin, *Rethinking the Good.*

[11] The Condorcet Paradox is the core case of this. If, however, individuals are evaluating the options $\{x, y, z\}$ in terms of a single dimension of evaluation (say, on a left-right continuum), intransitive social preferences over the triplet cannot arise. See my *On Philosophy, Politics, and Economics*, pp. 154–64. See also D'Agostino, *Incommensurability and Commensuration.*

[12] Somewhat weaker conditions than full transitivity would suffice to avoid this outcome. See Sen, *Collective Choice and Social Welfare*, pp. 7–20.

domain {X}, as well as a consistent set of comparative rankings of less-than-optimal elements. And if we are to make sense of the metaphor of a mountain range with "high peaks" we would do best to suppose some sort of cardinal-like scale, if only to understand the pure logic of ideal theory.

A quintessential philosopher may insist that something is lost in this comparative (noncategorical) approach: we have only comparisons of degrees of justice rather than two categories, "just" and "unjust," which call for very different responses. Thus the quintessential philosopher may wish to at least introduce a "positive" and "negative" range in the justice scores, identifying classes of "just" and "unjust" societies. Now while in some contexts a binary contrast between justice and injustice may be critical, in a theory of the ideal we are seeking to chart a course from where we are to increasingly just social states. Along the way, we wish to avoid getting much less just than we are presently, while finding a way to reach the heights of justice. To understand this quest for the ideal, a distinction between the areas of the unjust and of the just is not necessary. That said, within a strictly scalar approach (ranging, say, from 0 to 100), a theory of the ideal can have a mapping function such that, unless evaluative criteria are met to some threshold level very low overall scores of justice result, while above a certain threshold the scores become very high and perhaps compressed.[13] Our conception of a perspective on ideal justice allows, but does not require, this type of evaluation.

The mapping function has a number of critical tasks. Supposing that there are multiple evaluative standards, the mapping function must specify some sort of weighting system; it takes these multiple criteria and employs them to evaluate a social world.[14] In Rawls's

[13] Which is to say that the mapping function, MP (part *ii*), need not be linear with respect to the satisfaction of the evaluative standards. This is another reason to distinguish the mapping relation (MP) from the evaluative standards (ES); two theories could share the same evaluative standards and the same understanding of the relevant features of social worlds (WF), but one evaluates worlds in a strictly linear way in relation to their satisfaction of the principles while another is distinctly nonlinear, yielding very different perspectives on justice.

[14] See here Hamlin and Stemplowska, "Theory, Ideal Theory and the Theory of Ideals," pp. 53ff.

theory the mapping function can be understood as the original position.[15] Recall that in chapter I (§§2.1–2) I was skeptical of principle-defined ideals: even Rawls, who was so devoted to his two principles of justice, thought that the General Conception was more appropriate in some social worlds. Suppose, then, that we wish to evaluate two social worlds: *a*, whose features and their realization include severe economic deprivation of the entire society and *b*, with far more affluence. Rawls suggests that the justice of *a* should be determined by the General Conception while *b* should be evaluated in terms of the Special Conception. As both are part of the same theory of justice, there must be a set of underlying values (liberty, equality, reciprocity, quality of life prospects) that regulates this choice; the parties to the original position, in deciding that world *a* is to be evaluated by one principle and *b* another, are, in effect, applying different trade-off rates between liberty and income in the two worlds: in world *b* no inequality of liberty for the sake of greater resources is allowed, while in world *a* such trade-offs are allowed. The model device of the original position thus is part of what I have called the "mapping function," taking a set of underlying values and applying them to the evaluation of different social worlds.

That said, the model to be developed here does not depend on taking the set of underlying values and ideals—part of what Hamlin and Stemplowska call a "theory of ideals"—as more basic than the principles of justice. A theory might take the opposite approach. Instead of seeing principles as ways of commensurating underlying values in different social worlds, a perspective could insist that "in political philosophy as much as in aesthetics, the comparison of certain objects regarding their value (such as societies or paintings) depends on certain principles."[16] Such a perspective could put principles of justice at the foundation of the set of evaluative standards. So long as the principles were specified in a way such that they apply to all social worlds in the domain {*X*} to be evaluated,[17] and the mapping function could

---

[15] I have greatly benefitted here from Wiens, "Against Ideal Guidance."

[16] Gilabert, "Comparative Assessments of Justice, Political Feasibility, and Ideal Theory," p. 45.

[17] See Wiens, "Will the Real Principles of Justice Please Stand Up?"

score social worlds on how well they satisfied these principles, a principle-based perspective can be modeled. What is required is that, in some way, the perspective seeks to optimize the satisfaction of the evaluative standards, with the global optimum (the best in $\{X\}$), identified as the ideal. The evaluative standards, as weighted by the mapping function, yield a justice score for social worlds and thus define the ideal (as the optimum), as well as allowing comparisons of less-the-ideal conditions.[18] Something like optimization is required to meet the Social Realizations Condition.

We should not think of this as a "mechanical" optimization according to some obvious formulae. The mapping function can include weights and lexical principles, can allow for a number of ties, and can be context sensitive.[19] Different weights can be used in different circumstances (think again of Rawls's General Conception).

Also critical to a mapping relation must be a predictive model or models (part [ii]), which yield an estimate of the social realization of the set of justice-relevant features in a social world. As we have seen (§I.3.1), every set of world features will be associated, within a given model or models, with a probability distribution of social realizations. It is simply implausible to suppose that our understanding of nonexistent social worlds is so refined that for each set of features (WF), there will be one and only one possible justice-relevant social realization.[20] That is why we suppose that each well-developed perspective on ideal justice must include a model or models of the social realizations of a set of world features. Supposing this, the mapping function must take the range of possible social realizations for any given set of relevant features (WF), and generate some sort of expected justice score. We can imagine optimistic functions that identify the justice of a set of features (a social world) with the best social realizations that might

---

[18] The case for an optimization model of the ideal has been powerfully advanced by Wiens. See his "Against Ideal Guidance" and "Will the Real Principles of Justice Please Stand Up?" In this latter essay Wiens seeks to identify principles of justice with the widest possible application to, as I put it, the domain of worlds to be evaluated.

[19] As I pointed out at note 13, it could be nonlinear, giving very high scores to "pretty just situations" and very low scores to "less than pretty just social worlds."

[20] This would imply a one-to-one mapping of social worlds on to realizations. Should an ideal theory have such confidence, it can be included in the model.

arise from it,[21] and pessimistic ones that focus on the nastiest ones.[22] And of course some theories seek to weigh the risks.[23]

1.2 Meaningful Structures and the Orientation Condition

Recall the Orientation Condition:

> T's overall evaluation of nonideal members of $\{X\}$ must necessarily refer to their "proximity" to the ideal social world, u, which is a member of $\{X\}$. This proximity measure cannot be simply reduced to an ordering of the members of $\{X\}$ in terms of their inherent justice.

The Orientation Condition requires that a theory of the ideal must make sense of the idea of the "proximity" of social worlds a and b, and how far they are from the global optimum, u, and this proximity cannot simply express their overall inherent justice scores. As I have been stressing, unless the Orientation Condition is met, T could meet the Social Realizations Condition and yet be a simple "climbing theory" à la Sen's (§I.1.3), generating an ordering of social states (and in this sense proximity judgments) purely in terms of their inherent justice; the world closest to a would be the world in the domain $\{X\}$ with the closest justice score. The Orientation Condition requires that we make sense of proximity judgments of social worlds in a way that does not simply reflect their inherent justice.

---

[21] This is, perhaps, one sense in which a theory can be "utopian" without being "unrealistic"—when examining a set of features the theory assumes that they all work in, if not the best possible way, something very near to it. This, for example, is a manifest feature of Bacon's *New Atlantis*, where the ship arrives at what seems to almost be a "Land of Angells" (p. 12).

[22] Thus dystopias. In contrast to utopias, which are typically worlds far distant from our own (for an exception, see Bellamy, *Looking Backward*), dystopias are usually worlds (too) close to our own where things work out about as badly as we could fear. Orwell's *1984* is a prime example. In contrast to *1984*, in Rand's dystopic novel, *Anthem*, the hero's self is not destroyed; this could be understood as not depicting the worst possible realization, or a difference about the internal feasibility of thoroughly soul-destroying realizations.

[23] See Brennan's "Feasibility in Optimizing Ethics" for a model that seeks to weigh the probabilities of good and bad realizations.

I believe that by far the best way to think about the "distance" between two social worlds is in terms of how similar their underlying features are (see further §II.1.3). When I say that social world a is "very close" to social world b, I shall mean that it is very similar to it. This makes sense of the critical idea that the ideal orients our pursuit of justice by providing a direction of our endeavors. We move toward the ideal by making our world more like it, by changing our institutions and background facts so that they better align with the ideal world. The insight that the ideal is needed to give direction to our endeavors for reform cannot, as I have been arguing, simply be that we should reform so as to make our society more just; no doubt that is true, but, once again, Sen's climbing model can perfectly accommodate that. To say that the ideal gives direction for reform is to say that we know the sort of society (its world features) that characterizes the ideal, and this knowledge should help us in reforming the characteristics of our society.

Consequently, we need to add a fourth element to a perspective on justice that underlies a theory in which the ideal is ineliminable: the perspective must be able to generate consistent judgments of the form, that, with respect to the justice-relevant features, "social world a is more similar to b than a is to c," which I shall denote as $[(a\sim b)>(a\sim c)]$.[24] Given the underlying features (WF) of worlds a, b, and the ideal, u, an ineliminably ideal perspective must be able to judge whether a or b is more similar to u in its defining features. This seems intuitive. Those worlds that, according to the world feature (WF) element of perspective Σ, have nearly identical justice-relevant properties will be seen by Σ as very similar worlds; if the justice-relevant properties of a are almost identical to those of b, worlds a and b will be very close; if the justice-relevant properties of world a are very different from u, it will be very far from u. To say that utopia is far from our current world is to stress how different its features are from our own; if utopia (or dystopia) is close, only a few modifications of our present world would

---

[24] Similarity thus understood is a pairwise relation between overlapping pairs, a common idea. See Morreau, "It Simply Does Not Add Up," p. 484. Morreau's definition is somewhat different but also focuses on pairwise relations among pairs. See also Keynes, *A Treatise on Probability*, p. 36. For further specification of the properties of such an ordering, see appendix A.

bring it about. This is intuitively obvious at the limit: *a* is maximally close to itself because it has the precise same justice-relevant features as itself. The world closest to *a* will be that member of the domain {*X*} the justice-relevant properties of which are most similar to *a*. It is essential to stress that these similarity judgments are internal to a perspective: one of the things that defines a perspective on justice is not only what features of worlds it identifies as relevant to justice (WF), but which worlds it sees as very similar to others.

Understanding "distance" as an indication of likeness on pairwise comparisons conforms to the general literature on measuring "distance" between different systems. As Martin L. Weitzman stresses, "Distance is such an absolutely fundamental concept in the measurement of dissimilarity that it must play an essential role in any meaningful theory of diversity or classification. Therefore, it seems to me, the focus of theoretical discussion must be about whether or not a particular set of distances is appropriate for the measurement of pairwise dissimilarity in a particular context, not about whether or not such distances exist in the first place."[25] I assume that pairwise similarity is the basic relation, on which more complex measures of distance build. For simplicity's sake, I shall suppose that a theory of the ideal can array the domain of social worlds to be evaluated, {*X*}, as a consistent similarity ordering where the end points are most dissimilar from each other. (There are several ways in which such an ordering could be generated, and each has its distinct formal characteristics. For those who are interested in these matters, appendix A explores different approaches and some problems that arise.) I shall call this the Similarity Ordering (SO) of a perspective on ideal justice, Σ.

It might seem that this idea of an ordering of social worlds in terms of their overall similarity is artificial, and simply a result of accepting the Orientation Condition. Not so. In addition to identifying the relevant features of a social world and evaluating them (the tasks of evaluative standards, world features, and the mapping function of a perspective), a perspective on any optimization problem over a domain is useful only if it creates what Scott Page calls a "meaningful structure" or "meaningful relatedness" for that domain.[26] A perspective on a

[25] Weitzman, "On Diversity," p. 365.
[26] Page, *The Difference*, pp. 48, 33.

problem like seeking justice does not simply see the option space as a random collection of social worlds with diverse justice-relevant features, but rather as a set of options differentiated by systematic variations in their underlying properties. The organization of the option space in terms of systematic variation in underlying structures is how a perspective makes sense of the domain; given that certain properties are relevant to justice (WF), Σ then arranges the options in terms of their variations of these fundamental properties. And so it makes sense of the optimization problem confronting the theory. It is thus part and parcel of this view of the meaningful structure of the domain $\{X\}$ that Σ be able to make the sort of similarity judgments that the Orientation Condition requires.

The Orientation Condition refers to "proximity" to the ideal social world, u. An overall similarity ordering is a rough notion of "distance," but only very rough. If we have a set of five ordered social worlds $\{a, b, c, d, u\}$ in one sense we can say that b and u are far from each other, yet it may also be the case that the relations in figure 2-1 obtain. I thus suppose that a sophisticated perspective on ideal justice enriches its similarity ordering (SO) over the domain $\{X\}$ by applying a *distance metric*. Recall Weitzman's observation that "distance is such an absolutely fundamental concept in the measurement of dissimilarity that it must play an essential role in any meaningful theory of diversity or classification."[27] As he remarks, the real dispute between theories that seek to model similarity is not whether a distance metric will be used, but which one it will be. Different perspectives will, Weitzman suggests, arrive at different distance metrics; thus I do not suppose any specific metric for a perspective. However, to help fix the general idea of a distance metric, we can give a formal characterization. Let us say that Σ defines a metric space—an ordered pair (X, d), where $\{X\}$ is the domain of social worlds and d is a function on $\{X\}$ that defines the distance between all points in $\{X\}$. For now, at least, we assume that the distance metric (DM) is constrained by the prior complete similarity ordering (SO) of $\{X\}$. Again following Weitzman, we can say that such distances (X, d) must satisfy three core conditions. $\forall i, j \in \{X\}$: (1)

---

[27] Weitzman, "On Diversity," p. 365.

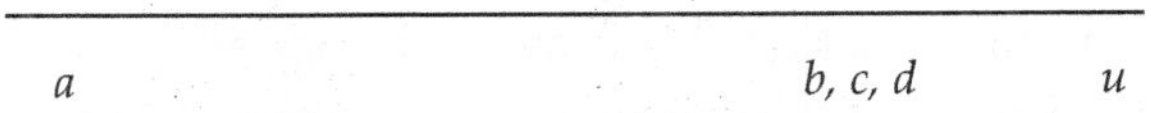

a   b, c, d   u

Figure 2-1. Orderings and metrics

$d(i, j)$[28] ≥ 0; (2) $d(i, i) = 0$; (3) $d(i, j) = d(j, i)$. To which we add (4) $\forall i, j, k$
$\in \{X\}$: $[(i{\sim}j) > (i{\sim}k)] \iff d(i, j) < d(i, k)]$.[29]

With these last two features of a perspective (the complete similarity ordering and distance metric) we now can fully meet the Orientation Condition. A perspective containing the final two elements can generate an overall evaluation of nonideal members of $\{X\}$, not simply by referring to their individual justice scores (as the Social Realizations Condition requires), but also by their similarity-distance to the ideal social world, u, which is a member of $\{X\}$. Social world u, we can say, is the global optimum in $\{X\}$—it has the greatest justice score. But the distance metric implies that some world i, whose justice score is close to that of u might not be close in this second sense—its underlying structure could be far from u's. Once again, it is important to stress that introducing the distance metric is by no means an artificial idea simply motivated by my statement of the Orientation Condition. If we seek to understand how our social world is similar to others, and which are most similar to the ideal, and this is not to collapse into Sen's nonideal climbing model (§I.1.3), some understanding of overall structural similarity is critical, and distance metrics are standard in modeling the similarity (or diversity) of different elements in a given domain (e.g., ecosystems).

We now have specified five elements of any evaluative perspective suited to ideal justice:

(ES) A set of evaluative standards;

(WF) An identification of the relevant features of social worlds;

---

[28] Read as "the distance between i and j." I assume in (4) that i, j, and k are different social worlds. See Weitzman, "On Diversity," pp. 364–65. Weitzman develops distance metric of similarity with attractive features.

[29] Condition (4) ensures that the distance metric is constrained by the similarity ordering.

(MP) A mapping relation from evaluative standards to the justice-relevant features of social worlds, yielding a justice score for each social world;

(SO) An ordering of the underlying structures as identified in WF that relates the social worlds in {X} in terms of a complete, consistent similarity ordering;

(DM) A distance metric applied to this similarity ordering.

Together ES, WF, and MP satisfy the Social Realizations Condition, while SO and DM satisfy the Orientation Condition.

1.3 Why Not Feasibility?

I have interpreted the Orientation Condition as requiring a second dimension of evaluation (in addition to the intrinsic justice of a social world), that of similarity of justice-relevant structures and background facts. No doubt some readers have been puzzled, assuming that this second dimension must be some sort of feasibility metric or space. Indeed, in Simmons's rejoinder to Sen's "climbing model," he insists that a mere ordering of states of affairs in terms of their intrinsic justice will not suffice because, in addition to the height (justice score) of a location, we are interested in "feasible paths to the highest peak of perfect justice" (§I.1.3).[30] So: why not feasibility rather than similarity?

I certainly do not deny that, in many respects and in many contexts, feasibility is critical. I have insisted that some notion of feasibility—no matter how optimistic—is always part of modeling a possible world and its justice (§I.3.1); because the mapping function includes such models of worlds, a notion of feasibility is intrinsic to our account of perspectives on justice. And, of course, to make sound action recommendations to a person, a political entity, or a collectivity, a different sort of feasibility consideration is critical—the feasibility of moves from one social world to another. The importance of feasibility in many contexts is undeniable.[31] Our present concern however, is

---

[30] Simmons, "Ideal and Nonideal Theory," p. 35.
[31] See Brennan and Pettit, "The Feasibility Issue."

whether something like a "feasibility metric" can satisfy the Orientation Condition in ideal theories of justice.

I think it is quite clear that, while recent work in political theory has focused on feasibility as central to the "ideal/nonideal debate," it is not an appropriate metric by which to satisfy the Orientation Condition. Gilabert and Lawford-Smith analyze feasibility as a four-placed predicate of the form: "It is feasible for X to ϕ to bring about O in Z," where X is an agent, ϕ a set of actions, O a set of outcomes, and Z a context, which "might be broad, ranging over all of human history, or narrow, limited to a particular time and a particular place."[32] Notice that feasibility is indexed to agents, time spans, and contexts. Thus outcome O may be feasible for Alf at time t_1 in circumstances C_1, but not at time t_2, but might be again feasible at t_3, though now the circumstances have changed. Perhaps it was feasible for Betty only at t_2 in circumstances C_2. For a theory of the ideal to specify a plausible feasibility space to orient our quest for justice, it would have to specify not only the agent (for example, feasibility could be defined in terms of the US Congress, the American people, Western society), but a time period. Suppose then a theory specifies Z as "any time within the next decade" and X = "US Congress and president." So only things that are feasible throughout the entire decade for the American Congress and president are in the feasibility space. But again, even *this* claim must be indexed to time. At the beginning of the decade, time t_0, it may be true that (*i*) Congress along with the president can ϕ to achieve outcome O any time during the time span t_0–t_{10}. But what Congress can achieve any time in the decade is apt to change as the decade proceeds, and Congress and the president take other actions that impact on whether ϕ can still achieve outcome O. Thus at time t_3, it may (*ii*) be false that Congress can ϕ to achieve outcome O during the remaining time span t_3–t_{10}, which would contradict claim (*i*), unless each is further indexed to a certain time for which it is true.

For example, in the American Civil War many in the North commenced the war to restore the union to something like its antebellum form, with slavery permitted in the southern states (but not federal territories). This was also the initial aim of Lincoln, and it certainly

[32] Gilabert and Lawford-Smith, "Political Feasibility," p. 812.

seemed feasible at the outbreak of the war; it is plausible to say that for most in the North the war was undertaken to achieve this end. But Lincoln decided that the Emancipation Proclamation was needed for successful prosecution of the war; after it, and after the years of bloody battles, it was very likely no longer feasible in 1863 that the union could be restored its antebellum form, even though the Democratic Party fought the 1864 election on a platform basically devoted to achieving it. In this case an aim O that was perfectly feasible in 1861 (and in 1861 would seem feasible throughout the next five years) became infeasible—interestingly, *because of events that were instigated to achieve O*, in 1864. Given the way feasibility changes as actors proceed through time, it seems important to always index feasibility judgments to the time of evaluation.[33] But, of course, then "feasibility space" is highly unstable, and that seems inappropriate for a theory of justice.

Additionally, feasibility judgments have many different dimensions, which operate over differing time spans, agents, and contexts. Wiens nicely sketches the many different dimensions of feasibility:

> We can make our assessment more tractable by grouping the relevant facts into analytically useful general categories. Some straightforwardly rigid constraints are logical consistency, the laws of nature and human biology. But we should also attend to less rigid, more malleable constraints. I only present a few salient examples here, leaving development of a full list as a practical exercise: ability constraints, which comprise facts about human abilities; cognitive constraints, which comprise facts about our cognitive capacity, including cognitive biases and computational limitations; economic constraints, which—if taken broadly—comprise facts about possible allocations of money, labour power and time; institutional constraints, which include facts about institutional structure and capacity (for example, the number and distribution of veto points in a collective decision procedure and the ways in which political officials are selected); and technological constraints, which include facts about the tools, techniques and organizational schemes available for bringing about new states of affairs. I [include]... motivational constraints, which identify the limits of what people can be

---

[33] See Wiens, "Political Ideals and the Feasibility Frontier," p. 12.

motivated to do given intrinsic features of human agents that affect motivation (including affective biases, prejudices and fears), as well as the extrinsic features of an agent's environment that interface with her intrinsic motivational capacities (including social norms and incentives).[34]

Wiens argues that different features can be aggregated into a general notion of feasibility (though he is somewhat skeptical about how accurate such general feasibility judgments might be).[35] He proposes aggregating all these facets into an overall "feasibility frontier," modeled on the economists' "production possibility frontier." According to Wiens, "we can say that a possible world is a member of the feasible set only if that world is circumstantially accessible from the actual world.... It follows that realizing a state is feasible only if there is at least one world at which the state is realized that is circumstantially accessible from the actual world; realizing the state is otherwise infeasible."[36] The idea of "circumstantially accessible" does not mean simply that no constraints exclude the move, but that given the resources and causal process obtaining in the present world, the feasible state of affairs can be brought about, much like the production possibility frontier tells us what level of production can be brought about in a given economy. Others are skeptical whether the many different layers of feasibility, differing according to time spans, and contexts, can be coherently brought together in this way.[37] Again, even if all this could be done, feasibility judgments must be time and agent indexed. Because the conditions that underlie feasibility are constantly shifting, the landscape of justice would be as well. While we may have to take account of these constant shifts for policy purposes, such a landscape would hardly orient our thinking about justice, providing what Rawls called "a long-term goal of political endeavor" (§I.1.2).[38]

Perhaps, it might be thought, a feasibility space that could satisfy the Orientation Condition could be constructed with some more fixed notion of feasibility, say "social engineering feasibility": social world i

[34] Ibid., p. 7.
[35] Ibid., p. 14.
[36] Ibid., p. 12.
[37] See Hamlin, "Feasibility Four Ways."
[38] Rawls, *The Law of Peoples*, p. 138.

is close to *j* just in case "we" (the agents still must be defined) have a social technology that could (under some parameters) reform *i* into *j*. I shall not explore this idea. But note that any space defined in terms of feasibility will behave oddly. Recall (§II.1.2) that we adopted a constraint on distance metrics: $d(i, j) = d(j, i)$, which requires that the distance between worlds *i* and *j* is the same as that between *j* and *i*. Our similarity metric (DM) satisfies this general condition. A feasibility-based similarity metric would not. As Geoffrey Brennan and his coauthors point out, some social states are "absorbing" in the sense that once a society is in that state, it may be very difficult to get out—such states are "sink holes."[39] Thus a move from *i* into the "sinkhole" *j* may be highly feasible (so, not distant in feasibility space), but moving back from *j* is not at all feasible, thus undermining symmetry: *i* is close to *j*, but *j* is not close to *i*. Note also that "feasible to move" is, at least in one sense, not a transitive relation: that it is feasible to move from *i* to *j*, and that it is feasible to move from *j* to *k*, does not mean that it is feasible to move *directly* from *i* to *k*; in fact that might be impossible.[40] Jon Elster believes that a utopian theory must advocate such transitivity. "Utopianism says that what can be done in two steps can also be done in one step."[41] Elster thinks this is false on its face, but unless some sort of transitivity holds an ideal theory may well be committed to the much-dreaded "incrementalism";[42] in order to get to the ideal, the theory may require that we proceed through the worlds "on the way" to the ideal, in something like a step-by-step fashion. Moreover, the time indexicality of feasibility leads to other relations that look intransitive. If at time *t*, it is feasible to move from *i* to *j*, and at time *t*, it is feasible to move from *j* to *k*, it does not follow that at time *t* it is feasible to move from *i* to *k*, either directly (as noted above) or indirectly (because by the time we move from *i* to *j*, time *t* will no longer

---

[39] Brennan, Eriksson, Goodin, and Southwood, *Explaining Norms*, pp. 107, 128–29.

[40] See here Gilabert, "Comparative Assessments of Justice, Political Feasibility, and Ideal Theory," pp. 47ff.

[41] Elster, *Logic and Society*, p. 57. For a discussion see Goodwin and Taylor, *The Politics of Utopia*, pp. 213–14.

[42] As I pointed out in §I.1.3, ideal theorists often wrongly charge Sen's "pairwise" comparison approach with being "incrementalist." I *do* defend incrementalism in chapter IV, so this lack of transitivity of feasibility is entirely consistent with the view I shall defend.

obtain, and we may not know whether a move from j to k is feasible at time t_2). Whatever else may be the case with this complicated idea, feasibility space is certainly oddly behaved and shifting—indeed rather *dis*orienting.

For a number of reasons, then, the Orientation Condition should not be interpreted in terms of feasibility. As Juha Räikkä observes, "To construct a political theory is not necessarily to engage in politics.... A political theory concerns the issue of what one is justified in *thinking* about the moral status of societal institutions, and it does not follow that what one is justified in thinking, one should do at the moment."[43] All this is entirely right, so long as we stress his final words—"at the moment." An ideal theory of justice seeks to orient our long-term quest for justice, not its time/agent-indexed best feasible moves. But this is not to say that even an ideal theory is about only what we should think, not what we should do. They are not ultimately separable, for to think about justice is to think about where we should *move*, and how to engage in this *quest* (§I.1.5). Note that our similarity ordering (SO) is by no means irrelevant to a type of feasibility: we would expect a reasonably high correlation between similarity as I have characterized it and many judgments of feasibility. If a world is very close to our own, and only a few changes needed to bring it about, it is *likely* to be feasible, at least in the middle term, for political institutions and social movements to bring it about. I hasten to add that this will not always be the case, but it often will be, and in most cases we can readily see how we possess the "social technology" to bring the new state about—we can identify a modest number of changes that would need to be made.

2 RUGGED LANDSCAPE MODELS OF IDEAL JUSTICE

2.1 Smooth v. Rugged Optimization

An evaluative perspective, then, allows us to make judgments about the justice and structural similarity of a set of social worlds. Sometimes, as figure 2-2 indicates, a perspective can show us that our search

---

[43] Räikkä, "The Feasibility Condition in Political Theory," p. 30. Emphasis in original.

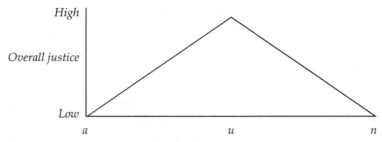

Figure 2-2. A Mount Fuji optimization landscape

for the ideal will be easy. Here the *x*-axis represents Σ's understanding of the underlying structure of social worlds *a* through *n* in {*X*}, based on their similarity (as Σ sees it), as required by the Orientation Condition. The *y*-axis represents Σ's evaluation of the inherent justice of these worlds satisfying the Social Realizations Condition. On this fortunate perspective, often called a "Mount Fuji" perspective, marginal changes in the underlying structure are always associated with marginal changes in their justice. As we move from social world *a* toward *u*, every small change in social structure leads to a small increase in justice. Similarly, as we move from *u* toward *n*, each small change yields a small loss in justice. Finding the ideal, *u*, is theoretically simple. First move from where you are. If you get to a more just social world, keep going in that direction. If and when you get to a less just social world, stop, and move back in the opposite direction: keep on moving in that direction until a marginal change yields a less just world. Finally, move one step back and you will have arrived at the ideal, the most just social world!

Notice that under these conditions, even if we add the similarity and distance metrics to our model so as to satisfy the Orientation Condition, securing justice is essentially captured by Sen's "climbing" model (§I.1.3). We really do not have to know that the highest "peak" is world *u*; all we need to know is which way is "up." There really is no important sense in which the ideal orients our efforts to seek more justice. Thus we see that a model that includes the Orientation Condition does not prejudge the dispute between Sen and Simmons (§I.1.3), it merely allows us to make sense of it. We should read Simmons as maintaining that the ideal theorist seldom faces such a straightforward optimization problem.

Now it may be thought that, *pace* Simmons, ideal theory does, in the end, confront relatively "Mt. Fuji-ish" problems. The thought is this: as we have seen, an evaluative perspective arrays social worlds in terms of their justice-relevant properties—world *a* is closer to world *b* than to *c* if and only if its justice-relevant features are more similar to *b* than to *c*. Suppose that *b*'s justice-relevant features are very much like *a*'s; we would expect that the justice score of *b* would, then, be very much like *a*'s. As we move further away from *a*, we might expect the justice score of *c* would be closer to *b*'s than *a*'s, while the justice score of *d*, the next world out, would be closer to *c*'s than to *b*'s, and closer to *b*'s score than to *a*'s. And so on. If so, it looks like a smooth justice score curve up (or down) from *a*, perhaps peaking at world *u*. On the face of it, minor changes in the justice-relevant features of the social world (WF) should be closely correlated with the social world's justice as measured by the evaluative standards (ES) and mapping function (MP).

Alas, this attractive picture is misleading. As I pointed out above, Rawls insisted that the "idea of realistic Utopia is importantly institutional,"[44] and indeed the importance of institutions is a theme throughout utopian thought (§I.1.2). This is crucial: the justice of an institution, practice, or policy can be dependent on what other institutions or policies are in effect, as shown in figure 2-3. Here I consider what might be described as a "bleeding-heart libertarian perspective"—that is, a perspective on justice that places great weight on free markets and small states, but also values basic government aid to the less well-off.[45] Now:

Let x = Prohibition of deficits;

Let y = Prohibition of tax increases;

Let z = Prohibition on cutting vital services.

[44] Rawls, *The Law of Peoples*, p. 16.
[45] See, for example, Tomasi's *Free Market Fairness*.

Worlds	World with x	World with y	World with z	Total justice
a	✓			10
b	✓		✓	12
c			✓	4
d		✓	✓	8
e	✓	✓	✓	2

Figure 2-3. The interactions of policies and resulting justice

Suppose we start out in social world *a*, which has limits on deficits. Our libertarian may judge this world to be reasonably just because current generations cannot push the costs of their consumption on to the future, and so will be apt to be more cautious about governmental expenditure. But recall that our libertarian is concerned with the less well-off members of society. The libertarian may therefore judge society *b* to be more just than *a*, since *b* protects vital services on which the least well-off depend. However, suppose we move to world *c* that keeps the prohibition on cutting vital services, but drops prohibition on deficits. On this perspective, the social realization of world *c* is a less just world than either *a* or *b* (with a score of 4 compared to 10 or 12), as the prohibition on cutting vital services is likely (given the model used by the mapping function) to inflate the size of the state whose costs will either be pushed onto future generations or funded through increases in taxation. Introducing a limit on taxation in world *d* at least mitigates some potential injustices, raising the justice of *d* compared to *c* (8 compared to 4), but still leaving *d* less just than *a* or *b*. Now suppose that in *e*, as in world *d*, there is a prohibition on increased taxation, but also, as in world *b*, prohibitions both on cutting vital services and on deficits. One might think that the libertarian would judge this to be the best of all worlds. However, now the libertarian's model of how this set of institutions will work out may lead to a "California syndrome," in which expenses can neither be cut nor paid for, giving rise to the real possibility of default on the state's obligations, which may pose the greatest threat to justice of all, leaving *e* the least just social world.[46]

---

[46] Thanks to Fred D'Agostino for suggesting this case.

Note that in figure 2-3, as we move from *a* to *e*, we have "justice peaks" at *b* and *d*, with "gullies" in between. Accordingly, the perspective generates an optimization problem more akin to the rugged landscape of figure 2-4 than to the Mount Fuji landscape of figure 2-2. If the various dimensions (institutions, rules, etc.) of the social world that a perspective is judging in terms of justice interact (on the perspective's preferred model or models, included in MP) as in our bleeding-heart libertarian toy example, then we are confronted with an *NK* optimization problem—one in which we are optimizing over *N* dimensions with *K* interdependencies among them.[47] When $K = 0$, that is, when there are no interdependencies between the justice scores of the individual institutions, we are apt to face a simple sort of optimization problem depicted in figure 2-2. When we face a simple optimization problem, the more of each element the better, and each act of local optimization puts us on a path toward global optimization, or the realization of an ideal. Not so when *K* begins to increase (as in evolutionary adaptation). When multiple dimensions (in our example, institutions) interact in complex ways to produce varying justice scores, as we saw in figure 2-3, we are faced with a rugged landscape in which optimization is much more difficult.

I believe that the *NK* characteristics of the justice of social institutions—that they have multiple dimensions on which they are evaluated and these display interdependencies as in figure 2-3—are critical in creating the rugged justice landscape of figure 2-4. However, this "justice as an *NK* problem" hypothesis is (roughly) sufficient to create rugged optimization problems, but by no means necessary. Even if justice were a simple unidimensional criterion (e.g., justice depended on only one institution and was itself a simple criterion), searching for the global optimum would still confront a perspective with a rugged landscape if the underlying structure that the perspective discerns in the similarity ordering of social worlds (the *x*-axis) is not well correlated with *y*-axis scores. To see this, take the simple unidimensional *y*-axis value of height, and arrange a group of one hundred people according to the similarity criterion of alphabetical ordering of first

[47] The classical work exploring these problems is Kauffman, *The Origins of Order*, especially chap. 2.

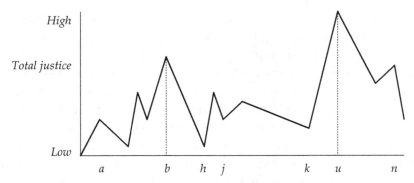

Figure 2-4. A rugged optimization landscape

names. If we array our one hundred people on a line, their heights will be rugged indeed—the diminutive Willamina may be standing between Big Wallace and the 7′1″ Wilt the Stilt. Whenever a perspective arrays on the *x*-axis the elements in the domain in a way that is badly correlated with the relevant *y*-axis scores of the elements, that perspective will generate a rugged optimization landscape (§III.1.2 considers three examples of such ruggedness relating to the pursuit of justice). However, in our model of a perspective on justice, the way a perspective Σ arrays social worlds—the structure it discerns among them—is based solely on the world's justice-relevant features; it is the evaluation of these and only these features that give rise to justice evaluations. Consequently—in marked contrast to our height example in which the scores and underlying structure are not remotely related—if we assume a simple theory of justice (whether there is only one factor in determining justice, or several factors that can be simply aggregated because they do not manifest interdependencies) we would expect the array of social worlds to be correlated with their justice, and so the justice optimization problem to be relatively smooth. That is, we would expect that the variation in the total justice scores of social worlds to be fairly well correlated with variation in their justice-relevant features, approaching figure 2-2. However, when our modeling of the social realizations has significant *NK* properties (such as in figure 2-3), the correlation of similarity with inherent justice is almost certain to be highly imperfect, and so we are almost certain to confront a rugged optimization problem (but see §III.2.3). Of course that a perspective judges that the features of a social world (WF) have interdependencies is a consequence of how it models the interaction of those features; thus we again see the central importance of the often-overlooked mapping function (MP). The *NK* features of institutional justice help explain why it is so difficult to avoid seeing the pursuit of ideal justice as a rugged optimization problem. Nevertheless, much of what I say in the remainder of this book applies even if one rejects the justice as an *NK* problem supposition, so long as the underlying x-axis structure of the social worlds in domain $\{X\}$ is not highly correlated with their y-axis justice scores.

Having now set aside the suggestion that the core orientation point is about feasibility (§II.1.3), Simmons can be reinterpreted as making a point about justice as a rugged optimization problem. *Pace* Sen, in rugged landscapes such as figure 2-4 a constant series of pairwise improvements can (*i*) lead to a local optimum (a low peak on figure 2-4) that is far inferior to the global optimum and (*ii*) lead us *away* (on the x-axis) from the globally optimal social world. If we are at world h in figure 2-4 we could move toward the nearby peak (a higher justice score) at world b, but this would take us further away from the ideal social world, u. *Whether theories of justice are tasked with solving optimization problems in rugged or smooth landscapes is, then, the point on which a critical issue in ideal theorizing turns—whether the climbing or orientation model is most appropriate* (§I.1.3). When landscapes are smooth the Orientation Condition is essentially otiose; Sen's insistence that improvement does not require knowledge of the ideal is then sound.

2.2 How Rugged? High-Dimensional Landscapes and the Social Realizations Condition

I am supposing, then, that rugged landscapes are created by *NK* features of the pursuit of just institutions; a theory of justice is seeking to optimize over N dimensions with K interdependencies between the dimensions. Recall that if $K = 0$, the N dimensions are independent, the theory is faced with a simple aggregation problem: as we increase our success on any dimension we move higher on the landscape. However, as Stuart Kauffman stressed in his groundbreaking analysis, if there are many dimensions and interdependencies are very high, the landscape will be fully random.[48] Let us use the term *high-dimensional optimization landscape* for one in which many dimensions display a large number of interdependencies; at the limit each dimension is affected by all others. In terms of our ideal theory model, in a maximally high-dimensional landscape there is no systematic relation between the justice of social world i and the justice of the worlds that are adjacent to it. Note that in such a landscape there is no point in getting *close* to the ideal point, u, but not achieving it: its near neighbors may not be at all just.[49] Any change of any institution (or rule) in any given world i produces a new social world, the justice of which has no systematic relation to the justice of i. Such landscapes have a very large number of poor local optima.[50] The crux of maximally high-dimensional landscapes is that the justice of any one rule or institution is a function of all others, producing what Kauffman called "a complexity catastrophe."[51]

Because many philosophers are committed to a type of holism, they seem committed to modeling the Social Realizations and Orientation Conditions in a way that results in high-dimensional optimization problems. "A sensible contractualism," writes T. M. Scanlon, "like most other plausible views, will involve holism about moral justification."[52] According to holist views, the justification of every element of a system of values or beliefs is dependent on many others—such systems

---

[48] Kauffman, *The Origins of Order*, pp. 45ff.

[49] In this case the reliance on the "theorem of the second best" (§I.1.4) is appropriate—arranging a world so that it *almost* instantiates ideal social structures does not tend to yield an *almost-ideally* just social world. However, in other cases, such as low-dimensional optimization problems (§II.2.3), it is by no means a fallacy to suppose that coming close to ideal structures will approximate ideal justice. One of the great benefits of the model developed here is that we can distinguish when it makes sense to seek an approximation to the best and when it does not, going beyond rather vague invocations of the theorem of the second best. Note also that our model is derived from the analysis in chapter I of the inherent structure of ideal theories, rather than simply seeking to import analysis of economic efficiency into a theory of ideal justice.

[50] Kauffman, *The Origins of Order*, p. 47.

[51] Ibid., p. 52. See also McKelvey, "Avoiding Complexity Catastrophe in Coevolutionary Pockets," esp. pp. 301–2.

[52] Scanlon, *What We Owe Each Other*, p. 214. See also Estlund, "Utopophobia," p. 121.

are often depicted as "webs," indicating a very high degree of interdependence among many elements. At the limit, the value of every element depends on the values of all other elements. It is precisely such systems that give rise to complexity catastrophes; a variation in the value of one element jumps the system to a radically different state.

Some models of evolutionary adaptation show how such high-dimensional landscapes can be successfully traversed (a species can avoid getting stuck at one of the numerous poor local optima—low peaks on a rugged landscape).[53] However our concern here is a political theory that seeks to judge the justice of various social worlds, and recommends moves based on its evaluations of these worlds. In this context, the idea of a complexity catastrophe is entirely apropos, for the system will be too complex—really chaotic—for the theory to generate helpful judgments and recommendations.[54]

Again, it should be pointed out that while the high dimensionality of an optimization problem can be the basis of a maximally rugged landscape—and so can help us to understand why maximally rugged optimization landscapes are so difficult to avoid for some perspectives—it is by no means necessary. Recall our example of arraying people's heights by the alphabetical order of their first names; here the root of the problem is not the high dimensionality of our concept of height, but the fact that the perspective's underlying structure (alphabetical ordering of first names) is entirely uncorrelated with height values. Whenever the underlying structural array of a perspective that orders the domain {X} is entirely uncorrelated with the justice values (whatever the root explanation) of the members of {X}, a perspective

[53] See Gavrilets, "High-Dimensional Fitness Landscapes and Speciation." The issues here are complex. If we consider landscapes in which data points are individuals and species are groups of points spread over an *N*-dimensional area, high-dimensional landscapes can display fitness ridges that provide paths from one optimum to another. I have greatly benefitted from discussions with Ryan Muldoon about these matters.

[54] Complexity is often defined as existing at the "edge" of chaos. For an especially clear and up-to-date analysis, see Page, *Diversity and Complexity*, esp. chap. 1; Waldrop's popular treatment, *Complexity*, is a classic, yet still enlightening. For a good overview of complexity applied to different fields, see Auyang, *Foundations of Complex-Systems Theories in Economics, Evolutionary Biology and Statistical Physics*. For a philosophically informed analysis of chaos, see Peter Smith, *Explaining Chaos*; for a very accessible (and another classic) treatment, see Lorenz, *The Essence of Chaos*.

will face a maximally rugged optimization problem. For any element i ∈ {X}, its place in the perspective's underlying structure tells us nothing about its score (on the y-axis) relative to its x-axis neighbors.

For the purposes of political theorizing, the problem such systems pose can be expressed in terms of:

> *The Maximal Precision Requirement*: A political theory T, employing perspective Σ, can meet the Social Realizations condition in a maximally rugged optimization landscape only if Σ is maximally precise (and accurate) in its judgments of the justice of social worlds.

Let us say that a judgment of a social world i is maximally precise (and accurate) if and only if that judgment correctly and precisely distinguishes the justice of i from proximate social worlds. A straightforward if somewhat rough way of interpreting this requirement is that a judgment that world i is just to level α is maximally precise only if Σ's judgment of world i does not attribute to it any features that proximate social worlds possess (say $i\pm1$), but which i does not possess. But while this is the basic idea, appealing directly to the features i "truly has" begs an important question, for a critical function of a perspective is to determine the relevant classificatory scheme—what the relevant features of each social world are. To say that world i truly has justice-relevant feature f would be to adopt a certain perspective, and this perspective may clash with Σ, which denies that f is a relevant classification applying to world i. As we shall see in the next chapter, different perspectives endorse different classificatory schemes, each of which insists that its is superior. If we could directly determine which is true, we would have no need to adopt a perspective on the world, but simply to report the truth about it (§I.3.3).

Rather than defining a maximally precise judgment of perspective Σ about i in terms of one that truly identifies the features of i, we can formulate a criterion that is internal to Σ. There is nothing more common in social theory than that our predictions about how a social world will function and its resulting justice end up disappointing us— we who made the prediction. Using Σ, we evaluated social world i as having features {f, g, h} with a resulting justice of α; when we actually sought to bring about that social world, we found either that all these features did not cohere (say, h was inconsistent with f and g, so we ended up with f, h^*, g), or else our efforts to bring about i went astray, and we actually ended up with a neighboring social world with f, h, g^*) with justice β. In this case Σ's evaluation of i (or the move to i it recommended) was not stable before and after the move; on Σ's own lights, it was wrong about i. Let us, then, say that Σ is maximally precise and accurate in its judgments about a social world if its judgments would be stable after moves to that world (or, we can say, Σ's predictions would be precisely confirmed by Σ after the move).[55]

Now because in a maximally rugged landscape the justice value of any social world (as measured on the y-axis) is uncorrelated with the justice of its neighbors (as measured on the x-axis), unless a perspective's judgments of social worlds are maximally accurate and precise, they do not convey useful (reliable) information. Suppose that a perspective's judgment of a given social world is precise and accurate (in the way we have defined it) plus or minus one social world on the x-axis. Its error is in a very tiny range; it is accurate to plus or minus one feature ($g-$ or $g+$ rather than g). This would imply that, given this reliability range, the justice of the world could be of *any* value in the entire range of justice (i.e., y-axis scores). But this, in turn, implies that the perspective cannot generate a useful ordering of the justice of the social worlds in the domain, and so a theory employing this perspective would not meet the critical Social Realizations Condition of an ideal theory (§I.4). More generally, even if we relax the assumption of maximal ruggedness, it remains the case that in high-dimensional landscapes the (x-axis) areas in which proximate social worlds have correlated justice will be very small, and so useful judgments of justice will require great, if not maximal, precision. For reasons to be explored presently (§II.3), I take it that maximally (or approaching maximally) precise and accurate judgments of near, much less far-off, alternative social worlds is a will-o'-wisp; if so, a plausible ideal theory cannot suppose that the quest for justice is a high-dimensional optimization problem.

---

[55] There are complications that might be explored here: for example this might seem to imply that Σ is always correct about the current social world. We could develop more conditions (say, some required reflection or information condition), but this basic idea suffices for present purposes.

This is not an inconsequential result.[56] Philosophers often combine commitments to justificatory holism with the aim of working to an ideal through a series of improvements. We now see that these two commitments do not cohere (at least not without a *very* complicated story). Consider, for example, the recent interest in so-called property-owning democracy as a core of a more just social world.[57] Suppose that a perspective's modeling of how such an economy might work is almost spot-on, but misses one significant institutional fact or relevant psychological consideration; if the optimization landscape is maximally rugged (holistic), then the perspective's evaluation, however sophisticated it may seem, tells us nothing about the justice of property-owning democracy.

2.3 How Rugged? Low-Dimensional Landscapes and the Orientation Condition

As K (the interdependencies between the dimensions to be evaluated) decreases (*i*) the number of local optima (peaks) decreases, (*ii*) the slopes lessen, so that the basin of attraction of the optima are wider (the same optimum is reached from a wider array of starting points), and (*iii*) the peaks are higher.[58] Additionally, in low-dimensional landscapes (*iv*) the highest optima tend to be near each other[59] and (*v*) the highest optima tend to have the largest basins of attraction.[60] As K decreases the landscape becomes correlated within itself. More generally, in smoother optimization landscapes the underlying structure (*x*-axis) is correlated with the (*y*-axis) values of any element. In a smooth

[56] Neither is it new. Popper insightfully analyzes the way that holism undermines social experimentation in *The Poverty of Historicism*, chaps. 20–25.

[57] Rawls identifies such a system in *A Theory of Justice*, pp. 241ff.; see also Rawls, *Justice as Fairness*, pp. 135ff. Rawls credits the economist J. E. Meade with the idea, citing a 1964 work. For a later treatment of Meade's, see his *The Just Economy*. For a recent collection of essays aimed at philosophers, see O'Neill and Williamson, eds., *Property-Owning Democracy*. For a critical treatment, see Vallier, "A Moral and Economic Critique of the New Property-Owning Democrats."

[58] Kauffman, *The Origins of Order*, p. 243. D'Agostino notes these features in *Naturalizing Epistemology*, pp. 118–19.

[59] Kauffman, *The Origins of Order*, p. 60.

[60] Ibid., pp. 62–63.

optimization landscape slight variants in current institutional structures (neighbors along the similarity array) produce new social worlds the justice of which is highly correlated with the current social order. As can be inferred from what has been said about smooth landscapes (§II.2.1), as the landscape approaches an entirely smooth optimization problem, Sen's climbing model is adequate. That is, we do not really need an ideal to orient our improvements, for our underlying similarity ordering (SO) of the alternatives is an excellent indication of their justice: we are, essentially, always simply climbing gradients. Solving very smooth optimization problems does not require meeting the Orientation Condition, in which case Sen is right: we can do well without knowledge of the ideal.

2.4 Ideal Theory: Rugged, but Not Too Rugged, Landscapes

Formalizing the pursuit of the ideally just society as a complex optimization problem leads to an insight: ideal theory has appeal only if this pursuit poses a problem of a certain level of complexity. This point is, I think, barely recognized in the current literature, which supposes that whatever attractions "ideal theorizing" might have are independent of the complexity of the pursuit of justice.[61] Recall Rawls's key claim: "by showing how the social world may realize the features of a realistic Utopia, political philosophy provides a long-term goal of political endeavor, and in working toward it gives meaning to what we can do today."[62] If the problem of achieving justice is not sufficiently complex, Sen is right: all we need is to make the best pairwise choices we can, and we do not need to identify our long-term goal. If the problem is too complex, the ideal will not help, because any move "working toward" it is essentially a leap into the dark, which is not apt to provide much meaning. In these chaotic, high-dimensional landscapes a fear of movement is as reasonable as a relentless quest for the ideal.

In the remainder of this book, then, I suppose that a theory of ideal justice confronts a *moderately rugged landscape*. More specifically I assume there are a number of optima with significant basins of attrac-

---

[61] For an important exception see Satz, "Amartya Sen's *The Idea of Justice*."
[62] Rawls, *The Law of Peoples*, p. 128.

tion—so that in a significant proportion of the option space there are gradients to be climbed. Thus, also, a significant proportion of the option space is correlated within itself; within a certain significant space, the justice of a social world is correlated with the justice of other near social worlds. However, we must suppose that the landscape is sufficiently rugged such that the Orientation Condition is well grounded: all the high optima (which would include the ideal) are not closely related to each other, so we really do need to locate the ideal before we can arrive at confident all-things-considered recommendations about which social worlds we should move to.

3 THE NEIGHBORHOOD CONSTRAINT AND THE IDEAL

3.1 Rawls's Idea of a Neighborhood

In a seldom-noticed discussion responding to Derek Parfit's objection to the difference principle, Rawls advances a conception of alternative social worlds in a "neighborhood." Parfit's objection is based on the example in figure 2-5.[63] The difference principle selects distribution (3) because the least well-off do best. But Rawls claims that a justification of the difference principle is that the shares of the better-off are not gained at the expense of the least well-off. As Rawls stresses in his later work, the difference principle expresses reciprocity, a commitment of the better-off not to gain at the expense of those who are already less well-off. Yet we see that under distribution (2) the Indians do better than they do under (3), so it would seem that the gains for British under distribution (3) do after all come at the expense of the Indians, who "lose" 5 units.

Rawls's reply is multifaceted. He insists that the difference principle does not refer to rigid designators such as "Indians" and "British" but to whomever the least well-off class might consist. However, he continues on:

> Ignoring the matter of names for a moment, consider what can be
> said to the Indians in favor of (3). Accepting the conditions of the

---

[63] Rawls, *Justice as Fairness*, p. 69.

	Indians	British
(1)	100	100
(2)	120	110
(3)	115	140

Figure 2-5. A "counterexample" to the difference principle

example, we cannot say that the Indians would do no better under any alternative arrangement. Rather, we say that, in the *neighborhood* of (3), there is no alternative arrangement that by making the British worse off could make the Indians better off. The inequality in (3) is justified because in that *neighborhood* the advantages to the British do contribute to the advantages of the Indians. The conditions of the Indians' being as well off as they are (in that *neighborhood*) is that the British are better off.

This reply depends, *as does the difference principle itself,* on their being a rough continuum of basic structures, each very close (practically speaking) to some others *in the aspects along which these structures are varied* as available systems of social cooperation. (Those close to one another are in the same *neighborhood*). The main question is not (3) against (2), but (3) against (1). If the Indians ask why there are inequalities at all, the reply focuses on (3) in relation to reasonably *close and available* alternatives in the *neighborhood.* It is in this *neighborhood* that reciprocity is thought to hold.[64]

In explaining the idea of a neighborhood Rawls explicitly relies on a distance metric—"a rough continuum of basic structures, each very close (practically speaking) to some others in the aspects along which these structures are varied as available systems of social cooperation." We might take the idea of being "close (practically speaking)" as simply about feasibility, but that interpretation would suggest that distribution (2) is irrelevant simply because it is infeasible, but Rawls never defends that claim (also, the idea of "close *and* available alternatives in the neighborhood" would be redundant if the neighborhood is simply defined by the available alternatives). Rawls's basic claim is that there

---

[64] Ibid., p. 70. Emphasis added.

is a continuum of structures that are close in terms of the variance in their structure, but not necessarily from the perspective of their inherent justice. A natural interpretation of this idea, given the analysis thus far, is that there is a continuum of basic structures (the x-axis in figure 2-4), on which some are close to others, but we should not confuse this type of practical closeness with close in terms of justice scores (as shown by the very different y-axis scores of many close x-axis worlds). This makes perfect sense if we model the problem of justice in terms of moderately rugged landscapes, in which it does not follow that those that are close in terms of basic structures are necessarily also close in terms of justice.

Rawls thus paints an especially interesting picture: there is a continuum of basic structures, somewhere on this continuum we can locate an ideal that orients our quest for justice, but at any given time, the recommendations of the principles of justice are confined to a neighborhood within this continuum. I believe that this idea of a neighborhood of related social worlds is fundamental to political philosophy and to the evaluation of ideal theory, as I shall now endeavor to show.

3.2 The Social Worlds We Know Best

The initial presentation of an evaluative perspective Σ (§II.1.1) and an array such as figure 2-4 presupposed that evaluative perspective Σ yields an evaluation of all social worlds in the domain $\{X\}$, which according the Social Realizations Condition must include the ideal. The discussion of the Maximal Precision Requirement (§II.2.2) introduced another variable: the precision (and accuracy) of Σ's judgment for any social world. Now on what we might call the Comprehensive Knowledge Assumption, whatever level of precision (and accuracy) Σ's judgments possess is, roughly, invariant across all social worlds. Given any two social worlds (i and m) in the domain $\{X\}$, Σ's judgments are (again, approximately) equally precise and accurate. But this simply cannot be right: our current social world is in the domain, and the evidential basis for judgments about the justice of the world we actually live in must be greater than judgments about merely possible worlds. For all nonexistent social worlds, we must rely for the most part (but see below) on predictive models to judge their social realizations; for our current world we can employ our best models to understand it, but we also have masses of direct evidence as to its realization. Indeed, our models are often developed from our current data, or at least with the constraint that they must cohere with what we know about our social world (think how important reports of the Factory Commission were to Marx's theory in *Capital*).[65]

I realize that some deny this: there is a persistent strain in political philosophy that the ideal world would be organized along straightforward and simple lines. In his utopian novel *Looking Backward* Edward Bellamy described "a social order at once so simple and logical that it seems but the triumph of common sense."[66] Or, as Cohen seems to suggest, the motivational structure underlying a socialist economy in an advanced technological society can be crystallized in the ethos of a friendly camping trip.[67] The supposition that the social institutions of the ideal will be simple and predictable is by no means restricted to socialist utopias—anarcho-capitalists seem to truly believe that actual societies will function as predicted by relatively straightforward microeconomics and the theory of the firm.[68] We must not confuse simple models of the ideal (they are extraordinarily easy to create) with plausible predictions of the social realizations of a set of institutions for large-scale societies. Those confident that they know the "simple and logical" workings of ideal mass societies should, perhaps, reflect on the surprising intractability of social norms in small-scale societies in the face of concerted, well thought out, and well-funded interventions by the United Nations and other agencies. While there have been some notable and important successes in altering specific norms such as female genital cutting in some locations, in other places these interventions have not met with success, and sometimes initial success has faded as targeted norms were readopted.[69] And this concerns a few

[65] Marx, *Capital*, vol. 2, pp. 613ff.

[66] Bellamy, *Looking Backward*, p. 1.

[67] Cohen, *Why Not Socialism?* I have argued that Cohen's small-scale camping trip model does not capture the egalitarianism of small-scale societies—it is not, I think, credible that it models a viable large-scale egalitarian order. See my "The Egalitarian Species," pp. 18–19.

[68] E.g., David Friedman, *The Machinery of Freedom*.

[69] See Bicchieri, *Norms in the Wild*.

specific norms in villages whose population is measured in the thousands. And as we shall see in more detail presently, actual socialist utopian experiments were unable to achieve their sought-after social realizations (§II.4.1). When we realize new social worlds we are always struck by features we did not quite anticipate; important causal relations emerge that even our best models did not include.[70] This is not to dismiss the pursuit of ideals; it is, however, to dismiss the claim that we can be confident about a social realization of a far-off ideal because it will be such a simple and predictable world. And even if we granted this outlandish claim, it surely could not be said that all the worlds on the way to the ideal are likewise simple and knowable (unlike the world we actually live in, which is far less knowable *because* we have so much *more* information about it?). Moreover if we granted *all this*— if it were simple worlds all the way from here to utopia—then we would be facing a simple, not a complex, optimization problem, and the ideal would not be necessary (§II.2.3). It is the very complexity of the interactions of justice-relevant institutions that is the most plausible basis of the rugged optimization problem, which, in turn, *requires* orientation by an ideal.

I take it as a given, then, that the precision and accuracy of judgments of justice of our current social world are greater than yet-to-be realized worlds, most especially ones that are far off. We also know that in the sort of moderately rugged landscapes presupposed by ideal theory, the justice value (as measured on the y-axis) of a world is correlated with its x-axis (i.e., similar) neighbors; simply knowing the justice of world i is informative about the justice of worlds plus or minus some x-axis distance ∂ (the smoother the landscape, the larger ∂, §II.2.3). Take, then, our current social world, j, and consider social worlds $j \pm$ distance ∂ (we also assume that the terrain is moderately rugged, so that ∂ is considerably less than the range within the domain $\{X\}$)—the entire landscape is not correlated throughout as it is on the climbing model.[71] For these possible social worlds, not only do we

---

[70] This includes even relatively close worlds. Tanner concludes his overview of policy interventions by observing, "What is almost a constant, though, is that the real benefits usually are not the ones we expected, and the real perils are not the ones we feared." *Why Things Bite Back*, p. 272.

[71] In Sen's climbing model (§I.1.3), every social world (except those at the top and

have modeling information as to the extent they would realize justice, but we have correlation information based on our great knowledge of our present world, j; the justice of our present world's neighbors (as determined by SO, the similarity ordering) is correlated with the justice of our present world, j. Only in high-dimensional landscapes is this not the case (§II.2.2). So we have a larger evidentiary base for conclusions about the justice of $j \pm \partial$ than for social worlds a greater distance than ∂ from j. "Experience and information," Xueguang Zhou concludes, "gained in the past decrease the cost of learning in the neighborhood of the familiar area and put a higher price tag on explorations into unfamiliar territory."[72] Again, this provides powerful evidence that our judgments about the social worlds $j \pm \partial$ have greater precision and accuracy than those outside our neighborhood, where we do not possess correlation information. In a moderately rugged landscape the area outside our neighborhood (i.e., $j \pm \partial$) almost surely encompasses many social worlds.

Another consideration should lead us to reject the Comprehensive Knowledge Assumption. As I have said, our models of social worlds are attuned to our current world, in which they have been developed. Given this, a natural way to predict other social worlds is to predict the nature of the most proximate social world, which, by the very nature of a perspective, is the world with the relevant features most similar to our current world (§II.1.2). A model attuned to our j world will have to be only minimally adjusted when applied to an almost identical world; its reliability in worlds $j \pm 1$ thus should not be terribly far from j. Having done this, we can then apply the revised model to worlds that are $j \pm 2$, and so on, each time adjusting for some slightly different features of the new social world. Now despite its obvious attractions, this procedure leads to rather quickly dropping reliabilities as we move away from j. Again, it needs to be stressed that for ideal theory to be a plausible alternative to Sen's climbing model, determining the justice of social worlds must be a modestly complex problem insofar as the

---

the bottom of the ordering) is one rank more just than the social world below it, and one rank less just than the world above it, hence the perfect correlation of justice and rank.

[72] Zhou, "Organizational Decision Making as Rule Following," p. 262. See also D'Agostino, *Naturalizing Epistemology*, p. 53.

relevant dimensions of evaluation are interconnected.[73] This means, though, that as the mapping function understands them, the justice of different features are coupled; varying one will result in changes in the way other features contribute to the overall justice score.

Our models of such complex, interconnected, systems are characterized by error inflation.[74] An error in predicting the workings of one feature will spread to errors in predicting the justice-relevant workings of interconnected features, magnifying the original error. As this new erroneous model is used as the basis for understanding yet further social worlds, the magnified errors become part of the new model, which is then itself subject to the same dynamic. In complex systems small errors in predicting one variable at an early application of the model lead to drastic errors in predicting the overall system state a rather small number of iterations out (depending on the complexity— ruggedness—of the system), as errors in the initial estimate of one variable both propagate to other variables and become magnified in subsequent periods (i.e., further-out social worlds). The quintessential example of this is weather forecasting. Our predictive models of weather systems ten days out are drastically inferior to our models predicting tomorrow's weather (which in turn is much inferior to looking outside and observing the current weather). It is crucial to stress that this problem of error inflation is part and parcel of the very complex interdependencies that create rugged optimization landscapes, and only if we have such a rugged landscape is there good reason to move beyond Sen's climbing model (§II.2.3). So the problem of error inflation is intrinsic to the ideal theorizing project. The only way to avoid it is to have a simple, aggregative view of the features related to justice, but then Sen is entirely right—in such smooth optimization landscapes the ideal is otiose.

3.3 The Neighborhood Constraint and the Ideal

We are now in a better position to understand the importance of a neighborhood of basic social structures or, as I have been saying, of

---

[73] Unless the perspective is a relatively "dumb" one, as in our height example. See §III.1.3.

[74] The analysis here draws on my "Social Complexity and Evolved Moral Principles."

social worlds. A neighborhood delimits a set of nearby social worlds characterized by relatively similar justice-relevant social structures. In this rough continuum of social worlds some are in the neighborhood of our own social world (and many are not); our understanding of the justice of alternative social worlds in the neighborhood of our own social world is far deeper than outside it. This neighborhood will include those social worlds whose justice is significantly correlated with that of our current world; if our predictive models are powerful, it may extend somewhat further. For simplicity, I assume that there is a clear boundary between the worlds that are in our neighborhood and those that are too dissimilar for us to make as firm judgments about, though of course this is an idealization (§I.3.3), which we will relax (§II.4.2).

Figure 2-6 incorporates the idea of a neighborhood into a rugged landscape model, with some indication in the shaded areas that our knowledge fades (and does not abruptly halt) when we leave our neighborhood, as our models become increasingly error prone. Here, our current world is j, our neighborhood runs from b to d, and b is the "local optimum" (LO)—the most just alternative in our neighborhood. We can immediately see the difficulty of pursuit of the ideal given the Neighborhood Constraint. While moving from j to b takes us to a more just social world, it also moves us further away from the global optimum (GO). So we face a dilemma. On the one hand, our understanding of the alternatives to our present world is limited. As we leave our neighborhood the precision and accuracy of our estimations of the justice of social worlds drops off sharply: we must rely solely on our predictive models (since outside our neighborhood the justice of other social worlds is not correlated with our present justice), and the reliability of these models rapidly decreases as we move to increasingly unfamiliar worlds. In contrast, within our neighborhood there may be relatively obvious local optima, about which our judgments are reasonably reliable, and we are in a position to make well-grounded recommendations that moves to them will increase justice.[75] And this is manifestly important. To make a reasonable recommendation that a

---

[75] Though, of course, we cannot assume that all moves in our neighborhood are feasible in all the various senses of that protean concept. However, we do have better grounds for concluding that intervention ϕ would produce outcome O, part of Gilabert and Lawford-Smith's analysis of feasibility (§II.1.3).

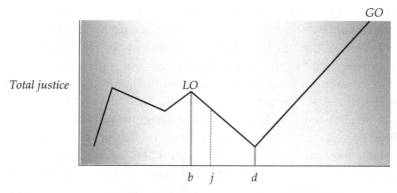

Figure 2-6. An idealized neighborhood

society or polity should work toward creating a new social world, a theory must have reasonable grounds for predicting what that world would be like.[76] On the other hand, ideal theory is intended to orient our quest for justice, but if the ideal (i.e., global optimum) lies outside our neighborhood, we do not know a great deal about it. To be sure, we may have some suspicion as to the direction in which the ideal lies, but we must remember that judgments outside of our neighborhood are not very reliable; if the ideal is not near (and almost all ideal theorists suppose it is not)[77] we are apt to have only rather vague ideas as to how it will work. But then an ideal theory is faced with what I shall call

> *The Choice*: In cases where there is a clear optimum within our neighborhood that requires movement away from our understanding of the ideal, we often must choose between relatively certain (perhaps large) local improvements in justice and pursuit of a considerably less certain ideal, which would yield optimal justice.

It is important to stress that The Choice is not an outlying hard case for the ideal theorist; it is precisely the sort of situation with which

---

[76] To be sure, there have been some "political theories" according to which what is important is not knowledge of what we are getting ourselves into, but following the will of the leader. Goodwin and Taylor judiciously consider whether such theories can be considered "utopian"—I shall simply set them aside. *The Politics of Utopia*, p. 18.

[77] But see §III.2.3.

ideal theory is designed to deal. If local improvements never led us away from the ideal, Sen's climbing model would be adequate; essentially, all we would need to do is to move toward the global optimum. But as Simmons's reply to Sen (§I.1.3) makes clear, the Orientation Condition—and so ideal theory—gets traction when local climbing can move us away from the ideal. Nevertheless, though this is manifest, implicit in writings of some ideal theorists is that we never face a significant instance of The Choice. Recall Rawls's conviction that ideal justice provides guidance for thinking about justice in our nonideal societies, assisting to "clarify difficult cases of how to deal with existing injustices" and to orient the "goal of reform," helping us to see "which wrongs are more grievous and hence more urgent to correct" (§I.1.2). But implicit in The Choice is that to pursue the goal of the ideal we must forego some obvious increases in justice in our neighborhood; rather than the ideal informing us about urgent matters that we must correct, it must sometimes encourage us to turn our backs on some increases in justice—to recommend that we do *not* move in that direction, as it will take us further from the ideal. This is inherent in the very idea of an ideal theory that is distinct from Sen's climbing model. If alleviating the most pressing problems of justice was always part of moving toward the ideal, we would not need the Orientation Condition, because we would not require the ideal to orient our search for justice: the ordering of social states by the Social Realizations Condition would suffice. Our model allows us to see that the ideal theorist cannot have it both ways: that we must orient ourselves by the ideal yet never forgo local opportunities for significant, perhaps great, increases in justice. It is inherent in the project of ideal theory that we must confront The Choice.

Many of the remarks made by ideal theorists strongly suggest that The Choice is relatively easy—to achieve "reconciliation[,] ... to calm our frustration and rage against society and history," "to accept and affirm our social world positively, not merely be resigned to it,"[78] we should orient ourselves by the ideal. But now we see that this is not obvious; by its very nature, when ideal theory is distinctive and plausible, it requires us to forgo local optimization, which typically has much clearer consequences. In the sort of moderately rugged land-

---

[78] Rawls, *Justice as Fairness*, p. 2.

scapes that ideal theory implicitly assumes, there are highish peaks throughout the landscape (§II.2.4); so confronting The Choice should be understood as the standard case with which ideal theory is designed to cope. To forgo relatively clear and perhaps great improvements in justice so that we can seek out an ideal that one's theory tells us lies away from these improvements is by no means an obvious way to reconcile ourselves to our social world. The Choice is by no means a trivial one.

In figure 2-6 the ideal is outside of our neighborhood, and it lies in the opposite direction of the local optimum. This may seem simply an unfortunate case. Suppose instead that the global optimum is identical with the local optimum. Now the rankings derived from the Social Realizations Condition converge with the advice of the Orientation Condition. Surely this is the happiest of all cases for ideal theory.[79] But a worry remains even here: how can we be confident that what we take as the global optimum is truly the global optimum? We know that we have a local optimum that seems ideal—presumably it scores very high on justice—but until we have good knowledge of the entire landscape, it will be exceedingly difficult to determine whether it is truly the global optimum, or whether it is a high local optimum that we have mistaken for the ideal, since the true global optimum lies beyond our ken. True utopia may well lie just beyond the horizon; as long as we are significantly constrained by our own neighborhood, we might never know.

3.4 Progressive v. Wandering Utopianism

Karl Popper recognized this problem and claimed it undermined utopian thought. If we accept that any perspective's vision of an ideal that lies outside our current neighborhood is vague and subject to revision as we move toward it, we are apt to find that utopia moves as we approach it. The social world that we thought was the global optimum turns out to be on a gradient, and so we must revise our judgment as to where the ideal lies. But, Popper continues, as we learn more about

---

[79] Though it is, alas, a case where the ideal is not needed—Sen's climbing model would suffice.

the ideal we might well conclude that we must "change our direction."[80] Elster advances a similar criticism, implicitly drawing on the idea of a perspective. "From my present point of view," he writes, "I have a full awareness of the front of all the objects in my visual field, but only a formal and empty awareness of the side that is hidden from my view. I know, that is, that they must have a backside, but I do not know how it appears in specific detail. Also from my present point of view I know that if I were to deplace [sic] myself to some other point in the field, new objects would become visible to me, even if I do not know which objects."[81] Applying this to the utopian analysis of seeking ideal possible worlds, Elster argues that one may know that worlds even better than the currently postulated ideal world most likely exist, but this fact is graspable only "in an empty and general manner." Once we reach our current ideal, however, we will have a new horizon of possibility, with new possible ideals accessible us. Thus, he argues in support of the inherent intransitivity of reform (§II.1.3): we cannot jump directly to ideal u^* from our current world, because until we get to the "proximate ideal" u, which we now appreciate given our current perspective as a describable ideal, we cannot even really see the better-than-that ideal u^*. Thus we need to pass through u to even know what u^* is.[82]

Some utopians have accepted this and thus upheld what we might call progressive ideal theory. To complete chapter I's epigraph from Oscar Wilde, "A map of the world that does not include Utopia is not even worth glancing at, for it leaves out the one country at which Humanity is always landing. And when Humanity lands there, it sees a better country, and sets sail. Progress is the realization of Utopias."[83] This image of progress qua going from one ideal to the next makes sense if the search meets two constraints. (i) The new, even better ideal, must be visible once we reach our current ideal. In my explication of Elster's analysis in the previous paragraph, I supposed that once we reach our current ideal, u, the next ideal, u^*, will be graspable.

---

[80] Popper, *The Open Society and Its Enemies*, vol. 1, p. 160.

[81] Elster, *Logic and Society*, p. 57.

[82] Ibid., pp. 57–58.

[83] Wilde, *The Soul of Man under Socialism*, p. 40. See also Goodwin and Taylor, *The Politics of Utopia*, pp. 213ff.

Here progress from one utopia to the next seems intelligible. But it also could be that u^* is not graspable from u; perhaps, say, our current ideal stressed social harmony to such a point that intellectual disagreement was lessened, and so we will miss the better ideal, u^*, if—to employ the standard voyage imagery—we first land at "land" at u. If we fell short of u, our current ideal, and landed instead at some less-than-ideal world, perhaps we *could* glimpse u^* from *it*. How, though, could we know this when we set out for u?

(*ii*) The idea of "progress," as opposed to wandering, requires that the new and better ideals are in some sense in the same direction as the ideal we are presently seeking. Again, the conception of a perspective on ideal justice is enlightening. If the new horizons of ideals are worlds where the world's features (WF) are developments of the institutions and other features that we have brought about in our current quest for ideal justice, then Wilde's image of setting sail again looks like "pushing onward."[84] But if, from our new vantage point, we see that we misunderstood the structures that we earlier rejected, which now must be reinstituted, our quest for the ideal looks more like wanderers searching back and forth across the landscape for the Holy Grail. In Sidgwick's imagery, the pursuit of the ideal confronts us "with an illimitable cloudland surrounding us on all sides, in which we may construct any variety of pattern states."[85] It can pull us first in this way, and then in that, as we change our orientation to the ideal. This is no mere theoretical possibility. Up to the middle of the twentieth century mainstream socialism resolutely rejected markets: states that moved toward that socialist ideal developed state structures with tremendous authority and shrunk markets as far as was consistent with medium-term economic viability. When analytically and economically informed socialists (such as Elster) rediscovered market processes, two facts became evident. First, the states that had continued furthest along the old socialist path were less likely to appreciate these new insights, having systematically trained generations that they were illusions (point [*i*] above). Second, when they did appreciate economic analysis, these states were committed to reinstituting many

---

[84] Or, as Bellamy puts it, "ever onward and upwards." *Looking Backward*, p. 1.
[85] Sidgwick, *The Methods of Ethics*, p. 22.

of the features of market systems that the Soviet and Eastern European "People's" regimes spent so much time and effort destroying. An ideal theory must be able to identify with great confidence the neighborhood in which the ideal lies. If it cannot do so, then we must wonder why, when we confront The Choice, we should turn our back on relatively clear local optimization to pursue what may well be a wandering search for the ideal—perhaps in the end the global optimum lies in the opposite direction we initially supposed, and so toward, not away from, our local optimum. Making The Choice to pursue the ideal looks irresponsible.

This line of analysis led Popper to conclude that "the Utopian approach can be saved only by the Platonic belief in one absolute and unchanging ideal, together with two further assumptions, namely (*a*) that there are rational methods to determine once and for all what the ideal is and (*b*) what the best means of its realization are. Only such far-reaching assumptions could prevent us from declaring the Utopian methodology to be utterly futile."[86] This, I think, is rather too strong: a theory of the ideal need not identify at the outset a specific, unchanging, destination. Simmons is entirely correct that "for a while we can just aim ourselves in the general direction of the Himalayas, adjusting our paths more finely—between Everest and K2, say—only when we arrive in India" (§I.1.3).[87] We do not need the precise location of the ideal before we set out, nor do we need to know every one of its features. However, a theory of the ideal that accepts the revisability of the ideal, but avoids wandering utopianism, must give strong grounds for believing that there is some neighborhood that contains the global optimum in which further searching should be concentrated, and that this will be so for a considerable period of time.

Popper is, though, correct that all too often political theorists have been insufficiently attentive to integrating revisability into their theo-

---

[86] Popper, *The Open Society and Its Enemies*, vol. 1. p. 161. Compare Bacon. We are informed by the lawgiver of New Atlantis: "And recalling into his Memory, the happy and flourishing Estate, wherein this Land then was; So as it might bee a thousand wayes altered to the worse, but scarce any one way to the better; thought nothing wanted to his Noble and Heroicall Intentions, but onely (as farr as Humane foresight miught reach) to give perpetuitie to that, which was in his time so happily established" (*New Atlantis*, p. 22).

[87] Simmons, "Ideal and Nonideal Theory," p. 35.

ries of the ideal, being consistently attracted to principles and institutional schemes that settle matters of justice "once and for all."[88] The claim to accurate and precise knowledge of an unchanging ideal struck Popper as both absurd and dangerous—absurd because our limited knowledge of the workings of social institutions is always open to revision and what is best depends on circumstances;[89] dangerous because those who are convinced that they have a perfect vision of an unchanging utopia are all too likely to give into the temptation to march us toward their promised land of justice, their "Paradise Island." John Stuart Mill, another philosopher keenly sensitive to the limits of our knowledge and the need for experimentation, also was deeply wary of such utopian projects. In referring to the "revolutionary socialists" of the nineteenth century, possessed of a clear vision of the ideal that they sought to immediately implement (i.e., without tentative experimentation), Mill writes:

> It must be acknowledged that those who would play this game on the strength of their own private opinion, unconfirmed as yet by any experimental verification—who would forcibly deprive all who have now a comfortable physical existence of their only present means of preserving it, and would brave the frightful bloodshed and misery that would ensue if the attempt was resisted—must have a serene confidence in their own wisdom on the one hand and a recklessness of other people's sufferings on the other, which Robespierre and St. Just, hitherto the typical instances of those united attributes, scarcely came up to.[90]

A century witnessing Stalin, Mao, and Pol Pot disastrously confirmed Mill's judgment; Robespierre is insignificant compared to this utopian

---

[88] See, e.g., Rawls, *Justice as Fairness*, pp. 105, 115, 118n, 119, 194. Despite the repeated use of this phrase, Rawls probably does not have in mind anything quite so Platonic. "Political liberalism... does not try to fix public reason once and for all in terms of one form of favored conception of justice." "The Idea of Public Reason Revisited," p. 582. See further §IV.1.3.

[89] Consider how quaint the utopias of Plato, More, Bacon, or Bellamy strike us today. Of course some believe that we are at the end of history, and their theory of the ideal has glimpsed the owl of Minerva. Popper was quite right to see historicism as a complement to Platonism (*The Open Society and Its Enemies*, vol. 2).

[90] Mill, *Chapters on Socialism*, p. 737.

trinity. The worry that certain judgments of the unchanging ideal will give rise to recommendations for immediate implementation is by no means a "utopophobia" of the liberal fallibilist.

4 INCREASING KNOWLEDGE OF THE LANDSCAPE AND EXPANDING THE NEIGHBORHOOD

4.1 Experiments in Just Social Worlds

The problem confronting epistemically bounded creatures (and even ideal theorists are so bounded) is to devise ways to explore different parts of their perspective's justice landscape without actually setting real societies and their populations on potentially wandering and destructive searches. A perspective worth taking seriously seeks reliable information about the justice of as many different social worlds as possible and hopefully gives good grounds for identifying the ideal or its neighborhood. The most straightforward method—one favored by Mill—is actual social experimentation. Given the variety of social worlds in the domain $\{X\}$, small-scale experiments might be conducted that seek empirical information about the ways in which principles, sets of rules and institutions, work out under certain background conditions.

We might think of social experiments as starting with an initial situation: a set of initial parameters within which the experiment commences (§I.3.1). This can be seen as setting up a small-scale social world. This initial situation need not be in our current neighborhood: we might commence our experiment seeking to institute a rather distant social world (e.g., a social system designed along the lines of Cohen's camping trip). Commencing from this initial situation, different experimental social systems (e.g., utopian communities) might then search alternative social worlds in the neighborhood of the initial situation and, perhaps, beyond, and so together, effectively explore significant areas of the perspective's justice landscape. Each group may employ different procedures for selecting what they see as viable changes in the initial situation, which, they believe, will lead closer to the perspective's ideal.

Mill was a strong advocate of these sorts of social experiments in living. In contrast to his condemnation of "revolutionary" socialism (§II.3.4), Mill was supportive of socialist experiments along the lines of Robert Owen's New Lanark community, and those inspired by Charles Fourier. All these proposals, he stressed, had the advantage of being subject to relatively small-scale experiments: they can be "tried first on a select population and extended to others as their education and cultivation permit."[91] Ideal theorists who appreciate the difficulties of knowing their entire justice landscape, and who agree with Mill that actual experiments are useful, will come to think of ideal theory as less of a political program than as a research agenda. Coping with the Neighborhood Constraint requires a diversity of communities exploring different parts of a perspective's landscape and sharing their results. Here ideal theory does not suppose a fixed point providing a beacon in orienting improvements in justice, but conceives of itself as a quest to discover what and where the ideal—or at least the distinctly better—might be. If successful, over time Σ adherents' knowledge of the terrain of justice could be greatly enhanced as different groups see how different social worlds might work.

Despite Mill's—and many current libertarians'—great attraction to local experimentation, conducting and then drawing inferences from these "social experiments" is extraordinarily difficult. Consider, for example, the fascinating experimental efforts of Robert Owen and his followers. Lenark was a village in Scotland, consisting of mills and workers' dormitories, founded in 1786 by David Dale. Owen, Dale's son-in-law, became manager and part owner by 1810 and set about reforming the community on something akin to socialist principles.[92] Owen's evaluative standards (ES) stressed rationality, cooperation, and minimizing competition, and his conceptions of the relevant features (WF) focused on the importance of social institutions in shaping personality as well as in producing more cooperative people and, especially, educating citizens to make them more rational, which, in turn, would render them more social. Owen's fame from this initial experiment led to the establishment of a number of experimental

---

[91] Mill, *Chapters on Socialism*, p. 737.
[92] For Robert Owen's own account, see his *A New View of Society*.

Owenite communities in Great Britain and the United States—something like twenty-three in all.[93] The great American experiment was New Harmony, Indiana, founded in 1825. Like most Owenite communities it was characterized by internal disputes, effectively breaking into three communities in 1826, with the experiment effectively ending in 1827. The Lanarkshire community lasted from 1825 to 1827; the one in Ralahine in Ireland from 1831 to 1833; and the one in Hampshire from 1839 to 1845, but it was riven with division by the end.[94] Many other communities expired very quickly.

That the communities did not persist by no means shows that they were not valuable as experiments; we might think that a good deal was discovered as how *not* to organize an Owenite social world.[95] (Recall Thomas Edison's remark about his long search for the incandescent light bulb: "I have not failed. I've just found 10,000 ways that won't work.") The problem with drawing inferences from the communities' failures is rather subtler. In order to view these as experiments seeking to fill out the Owenite perspective's justice landscape, we have to see them as all seeking to base their pursuit of justice on Owenite evaluative standards and stressing the features of social worlds that Owen thought were relevant to achieving a just society. Thus the experimental aim would be to vary, say, the rules by which the various communities lived and the way they educated members, and then observe how well these realizations scored on Owenite standards. Owen clearly recognized that the variations and changes within communities needed to be constrained to social rules and not basic matters of justice (i.e., Owenite evaluative standards could not be challenged), and so he sought to restrict the ambit of committees running the experiments to nonbasic changes. But this restriction of the decision-making powers of the community—which was necessary if the experiments

[93] Haworth, "Planning and Philosophy."

[94] Kumar, "Utopian Thought and Communal Practice," p. 18.

[95] Ibid., p. 19. A grave problem, however, is to distinguish endogenous causes of collapse (which suggest problems with how the social world was ordered) from exogenous ones, e.g., the environment in which the experiments took place. That the Ralahine experiment failed after its "proprietor, John Scott Vandeleur, gambled away his fortune in the clubs of Dublin and fled the country to escape his creditors" can hardly be said to show us much about the viability of Owenism. Haworth, "Planning and Philosophy," p. 151.

were to genuinely explore the Owenite perspective—was a critical cause of disputes that unraveled the communities, as some members sought to revise the evaluative standards (as in New Harmony, where inequality was a cause of dispute, leading to a splinter community, the Community of Equality).[96] Thus in the end, restricting communities to exploring only the Owenite perspective, which was necessary to see them as actual Owenite experiments, was itself a critical source of failure. Residents rebelled against the limitations on their decision making that the very nature of a true experiment required. Perhaps Owen was not merely making excuses when, in 1840, he declared, "My principles have never been carried out."[97]

To generalize the lessons of the Owenite tale, in order for actual small-scale experiments to help the proponents of perspective Σ to better know the social worlds in domain $\{X\}$ almost all the elements of Σ's perspective would have to characterize each experimental group. They would have to concur on evaluative standards, on an understanding of the relevant features of the social world, on the trade-offs of values characterizing the (second part of the) mapping relation, on an understanding of the similarity of the underlying structures, and on the distance metric (§II.1).[98] They would, presumably, omit the modeling part of the mapping function (element $[i]$), as they are engaging in actual experiments to discover the social realizations of these worlds. Enthusiasts of social experiments often fail to perceive that the very value of the experiment depends on *not* permitting a number of variables to be altered; if the basic features of the perspective can be altered, the results of the experiment will not be helpful in orienting a particular perspective's pursuit of justice. It is noteworthy that Owenite communities such as New Lanark and Ralahine were owned by proprietors or subscribers; this sought to convert the social experi-

---

[96] Haworth, "Planning and Philosophy," p. 153; Kumar, "Utopian Thought and Communal Practice," p. 18.

[97] Quoted in Haworth, "Planning and Philosophy," p. 152.

[98] Without this prohibition the groups develop different perspectives, rather than exploring the same one. As we will see presently, and especially in the next chapter, different perspectives can be of great use in solving optimization problems, but their benefits and problems are different from models in which the teams share all the elements of a perspective, and simply explore different parts of the same optimization space.

ment into a management exercise, where the manager (owner) sets the criteria for success and leaves the employee teams to find the optimal solutions. Owen was prescient: these are precisely the cases where it can be shown that different teams exploring the same problem can yield real benefits.[99] The great barrier to social experimentation, as the fate of the Owenite communities suggests, is to stably maintain this model when the experiment is about the pursuit of justice.

Needless to say, the problems of small-scale social experimentation are even more daunting if it is supposed that these small-scale experiments are informative about the application of the perspective to large-scale societies. If they are so intended, it will often be doubtful that their results scale up; large-scale societies will have features that small-scale societies lack, so it will be uncertain how well their lessons apply to large-scale societies. Moreover, unless we have a rather large number of experiments, we will not be able to employ statistical techniques for judging our inferences, which will be based more on hunch. If we try to avoid the problem of inferences from small-scale experiments by conducting large-scale ones, then we know that the number of experiments will be very limited, and so drawing inferences from such small-n experiments will generally be uncertain.[100]

4.2 Improving Predictions: Diversity within, and the Seeds of It between, Perspectives

Perhaps Owen's son had it right: "the enjoyment of a reformer is... much more in contemplation than reality."[101] Not all investigations of alternative social worlds need to engage in actual social experimentation. As one scholar has put it, "Just as the artist invents imaginary worlds, so the social theorist invents pure states of society."[102] Of course our problem is that, while in one sense the social theorist is "inventing" a social world in the model, the theorist is also trying to

[99] For an extended discussion of an example from management, see D'Agostino, "From the Organization to the Division of Cognitive Labor."

[100] Although, of course, regression and other statistical techniques can allow us to draw some useful inferences from natural experiments.

[101] William Owen, *Diary of William Owen*, p. 129.

[102] Kumar, "Utopian Thought and Communal Practice," p. 1.

discover its justice so as to make sound recommendations about where utopia lies—and to do that, the theorist needs to figure out how the recommended social world will function. An ideal theorist seeks to understand far-off social worlds and then report back to the rest of us on how they function, and how just they are.

We saw that actual social experiments more or less bracket one part of a perspective on justice—the modeling of worlds and their social realizations—which is replaced with social experimentation. This suggests a way forward for the utopian: an ideal theory might employ multiple predictive models, and see when these different models agree and when they diverge. In this sense we can think of an *internally diverse perspective*, one that adopts a variety of ways of modeling social worlds, and which seeks to combine them to arrive at an overall prediction of the way a world might work. One case seems especially clear: namely, when the perspective's models almost converge on estimates in the same small range. To be sure, even here we can go wrong, but our confidence in our estimates will be much higher.[103] If we suppose the approach to understanding complex systems that we considered earlier (§II.3.2), convergence of models is most expected up to the borders of our neighborhood. Take again a case drawn from meteorology—hurricane prediction. Predictions typically draw on a number on models based on very different methods and assumptions. As those of us who have lived in New Orleans and have closely followed the models in the summer months know, they usually have markedly diverging results three to five days ahead but converge on one-to-two day predictions. This is precisely what we would expect in modeling complex systems: the further we get from the observed system the more even our best models diverge.

However, an internally diverse perspective can improve the reliability of its predictions even without such convergence. Scott E. Page has stressed what he calls the *Diversity Prediction Theorem*, according to which *collective predictive error = average individual predictive error minus predictive diversity*. The upshot of the theorem (explained in ap-

---

[103] For example, before the North American Free Trade Agreement was launched extensive and varied modeling was used to predict effects; even what seemed like consensus conclusions of the models often turned out quite wrong on critical matters. See Shikher, "Predicting the Effects of NAFTA."

pendix B) is that "individual ability (the first term on the right-hand side) and collective diversity (the second term) contribute *equally* to collective predictive ability. *Being different is as important as being good.* Increasing diversity by a unit results in the same reduction in collective error as does increasing average ability by a unit."[104] Although an excellent predictive model can still beat a collective prediction, the theorem tells us that we can compensate for an error in our predictive model by employing a greater diversity of models, and essentially averaging the result. This is an important theorem: even if our predictive models are not very good, a perspective that draws on diverse predictive models can significantly enhance its confidence in its estimates of the justice of alternative social worlds. Predictive diversity thus can expand the neighborhood by expanding the range of sound predictions, and so mitigate the problems posed by the Neighborhood Constraint. By drawing on a variety of models, diverse information can be put together to form a more adequate composite prediction.[105] Any ideal theory committed to the Social Realizations Condition and cognizant of the Neighborhood Constraint must value predictive diversity.

The ability of predictive diversity to expand our neighborhood by improving our predictions is of real importance, but it is in one respect critically limited. It remains the case that an excellent predictive model can beat the average of a mediocre collection, but how can we know which models are especially powerful and which are mediocre? "Finding out about" the terrain of justice and the social realizations of other social worlds is not so much about making a prediction about the justice landscape that a perspective can subsequently check as it is about, in a very real sense, constructing that landscape. Recall the idea with which we began this section—"the social theorist invents" social worlds. This is not to say that we are making justice up or constructing the principles of justice (though we could be), but that our only knowledge of a far-off social world is our models of it. We have no indepen-

---

[104] Page, *The Difference*, p. 208. Emphases in original.

[105] Surowiecki discusses the example of the search in 1968 for the lost United States submarine, the *Scorpion*, in which diverse predictions within a group as to its location were aggregated to arrive at group prediction that was accurate to within 225 yards. *The Wisdom of Crowds*, pp. xx–xxi.

dent measurement techniques to determine when a model has gone astray, or to decide what model performs best. We cannot, at the end of the day, compare the results of the model to how the world really is—at least, not until we have actually brought it about. As far as our theory right now is concerned, we are making up the landscape while we are investigating it.

So how should we "explore" landscapes where our exploration via a model in some sense also constructs them? Once we see that the social worlds are "being made up as we go, we can see, clearly, that there is nothing interesting to be said about how the space *should* be explored, except to say that it should be explored (as it is made up) in the various ways in which various enquiry teams think best. We should, in other words, devolve decision-making about enquiry to the enquiry teams and let them get on with it."[106] D'Agostino identifies this with a "*liberal* solution to the problem of enquiry in complex environments. Each team will construct and traverse that region of the space which they find interesting," using the tools and models they think best.[107]

This liberal solution is apt to encourage maximum discovery, as each team (or ideal theorist) seeks to model the possible social worlds it is studying in a way that it deems most fruitful. The likelihood that the most appropriate tools and information ultimately will be used is thus greatly enhanced. The drawback is that each "team" judges for itself whether it has been successful; in the absence of shared standards of evaluation, a genuine insight of one investigator is not apt to be taken up by others. In the absence of shared standards of success we cannot suppose that once an inquirer has modeled a far-flung part of the landscape, and announces the resulting heavily model-dependent results, the rest take the report as veridical. Thus, the liberal approach cannot be well integrated into a single perspective. Those using diverse models tend to go their own way. Given the controversies surrounding which models are most appropriate, rather than seeing modeling diversity as occurring within a perspective on justice, it seems more a diversity among those who understand the problem in differ-

---

[106] D'Agostino, *Naturalizing Epistemology*, p. 138.
[107] Ibid.

ent ways. We can discern here the seeds of a dynamic that we will observe in the rest of this, and the coming, chapter: as we seek to take increasing advantage of the fruits of diversity we find that we introduce diversity not simply within a perspective, but between perspectives. The way we see the world tends to influence the models that we think are best to understand it, and so one perspective has some tendency to see some models as more sensible and reliable than do other perspectives. As Page recognizes, a perspective encourages its proponents to employ a specific set of tools for understanding its social worlds and its problems.[108] To the extent this is so, maximum predictive diversity is apt to occur when many *different perspectives* ("crowds") interact, and bring very different tools to bear on a predictive problem. Overall, "the logic of collective intelligence is that different individuals will apply different 'theories,' or more appropriately heuristics, to the guessing task, the aggregate of which results in a highly precise estimate of the variable in question. While each 'theory' would only be able to predict part of the variance in the observed outcome, the collection of theories brought together can explain much of the variance and lead to a highly precise result."[109] As we move from a single perspective employing diverse models, to the interaction of diverse individuals with different perspectives, we move from the importance of internally diverse perspectives to the diversity *of* perspectives.

The alternative to the liberal, individualistic, and diversity-maximizing approach is what D'Agostino deems the "republican approach," where inquirers possess common standards of assessment.[110] Here we would expect agreement as to what constitutes a good model and how to interpret its results. The "republican" approach seems consistent with diversity within a perspective: when one announces to one's Σ-perspective colleagues that one has expanded our neighborhood by identifying the working of a new social world at its edges, they are apt to see this as a real advance, as they embrace the assumptions of one's search. Or, when one group develops a new model, others will grasp its usefulness, and so add it to the basket of models used

[108] Page, *The Difference*, p. 286.

[109] Wagner, Zhao, Schneider, and Chen, "The Wisdom of Reluctant Crowds." See also Sunstein, *Infotopia*, chap. 1.

[110] D'Agostino, *Naturalizing Epistemology*, pp. 138–41.

in the perspective. But while the republican approach enhances communication of results and mutual comprehension, in our case it does so by restricting the lessons that can be drawn from different models of any given social world: only models embraced by the republican community count as informative. On the liberal approach, in a rugged landscape rugged individualist investigators can use innovative techniques to understand the justice of far-off possible social worlds; in contrast, in a republican community that commences with agreement as to what constitutes the correct range of approaches and subjects of inquiry, insightful and highly innovative approaches may be excluded. Thus an exploration of a rugged landscape that is being constructed as we explore it (in the sense that our best models of a social world are the only way to know it—until we arrive at it) confronts the critical trade-off between innovation and communication, a theme that we will explore in some depth in the coming chapter. The greater the diversity of inquiry is embraced, the more apt we are to actually uncover the best insights; but many techniques might not be accepted as reliable by others, and so these insights may not be accepted as veridical. As approaches are constrained to those endorsed by a republican community, they achieve communication of insights, though at a cost of excluding some approaches and their insights.

4.3 Introducing Explicit Perspectival Diversity

The costs and benefits of employing different search strategies dominate much of the literature on exploring rugged landscapes.[111] However, once an inquirer seeks to evaluate social worlds beyond our neighborhood, our rationale for adopting the neighborhood constraint leads us to take these findings with more than a grain or two of salt. *Ex hypothesi*, the inquirer is making claims about the justice of social worlds about which we cannot be confident; the resulting model(s) is (are), in an important sense, creating the very world we are evaluating. If we are to search more widely and yet accept the reasoning behind the Neighborhood Constraint, then a theory of the ideal must explore

---

[111] This subsection draws on work that I conducted with Keith Hankins. I thank him for permission to use it.

ways to expand its ken within this constraint. Besides improving its predictive models, are there other ways it can do so?

Recall again the five elements of a perspective: (ES) a set of evaluative standards or principles of justice; (WF) an identification of the relevant features of social worlds; (MP) a mapping relation from the evaluative standards to the features of the social worlds, yielding an overall justice score; (SO) a similarity ordering of the underlying features that provides a meaningful structure to the domain $\{X\}$ of worlds to be evaluated; and (DM) a distance metric (§II.1). Thus far I have been supposing that everyone shares all these features except, perhaps, the modeling element of the mapping function. Such thorough agreement on the elements of a perspective is, however, an extreme assumption. Analytic results indicate that if we relax the assumption of a thoroughly common perspective, and consider searches among individuals who posses different perspectives, results can be greatly improved.[112] Let us, then, introduce a modest degree of diversity among perspectives more formally into the analysis. Suppose that the investigators now all agree on every element of perspective Σ except the *metric of distance* (DM) between social worlds (§II.1.2).

To illustrate the significance of this sort of perspectival diversity consider the idea of a *distance-contracting metric*. A distance-contracting metric is any metric that increases the effective size of our current neighborhood relative to some other metric. Consider for instance the most minimal and straightforward way in which two distance metrics, d_1 and d_2, might differ from one another, namely if d_2 were to be a scalar transformation of d_1. In this case if $d_2 = kd_1$ where $k \in (0,1)$, then d_2 would be a distance contracting metric relative to d_1. Thus a perspective Σ_2—identical to Σ_1 except for its distance metric, d_2—will view moves between certain social worlds (say, from our current socioeconomic system to property-owning democracy) as moves within our neighborhood, while Σ_1, employing the d_1 metric, will see these moves as beyond our ken. The result of this sort of difference is likely to be debate about the real size and scope of our current neighborhood. An upshot of this debate sometimes will be the effective ex-

---

[112] See Hong and Page, "Groups of Diverse Problem Solvers Can Outperform Groups of High-Ability Problem Solvers"; Hong and Page, "Problem Solving by Heterogeneous Agents."

pansion of our neighborhood. Should those with distance-contracting metrics like d_2 convince Σ_1 adherents that Σ_2 is a more plausible perspective, we take a small but significant step toward mitigating the Neighborhood Constraint.[113]

The point here is subtle and important: just what is within our neighborhood is partially a matter of how far away—how dissimilar—we view certain social worlds. For example, two metrics d_1 and d_2 might agree on the similarity of the underlying structure of social worlds, such that they both arrange them a–b–c–d–e. On d_1, though, a and b are very close social worlds, both considerably distant from c, which is nearer to d and e, while on d_2 c is much closer to b than to d (recall figure 2-1). Suppose we are at world a; d_1 will not see knowledge of a and its neighbor b as very informative about c, while d_2 will; as a result d_2 may include c in the neighborhood of a while d_1 will not. If Alf can convince Betty, who employs d_1, that his d_2 is the superior metric, then he will have somewhat mitigated the Neighborhood Constraint by bringing new social worlds into Betty's current neighborhood, and thus perhaps a better local optimum. This constitutes a minimal difference in perspectives: while the similarity ordering (SO) of the domain $\{X\}$ is the same, the distance metrics (DM) are different.

Once again, it is important to stress that the benefits of perspectival diversity are not merely an upshot of my formal representation of the problem. Consider again Mill's case for what he called "socialism." From Mill's perspective Victorian capitalism fell far below the moral optimum; a form of society centered on worker cooperatives was far better, and perhaps even the ideal. Mill did not simply analyze this

---

[113] On the other hand, even this very modest degree of diversity can lead to problems of communication, a worry that will occupy us in the next chapter. If we deeply disagree about how to measure similarity (or distance) between social worlds, a modification to some relevant feature of the world that I consider to be relatively minor might appear quite radical to you. For instance, I might ask you to imagine a world that is otherwise like ours, but in which people are slightly more equal, though at the cost of being slightly less free, and I might judge that world to be superior to our own. If you have a different conception of what counts as slightly less free, though, you might imagine an entirely different world—one which you, reasonably, might think is much less just than our own—and in this case, it is almost inevitable that we will find ourselves talking past one another.

ideal, though. Instead he sought to show how a society that might appear very far from the one he inhabited could be achieved via the institutions already in place. Mill insisted that the evolution of new forms of partnerships and corporations that render capitalism more efficient would also allow competitive market processes within capitalism to test the viability of socialist experiments. By connecting the idea of worker cooperatives to a series of intermediate social worlds, he sought to bring socialism into the neighborhood of Victorian capitalism. Rather than a leap into the dark, Mill depicted socialism as a form of industrial organization within the current neighborhood.

5 THE LIMITS OF LIKE-MINDEDNESS

As we saw in chapter I, for a theory of ideal justice to orient the search for improvements in justice and, simultaneously, for the identification of the ideal to be critical, two conditions must be met: Social Realizations and Orientation. The first ensures that our ideal theory will help us make the choices between less-than-ideal social worlds that usually compose our option set. When the Social Realizations Condition is met our theory can provide guidance as to whether one social world secures more or less justice than another. This allows us to form judgments of comparative justice as well as sometimes being in the position to recommend reforms that increase justice. As I stressed, however, the Social Realizations Condition alone does not require reference to an ideal; Sen's "climbing" model meets this condition, and it strenuously abjures any appeal to the best or optimal social realization of justice. The ideal is necessary to orient us not simply when we are concerned with ranking the options in terms of their justice, but when our choice confronts at least two dimensions: how just a social world is, and whether changing the features of the world moves it closer to the features of the ideal.

In this chapter I have explored a model of these types of searches—rugged landscapes, which have been developed in other contexts in different ways. Some model along these lines, I have argued, is implicit in the very idea of ideal theory as a distinctive and necessary approach to political theory. To be sure, the model I have developed is a simple one; for example, "directionality" has been assumed to be unidimensional (there is only one overall dimension of similarity). This, of course, is an "idealization" (i.e., simplification), but if we make the model more complex (say by assuming that we could move north, south, east, or west, rather than simply to the right or left),[114] the problems for the ideal theorist become more, not less, difficult. In this simple model I have supposed that ideal theory identifies a perspective on justice that, in principle, generates a terrain of justice for a set of possible social worlds; the aim is to find the global optimum while also making improvements in justice in the less-than-perfectly just social worlds that confront us.

The critical claim of this chapter is that in this terrain the ideal theorist confronts the Neighborhood Constraint: we have far better information about the realization of justice in our neighborhood than in far-flung social worlds. I have tried to show that a variety of considerations lead to this conclusion: the correlation of the justice values of proximate locations in moderately rugged landscapes (which are the sort that ideal theory must be supposing); error inflation as models of complex social dynamics depart from observed social worlds (and ideal theory must be assuming moderate complexity); the fact that our models are calibrated to our social world; the mass of empirical evidence about the dynamics of our social world; and the differential costs of discovery about our neighborhood and far-flung worlds. Despite all this I have found that philosophers often simply deny the Neighborhood Constraint (given the status of Plato in the profession, perhaps this should not be surprising). Distant possible social worlds, they have insisted, may be quite simple to understand and model, and so we know them better than our neighboring worlds. I know of no systematic analysis that supports this conclusion: it is at best a mere, not terribly plausible conjecture. The question, I have stressed, is not whether a philosopher can "invent" a simple world of perfect justice that looks like a camping trip or a perfectly competitive market in private security firms, but rather the philosopher's grounds for concluding that the realization of this social world, with the features as-

---

[114] See appendix A, point (iii).

cribed to it and the assumed parameters, will behave in the simple way that is predicted. Admittedly, the theorist can fix the parameters to ensure this result, while acknowledging that this simple world is unrealistic and could not be implemented. But even if this is acceptable for "the ideal" it cannot be acceptable for all worlds outside of our neighborhood, for if the parameters are not ones that are plausible for us to meet in any of these further-off worlds, then ideal theory cannot recommend movement outside of our neighborhood. The ideal becomes mere dreaming or lamentation, as it no longer orients our efforts at reform (§I.1.4).

Because of the terrain of justice, which motivates the Orientation Condition, local optimization often points in a different direction than pursuit of the ideal. We then confront what I have called The Choice: should we turn our back on local optimization and move toward the ideal? Given the Neighborhood Constraint our judgments within our neighborhood have better warrant than judgments outside of it; if the ideal is outside our current neighborhood, then we are forgoing relatively clear gains in justice for an uncertain prospect that our realistic utopia lies in a different direction. Mill's revolutionaries, certain of their own wisdom and judgment, were more than willing to commit society to the pursuit of their vision of the ideal; their hubris had terrible costs for many.

For the ideal theorist to make a reasonable Choice in favor of pursuit of the global optimum, it would seem that much better information is needed about the terrain of justice, at least mitigating the asymmetry of knowledge expressed by the Neighborhood Constraint. I have briefly examined two important proposals: actual social experiments and internal diversity of predictive models. In the context of pursuit of a given perspective's view of optimal justice, both have shortcomings. I concluded with the possibility of expanding the neighborhood, perhaps bringing better optima into our neighborhood.

Although this last inquiry—into how the boundaries of the neighborhood might be expanded—was in one way modest, in another way it was the first step to a more radical solution. In expanding the neighborhood we varied the distance metric, which was an element of the perspective. So rather than searching under simply one common, normalized perspective on justice, we now have multiperspectival searching. In recent years powerful analytic treatments have demonstrated that under some conditions multiperspectival searching has tremendous advantages over single perspective searching in rugged landscapes. We now turn to these results, and their application to the search for ideal justice.

CHAPTER III

The Fractured Ideal

Searching with Diverse Perspectives

> And they said, Go to, let us build us a city, and a tower, whose top
>   may reach unto heaven....
>
> And the LORD said, Behold, the people is one, and they have all one
>   language; and this they begin to do....
>
> Go to, let us go down, and there confound their language, that they
>   may not understand one another's speech.
>
> > —GENESIS 11

1 ATTAINING THE IDEAL THROUGH PERSPECTIVAL DIVERSITY

1.1 From Full to Partial Normalization

IN THE PREVIOUS CHAPTER WE SAW THAT A SINGLE, FULLY NORMALIZED perspective confronts The Choice: it must choose between local improvements in justice and the pursuit of the ideal. The necessity for The Choice follows from the very core of ideal theory, that the Social Realizations and Orientation Conditions can give different answers as to what social states are "closer" to ideal justice. The Social Realizations Condition measures the justice of a social world in terms of its inherent justice (so, in one sense, the more just a social world, the closer to the ideal), but the Orientation Condition measures proximity to the ideal in terms of the similarity of the underlying structure of the social world, and so a reform that moves us closer to the ideal on the Social Realizations Condition can lead away from it given the conception of proximity expressing the Orientation Condition. The Choice is made much more troubling by the Neighborhood Constraint. If we had comprehensive knowledge of the entire landscape of justice, we would at least know, when we turn our backs on local improvements, just where the ideal lies, and just how ideal it really is. Perhaps the main worry then would be the feasibility of getting to the ideal (§II.1.3).[1] But the Neighborhood Constraint implies that we almost certainly do not have such knowledge; we know near social worlds better than far-off ones. If the ideal is not in our neighborhood, no single perspective can be very confident just where, or what, it is.

As I have noted, all too often ideal theorists respond to this with sheer denial. We *do*, they assert, have comprehensive knowledge of far-off social worlds; we know how utopia would work as well as how America in 2016 does. I join Popper in dismissing this as sheer delusion; the case for deep uncertainty in our understanding of the workings of far-off worlds is overwhelming. However, there is a much more sophisticated response available to the ideal theorist. A proponent of the ideal may acknowledge that we do not have comprehensive knowledge of the landscape of justice—no single perspective on justice could ever have a complete knowledge of the justice of all social worlds. Every perspective is always learning, searching the landscape, trying to find better optima—better utopias. At the close of the last chapter we saw, though, that a diversity of perspectives can mitigate some of the constraints faced by a single perspective in searching the optimization landscape (§§II.4.2–3). This insight has been elegantly and powerfully developed by Lu Hong and Scott E. Page, who demonstrate that—under what, prima facie, seems to be a modest set of conditions— a certain group of perspectives that agree on some parts of perspective Σ but disagree on others will locate the ideal.[2] Specifically, what the work of Hong and Page suggests is that such a group of perspectives is one that concurs on the core elements of Σ's normative theory of justice, but disagree on how they understand the similarity of social

---

[1] Philosophers working on the debate concerning "ideal v. nonideal theory" have seemed to suppose that feasibility is the main worry about ideal theory. If I am correct, this is a problem pretty far downstream. Before we can know whether it is feasible to seek the ideal, we have to know where it is. It often seems to have been supposed that identifying the ideal is the purview of political philosophers, who can retreat into their studies and identify it; only when we come to implementation questions do social scientists enter. I hope it is clear that this common picture is woefully inadequate.

[2] Hong and Page's characterization of a perspective is not identical to that presented in §II.1; I consider crucial differences in §III.2.4 For his conception of a perspective, see Page, *The Difference*, chaps. 1, 3, and 5.

worlds in the domain $\{X\}$. Let us call such a group of perspectives *evaluation-normalized* versions of Σ. These perspectives all concur on the evaluative standards (ES), justice-relevant features of the worlds to be evaluated (WF), and the mapping function (MP). They disagree, however, in the similarity ordering of the worlds (SO) and the distance metric (DM), which determine the similarity of any two social worlds in $\{X\}$. Recall that ES, WF, and MP jointly satisfy the Social Realizations Condition, which requires that social worlds must be compared in terms of their inherent justice (§II.1.1); these have a sound claim to being deemed the core value elements of a perspective. Those who agree on these three elements agree on what each social world looks like (its justice-relevant features) and the overall justice of each world. Looking at some world, they would always agree on its features (WF) and on how just it is (ES, MP). Thus core normative agreement is secured by agreement on these three parts of a perspective. Let us denote all perspectives that share these evaluative elements of Σ, Σ^V. Perspectives that include Σ^V can have radically different similarity orderings of the domain of worlds to be evaluated and distance metrics; in terms of our basic landscape model, all perspectives in this evaluative core of perspective Σ agree precisely on the justice score of every world, so they concur about the placement of every world on the y-axis; but they may disagree about any world's location on the x-axis. Given this, Hong and Page's analysis would appear to show that members of Σ^V, working together, will outperform any single member of the Σ^V family in locating the ideally just social world, as all members of Σ^V understand it. Thus an ideal theory that refuses to fully normalize its perspective, but opts instead for only evaluation normalization (Σ^V), seems able to find the ideal without making claims that any single perspective (one composed of all five elements) has comprehensive knowledge of the landscape of justice.

1.2 Diversity of Meaningful Structures and Finding the Ideal

Before turning to the details of Hong and Page's analysis, we can get an intuitive grasp of how a team of sophisticated ideal theorists (who share an evaluative core of a perspective) might employ their work by considering a real-world example. Suppose that instead of searching

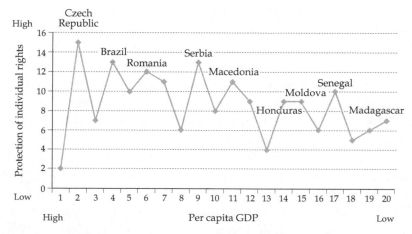

Figure 3-1. Searching for justice on an economic perspective

for the most just social world among a set of possible worlds, our team is searching for the most just state within a domain or set of actual states. If they are genuinely searching, of course, they do not yet know which is the most just state. They know that there is a most just state in the domain, but not what member it is. Because team members concur on the evaluative core of a perspective (state features, evaluative standards, and mapping function), they all concur on where any given state should be placed on the y-axis. However, because they do not share the similarity ordering and/or distance metric, they may disagree on a state's location on the x-axis. Suppose one member of the team has a straightforward economic similarity metric, which arrays states simply in terms of per capita GDP; a state is similar to another if and only if it has a similar per capita GDP.[3] Figure 3-1 uses this perspective to search for the most just state among a group of twenty selected current states: Brazil, Bulgaria, China (PRC), the Czech Republic, Guyana, Haiti, Honduras, Jordan, Macedonia, Madagascar, Mexico, Moldova, Pakistan, Romania, Russia, Saudi Arabia, Senegal, Serbia, Swaziland, and Zimbabwe. Justice is understood in the classical liberal sense of the best protection of individual rights and autono-

[3] Note that this example does not presuppose that justice is an *NK* optimization problem, but only that the underlying structure is not perfectly correlated with the justice of the states. See sections II.2.1 and III.2.4.

my.[4] (Note: figures 3-1 to 3-3 label only the states in the group that are "local optima" on a perspective—states at the top of a gradient.)

Note that on the economic perspective in figure 3-1 there are nine local optima. Although there is certainly some correlation between high GDP and protection of individual rights, seeking justice on this perspective does not create a smooth optimization problem. Suppose a perspective searches for the ideal via a simple climb-the-gradient strategy: if it finds itself on a slope, this strategy instructs it to climb up to the peak, but it will never go down a gradient.[5] Such a procedure will thus never embark on a path that leads to worse results—it "climbs" only "upward." The downside to this strategy, however, is that it will get stuck at the first local optimum it comes to, which are rather abundant on this perspective. To be sure, if the search commences with the very richest states, the global optimum (the Czech Republic) will be quickly hit upon; but from any other starting point there is a deep valley between the global optimum and all other states. Suppose that another member of the team has a different, more libertarian, perspective that arrays states according to their economic freedom, as in figure 3-2.[6]

Note that for every state, this perspective fully concurs with the first with regard to justice scoring. This perspective, however, employs a different similarity metric; as a result it eliminates local optima at Honduras, Moldova, and Madagascar, while adding optima at Mexico and Guyana. Assume the simple per capita GDP perspective is stuck at Honduras, Moldova, or Madagascar and it asks the economic liberty perspective, "Can you see any way that goes up from here?" The economic liberty perspective will, since it will still be on a gradient; in contrast, the GDP perspective will never get stuck at Mexico or Guyana, so the two perspectives can assist each other. Nevertheless, we have quite a few shared local optima; if they are both on one of these

[4] Rights protection data are drawn from the *Freedom House Freedom in the World 2014 Report*. GDP rankings are based on 2013 data and are available at http://knoema.com/sijweyg/gdp-per-capita-ranking-2013-data-and-charts.

[5] This is what Page calls a "heuristic." "Heuristics apply within a perspective. Given a perspective, a heuristic tells a person where to search for new solutions or what actions to take." *The Difference*, p. 53.

[6] Economic freedom data are taken from *Economic Freedom in the World 2013 Annual Report*.

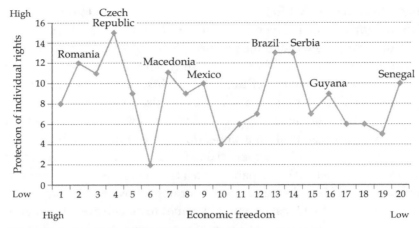

Figure 3-2. Searching for justice on a libertarian perspective

neither can see a way upward. Now add a third member of the team, employing a more political perspective. On this third perspective the underlying structure of the relevant aspects of states concerns how well their government functions, whether its elected leaders determine economic policy, whether the government is free from corruption, and so on.[7] Figure 3-3 gives this perspective on the problem.

The only optima shared by all three perspectives are the Czech Republic, Brazil, and Serbia: *if each perspective can rely on the other members of the team to get it over its own local optima,* (and, we shall see that is a very big "if"), our diverse team is bound to at least get as high as 13 on the individual rights protection scale. (At Brazil or Serbia none of the three perspectives can see a way upward.) Notice that alone, no single perspective can be assured of doing that well. This is true even though the third perspective is in an obvious sense the best perspective; its understanding of the similarity of states tracks the underlying structure of the rights protection problem better than the others (it has fewer local optima). As we shall see, this is an important point: under certain conditions a diversity of perspectives does better than even the best alone.

[7] Government functioning data are drawn from the 2014 *Freedom House Freedom in the World 2014 Report.*

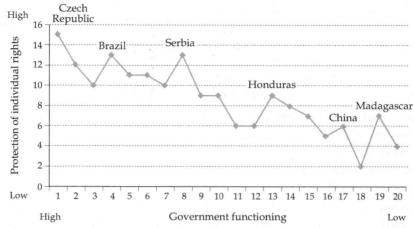

Figure 3-3. Searching for justice on a government functioning perspective

1.3 The Hong-Page Theorem

The crux of our example is how searching a rugged landscape can be improved by what we might call a *handing-off-the-baton dynamic*.[8] A perspective takes the baton (it takes charge of the search) and runs uphill as far as it can, to a local peak. But on some other perspective this is not a peak, so the baton can be handed off to it, and then it will run uphill until it comes to one of its local optima, where it will hand off the baton to yet another perspective that is still on an upward gradient. Hong and Page have identified conditions under which this general type of dynamic is *guaranteed* to find the global optimum—when the ideal is guaranteed to be discovered.[9] At least in some of its core suppositions, their theorem fits well with the model of ideal theory developed in chapter II, as they (*i*) suppose precisely the sort of rugged

[8] My example has the same structure as that given by Page, *The Difference*, pp. 139–43.

[9] Hong and Page, "Groups of Diverse Problem Solvers Can Outperform Groups of High-Ability Problem Solvers"; Hong and Page, "Problem Solving by Heterogeneous Agents." I am giving here an intuitive presentation of a complex formal model. Thompson ("Does Diversity Trump Ability?") has pointed out problems in a version of the proof. She also has made a rather extreme claim that "the attempt to equate mathematical quantities with human attributes is inappropriate" (p. 1029). The logic of the analysis discussed here is not affected by Thompson's critique.

landscapes that underlie ideal theory (§II.2.4.) while (*ii*) showing under what conditions a diverse community will locate the ideal. They thus appear to prove the conditions that guarantee locating utopia! No small feat.

Page provides an excellent informal discussion of the conditions of the proof.[10] (*i*) The optimization problem has to be sufficiently difficult such that no single perspective always finds the global optimum. I stressed this point throughout chapter II; if the optimization problem is smooth, then a single perspective will climb to the global optimum on its own. But then, as I have stressed, orientation via the ideal is not necessary for the search for justice. (*ii*) At the same time, the problem cannot be too complex. Page glosses this as "the problem solvers are smart," and this parsing is at the heart of Hélène Landemore's use of the Hong-Page theorem in her excellent account of democratic deliberation—indeed, as she puts it, the problem solvers cannot be "too dumb."[11] Recall our perspective on height, which sees the underlying meaningful structure in terms of the alphabetical ordering of first names (§II.2.1). This perspective created maximal ruggedness; the height measure (y-axis), is uncorrelated with the name ordering (x-axis). It thus gets constantly caught at local optima; a group of perspectives like this cannot make much progress on the problem of finding the tallest person. However, this assumption is not really only about whether perspectives are "dumb" but also about whether the problem is "easy enough." The real question is whether perspectives understand the problem as posing a very high-dimensional landscape (a maximally rugged one) (§II.2.2). In such landscapes there really are no gradients (each point's justice is uncorrelated with its neighbors), and so no one can really make progress in solving the optimization problem. In maximally rugged landscapes there are a great number of poor local optima at which the group can get stuck.[12] Under conditions of maximal complexity, then, increased diversity does not promote

---

[10] I am following Page, *The Difference*, pp. 159–65. The application of the proof to political life has been admirably defended by Hélène Landemore against a wide variety of objections in her "Yes, We Can (Make It Up on Volume)."

[11] Landemore, *Democratic Reason*, p. 102. Cf. Page, *The Difference*, p. 160.

[12] Landemore, *Democratic Reason*, p. 102.

optimization.[13] We can understand the gloss of this condition as the problem solvers are "not too dumb" in the sense that they find the problem sufficiently tractable—they possess perspectives in which the underlying structure is correlated with the optimization problem. Nevertheless, I believe it is better to focus on the question of complexity: if we are confronting Kauffman-like complexity catastrophes (§II.2.2) we may all be "dumb."

Notice that Hong and Page's conditions (*i*) and (*ii*) are essentially the conditions that, on other grounds, I have argued are presupposed by ideal theory: the landscape is not too smooth and not too rugged (§II.2.4). Too smooth and the optimization problem can be solved by simply "climbing" the gradient; Sen's climbing model is perfectly adequate to this task. Too rugged, and we are all "dumb." Given this convergence of the conditions of the proof with the underlying problem ideal theory presupposes, the proof appears manifestly apropos to the modeling of ideal theory.

(*iii*) The third condition supposes that in the relevant group of problem solvers, the only element of the domain that is an optimum for each and every member of the group is the global optimum. Think back to our searching for the best rights-protecting state (§III.1.2). By the time we included our third perspective, the team shared three optima: the global optimum (the Czech Republic), and two lower optima (Brazil and Serbia). Our team with three perspectives thus did not meet condition (*iii*), and that is why it is not certain they would find the global optimum. If we add other perspectives in which neither Brazil nor Serbia are optima, then the handing-off-the-baton dynamic will inevitably lead to the Czech Republic, as it would be the only optimum shared by all perspectives.

(*iv*) This brings us to the fourth condition: our collection of Σ^V perspectives, seeking to solve the problem, must be drawn from a large and diverse set of perspectives, in particular a diverse set of similarity orderings. Σ^V itself must be a goodly sized group; the more difficult the problem, the larger the group should be. This fourth condition allows that the group of problem solvers certainly need not be the whole

---

[13] Hong and Page, "Problem Solving by Heterogeneous Agents," pp. 149–51.

population (the transaction costs of joint problem solving in such a large group would be very high), but our collection of Σ^V perspectives must still be diverse and "contain more than a handful of problem solvers."[14]

Given conditions (*i*)–(*iv*), Hong and Page derive the "Diversity Trumps Ability Theorem": in our terms, a randomly selected group of Σ^V perspectives will outperform a more homogeneous group composed of the "best problem solvers"—those perspectives with the smoothest optimization landscapes. Moreover, Hong and Page's simulations show that even if these conditions are not perfectly met, "a random collection of agents drawn from a large set of limited-ability agents typically outperforms a collection of the very best agents from that same set."[15] For our purposes the crucial point is not the formal theorem's specification of the conditions under which randomly selected Σ^V perspectives are *guaranteed* to beat the best perspectives, but the dynamic that drives diverse groups to generally outperform homogenous perspectives, even very good ones.

When I analyzed the elements of a perspective in chapter II (§1), some may have thought that similarity and distance measures would be difficult to devise, and so are controversial. The Hong-Page theorem indicates that this is all well and good. If adherents of an ideal theory could agree on the evaluative standards, relevant world features, and mapping relations, but came to different conclusions about the similarity ordering and the distance metric, they could more effectively locate the ideal than if they had agreed on all five elements. The core lesson to be learned is that different ways of looking at an optimization problem are more effective than looking at it in the same way, even if that is the best way.

2 DILEMMAS OF DIVERSITY

Hong and Page's work on diversity is important and remarkable; I certainly do not wish to disparage it. Indeed, political philosophers

[14] Page, *The Difference*, p. 162.

[15] Hong and Page, "Groups of Diverse Problem Solvers Can Outperform Groups of High-Ability Problem Solvers," p. 16386.

should pay it much more attention. Landemore's excellent work has led the way, making a powerful case for the applicability of Hong and Page's work to political problem solving.[16] Nevertheless, as I shall show in this section, it relies on critical additional assumptions that are not always clear; when we interrogate these assumptions, we shall find that its implications for ideal theory are far less sanguine than first appears.

2.1 The Neighborhood Constraint (Again)

The most obvious limitation of its results for thinking about ideal theory is that it does not recognize a Neighborhood Constraint (§II.3). As was explicit in our example of the search for the best rights-protecting state, each perspective has full knowledge of the justice scores of each element in the domain. We supposed that each perspective, when some world is brought to its attention, knows how that world scores in terms of justice (the y-axis). And this is critical to the analysis: when the per capita GDP perspective proclaims that it is stuck at Moldova with a score of 9, the economic liberty perspective locates Moldova on its perspective, agrees that it is a 9, sees that it is not a local optimum, and so can carry the baton further than 9, and (as it turns out) can go up to Macedonia, which scores 11. Now if the set of worlds to be searched is itself a neighborhood on which all perspectives converge, then within that neighborhood the Hong-Page theorem is applicable to *our* problem; it nicely shows how diverse Σ^V perspectives can better explore a common neighborhood. But the rub here is that diverse perspectives tend to disagree on the neighborhood—which is precisely why they can help each other. A neighborhood of the domain $\{X\}$ is a function of a perspective's similarity ordering (SO) and its distance metric (DM). To put the point somewhat simplistically: it is precisely because diverse Σ^V perspectives concur on the ordering of the elements on the y-axis (the justice scores) while disagreeing on the ordering of the x-axis that the diverse group can climb up the y-axis. But the diversity of the x-axis, unless very constrained, inevitably produces a diversity of neighborhoods. If we again go back to our perspectives on

---

[16] Landemore, *Democratic Reason*, chap. 4.

rights protection, on the GDP perspective Brazil and Romania are neighbors, while on the economic liberty perspective they are far apart; it is this very diversity of neighborhoods that drives the result, but which severely limits its applicability to ideal theory. Let us call this:

> *The Neighborhood Diversity Dilemma*: Diversity of Σ^V perspectives improves the search within a neighborhood, but as we increase diversity of Σ^V perspectives, they disagree about what our current neighborhood is.

Given that the heart of the Hong-Page theorem is the benefits of *high* diversity, but high diversity almost surely means the perspectives disagree on the neighborhoods, its applicability to our problem seems limited indeed.

2.2 The Theorem and Actual Politics

It needs to be stressed that this does not imply that the Hong-Page theorem is of limited applicability in all political contexts, such as collective deliberation. If a group concurs on the domain of options and the scores of each option are known by (or agreed to by) all, Hong and Page's analysis gets real traction in explaining why collective decision making is apt to outperform individual judgments—even expert ones— in actual deliberative contexts. Landemore and Page have recently argued that consensus in identifying the best solution to a problem is a plausible assumption in many political contexts. "We assume then that participants have already reached consensus on the criteria for evaluation [ES] and how those criteria will be weighted [MP (part *ii*)]."[17] Note that they suppose agreement on some of the elements of a perspective as understood in this work, the evaluative standards and the mapping function's weighting task.[18] Given this, they argue that we

[17] Landemore and Page, "Deliberation and Disagreement," p. 6. They add: "This assumption can be equated with Habermas' claim that the 'unforced force of the better argument' will triumph in an ideal speech situation (that is, the superiority of the 'right answer' will appear as such to all)."

[18] To remind ourselves: a *mapping* function takes the evaluative standards (ES) and applies them to a social world, *i*, as specified by WF, yielding a *justice score* for world

should expect consensus on what constitutes the best solution (the global optimum); indeed, given how we have understood a perspective here, this may seem to follow.

The problem, however, is that agreement on simply the evaluative standards and the weighting procedure will produce agreement in the overall evaluation of options only if the evaluation does not depend on predictive modeling of how the features of the option will actually function together. As Landemore and Page note—and as we have seen in §II.4.2—in predictive tasks disagreement may lead to better results than consensus.[19] If, however, Alf's conclusion about the ultimate value of an option depends on predictions about how that option will function, and so how well its functioning will meet the shared evaluative standards, Betty will always agree with him on the global optimum (and the value of less-than-optimum solutions) only if she also shares his predictive models.

To see this better, consider Landemore's example in which she postulates a problem for the French government in selecting a city for an experimental program.[20] "Three *députés* are deliberating, one from Calvados, one from Pas de Calais, one from Corrèse. They are aware of different possible solutions…, each of which have a different value for the experiment. On a scale of 0 to 10, a city with a value of 10 has the highest objective value for the experiment. Each of the cities that a given *député* might offer count as a local optimum.… The goal is for the group to find the global optimum, that is, the city with the highest objective value."[21] The *députés* and their perspectival optima are summarized in figure 3-4. We can see that, as required by assumption (*iii*) of the Hong-Page analysis, the only optimum shared by all three is Caen, the global optimum. On something like Landemore's version of the story, as given in figure 3-4, Alfred might get stuck (indicated

---

i, the social world described by its world features. The mapping function has two parts. (*i*) It must employ a model or models that predict how the justice-relevant features of a social world (WF) will interact to produce a social realization. This is the *modeling task*. (*ii*) It must take the set of evaluative standards (ES) and determine their relative importance in such a way that they provide a single evaluation of this social realization. This is the *overall evaluation task*.

[19] Landemore and Page, "Deliberation and Disagreement," p. 10.

[20] This example is repeated in ibid., p. 7.

[21] Landemore, *Democratic Reason*, p. 99.

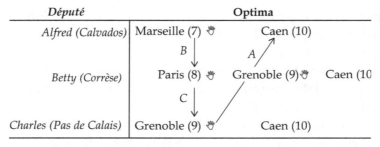

Figure 3-4. Landemore's example

by ✋) at his local optimum at Marseille; Betty can carry the baton to Paris, but she gets stuck at a local optimum there (✋); Charles can take it to Grenoble before halting at a local optimum (✋) but Alfred can take the baton back, and arrive in Caen.

The important assumption here is not simply that the *députés* agree on their evaluative standards and trade-off rates, but that all three *députés*, when they run their predictive models of how well each city will serve these agreed-on weighted evaluative standards, concur on the best city. This would be the case only if, as I have said, they all share an evaluation normalized perspective Σ^V, which includes the same predictive models, and so once a particular solution is pointed out, all members of Σ^V concur on the predicted value of the option. This is why, I think, the example looks a bit contrived as a case of actual politics. What we would expect is variance of predicted outcomes when they apply different predictive models. Even if they share the same fundamental values, then, people who employ different predictive models are apt to disagree on the value of options.[22] Their different predictive models will lead them to disagree on the overall value of the options—their ordering along the *y*-axis, not just how they array them along the *x*-axis. The assumption that they all share the Σ^V perspective, and so entirely agree about the scoring of each option in the domain, turns out to be very strong indeed, at least in many instances of actual politics.

At this point we might invoke the Diversity Prediction Theorem (§II.4.2), and hold that the *députés* could pool their predictive models.

[22] Page, *The Difference*, pp. 257–58.

As Landemore and Page consider, the *députés* might engage in a high-level deliberation about the comparative benefits of their different models, which can improve the toolkits of each. But Landemore and Page are hesitant about recommending a procedure that leads to consensus on predictive models: "it need not be more advantageous to reach a greater consensus following deliberation in the predictive context."[23] As they show, if each predictor moved a step closer to the average prediction, no gains in group prediction would be generated.[24] This is a consequence of the Diversity Prediction Theorem; even if Alfred's moving toward the average prediction increases his predictive reliability, the group as a whole has lost an element of predictive diversity, and given that a unit of predictive diversity is equal to a unit of predictive accuracy, the average predictive performance of the group will not be increased.[25] We might imagine a deliberation in which the *députés* would first make their models explicit, discuss how they work, pool them for some purposes, but also continue using their original, divergent, predictive models. Thus in one sense they agree (insofar as they are using the pooled results), and in another sense they disagree (because they continue to use their diverse predictive models), as to which city would work out best for the experiment. It is hard to see how this would work in practice, much less as an approximation of actual politics.

We thus must wonder about the broader persuasiveness of Landemore's claim that the "four conditions for this theorem are not utterly demanding."[26] Although this may be plausible if we restrict ourselves to simply the formal conditions (i)–(iv), the worry is about the supposition that all share, or can be brought to share, the full Σ^V perspective. For us to be confident that Hong and Page's model really applies in a case such as this, the different perspectives must employ predictive models that agree about the scores of each city. Of course it does not follow that as soon as any disagreement on the scoring of the elements is introduced the Hong-Page search model becomes irrelevant, but it does mean that the more it is the case that the perspectives score

[23] Landemore and Page, "Deliberation and Disagreement," p. 13.
[24] Ibid., pp. 9ff.
[25] See appendix B.
[26] Landemore, *Democratic Reason*, p. 102.

the options differently, the less applicable the theorem. When perspective Betty announces that she has moved from Marseille at 7 but is stuck at Paris with a score of 8, Charles might reply *"pas question!"*—you just moved from 7 to 6!

2.3 The Utopia Is at Hand Theorem

Although the Hong-Page Theorem does not recognize neighborhoods in which confidence about the terrain is much higher than in outlying areas, Page discusses a second theorem that can do so. According to what he calls the "Savant Existence Theorem... for any problem there exist many perspectives that create Mount Fuji landscapes."[27] There are always arrangements of the elements in {X} (social worlds) that create Mount Fuji landscapes. Showing this is trivial in our simple one-dimensional similarity space: take the ordering of scores on the y-axis from high to low, and rearrange the x-axis to correspond to this ordering. This will yield a Mount Fuji landscape. There are many such possible landscapes for any optimization problem. If we can show that our problem is a smooth optimization landscape, the conflict between local and global optimization is entirely obviated (§II.2.3). Note that in principle for any landscape, no matter how rugged, there exist alternative arrays of the x-axis that generate a smooth optimization problem. This is, I think, the motivation behind interpreting the second condition of the Hong-Page theorem in terms of the smartness of the perspective rather than the difficulty of the problem: there is, *in principle*, some perspective that turns every difficult problem into a simple one.

A more modest version of the Savant Existence Theorem might be called:

> *The Utopia Is at Hand Theorem*: There are in principle Σ^V perspectives according to which Σ's ideal is within our current neighborhood.

This is a "more modest" version of the Savant Existence Theorem as it does not require a reordering of the similarity dimension such that for all social worlds in {X} there is a smooth optimization landscape. It

---

[27] Page, *The Difference*, p. 47. On Mount Fuji landscapes, see §II.2.1.

requires "only" that a subset of $\{X\}$, which includes the current world and the global optimum (and we assume some other nearby social worlds) are ordered such that they form a neighborhood. Neither does it require that within this neighborhood there is a smooth, Mount Fuji landscape. "All" that is required is that Σ's global optimum is within our current neighborhood. We have a potentially compelling result: there is in principle always some Σ^V perspective on the problem of ideal justice that shows that Σ's utopia is in the neighborhood of our current social world. This would mean that The Choice (§II.3.3) may be avoided—pursuit of the ideal and of local justice can be one and the same.

In the abstract it may seem easy to rearrange the elements of a domain. What is not easy is to arrange them in a way that expresses an intelligible similarity ordering of the features of the relevant social worlds (WF)—to show that this new arrangement of the domain $\{X\}$ exemplifies a meaningful structure that relates social worlds (§II.1.2). If I think that, say, a socialist camping trip—like utopia—is far away from our current world, and you arrive at a perspective in which it is adjacent, this could be immensely enlightening—*if* I can agree that the way you have structured the worlds really does capture similarities that mine has missed. And then I may come to the conclusion that I can share your deeper knowledge of the ideal, as it is much more like our current world than I ever contemplated.[28] But if your perspective on $\{X\}$ seems arbitrary or implausible, or misses critical characteristics, I will dismiss your "savant" perspective, and its claims to have brought the ideal into my neighborhood. It is no mean feat to impose a meaningful structure on social worlds in a way that brings very close what looks, on my current perspective, to be very far away.[29]

In social thought such revolutionary changes in perspective have no doubt occurred. Perhaps liberalism itself was such a reconceptualization. At one point Western societies faced the problem of which false religions to tolerate. Even in his *Letter concerning Toleration,*

---

[28] Bellamy hints at this: "As every schoolboy knows, in the latter part of the nineteenth century the [socialist] civilization of to-day, or anything like it, did not exist, although the elements which were to develop it were already in ferment." *Looking Backward*, p. 3.

[29] Page is certainly well aware of this. *The Difference*, p. 48.

Locke still was struggling with this view. While he thought it would promote the good of the commonwealth to tolerate dissenting Protestants, extending toleration to Catholics might decrease justice (an England that tolerated Catholics was far from his own); and extending toleration to atheists would be even a further social world.[30] But, no doubt without being fully aware of it, Locke was pushing toward a more Mount Fuji liberal landscape, in which each additional right of conscience and speech advanced justice. Eventually the early modern problem of which false creeds to tolerate was transformed into the problem of increasing freedom of thought and belief, where the options of which creeds to tolerate were arrayed in something much closer to a smooth optimization landscape. Once one arrays the social worlds in terms of their liberty of conscience, the world in which Catholics are tolerated is very close to that in which Protestant dissenters are, and tolerating atheists is just a step beyond that.

However, this revolution was not simply rearranging worlds with a fixed set of justice-relevant properties and social realizations: it was coming to revise some judgments about the ways social worlds work (for example, social worlds that insist on uniform religious practice were not more harmonious and stable, as was traditionally thought), as well as coming to appreciate new evaluative standards, such as personal dignity. That is, the change did not just occur within a stable Σ^V perspective: it revised some of the core normative elements of the perspective itself—the evaluative standards, the world features, and the mapping relation. This example raises an important question: how radically can the similarity ordering of domain $\{X\}$ be rearranged without also revising the perspective's evaluative core (ES, WF, and MP)?

2.4 The Interdependence of the Elements of a Perspective on the Ideal

We have defined the Σ^V perspectives as agreeing on the standards of evaluation (ES), the properties of the social world (WF), and the mapping function (MP). These perspectives secure agreement on the over-

---

[30] See Locke, *A Letter concerning Toleration*, pp. 245–46. See also my "Locke's Liberal Theory of Public Reason."

all evaluation of the justice of all social worlds in the domain. The core results we have been examining derive from allowing the similarity ordering (SO) and the distance metric (DM) to freely vary while holding the other elements constant. It is important to stress that a great deal of variation in the similarity ordering is required to yield strong conclusions that we are very likely to find utopia, or that the ideal can be "brought" within our neighborhood.

Hong and Page's results manifestly presuppose that the similarity ordering can be varied freely without affecting the evaluative core of a perspective, including its overall justice judgments of a social world. This is the main lesson of our example of the search for the best rights-protecting states. The GDP, economic liberty, and political functioning perspectives radically rearranged the similarity ordering, but they had the same set of evaluations over the same set of options. However, this sort of complete independence of the similarity orderings from the evaluative core cannot occur on the model I have been developing, for the similarity orderings are based on the perspective's nonholistic evaluations of the justice-relevant features of social worlds.

To see why the model developed here is inconsistent with the assumption of *complete independence of the similarity orderings from the evaluative core*, suppose for the moment we accept the assumption. Assume further that we have an admissible perspective on the ideal, Σ^V. Such a perspective, it will be recalled, does not engage in holistic evaluation, as this would result in a high-dimensional, essentially random perspective on justice (§II.2.2). Admissible ideal justice landscapes are moderately rugged; very similar neighbors have correlated justice scores (§II.2.4). Take, then, three worlds from the domain $\{X\}$, a, b, k. Assume that on Alf's version of Σ^V b is a world with almost exactly the same world features as a, with only the slightest recognizable difference. Now because of interdependencies between the justice-relevant features of institutions and background facts, worlds that are structurally extremely similar may be significantly more divergent in their overall justice. Nevertheless, on Alf's version of the perspective two adjacent social worlds, a and b, have very similar justice-relevant features, and because the evaluation of a's and b's justice is based on nonholistic evaluations of these justice-relevant features, a and b must have correlated justice scores. Now take some randomly selected world k, and assume some version of the Σ^V perspective, Betty's, that adopts a similarity ordering such that k is between a and b. Our initial assumption (complete independence of the similarity orderings from the evaluative core) says that this is consistent with keeping the evaluative core of this perspective. But note that, because it is randomly selected, k can have *any* justice score in the entire range allowed by the Σ^V perspective. So on Betty's version of the Σ^V perspective, it would follow that even though worlds a and k are adjacent they need not have correlated justice scores. Even though world a is, on Betty's version of Σ^V, very similar to k, knowing the justice of world a tells Betty nothing about the justice of k. The evaluation of any social world is based on its features, but here we see almost identical features result in uncorrelated justice scores. By iteration we could ensure this is true of all pairs in the domain $\{X\}$ on Betty's version of the perspective. This would produce a maximally high-dimensional landscape, where there is no correlation between any adjacent elements, and so no neighborhoods (§II.2.2). Such a perspective can result only if (*i*) the evaluation of the justice of social worlds was not a function of their features (WF)[31] or (*ii*) the evaluation of those features was maximally holistic (any change in features produces entirely uncorrelated judgments). But our model of an admissible perspective on justice precludes both. It denies (*i*), since justice is indeed the result of the evaluation of world features, and our limitation on admissible perspectives on ideal justice prohibits (*ii*). Thus we have arrived at a contradiction: we assumed that that Σ^V was an admissible perspective, but Betty's version of it is not. Admissible perspectives cannot allow complete independence of the similarity orderings from the evaluative core.

It does not follow that a stable evaluative core cannot allow any differences in the similarity orderings on our model: differences within the same neighborhood are certainly allowed (§II.4.3). Consider the five economic systems sketched by Rawls, and much discussed in the current literature: "(a) laissez-faire capitalism [the classical system];[32]

---

[31] Think here of our height example, §II.2.1.

[32] "Laissez-faire" is a misnomer; as Rawls describes this system it includes a "rather low social minimum." Rawls, *Justice as Fairness*, p. 137. His description suggests the classical system in political economy, which was most definitely not a laissez-faire system—laissez-faire was characteristic of the Manchester School and French

(b) welfare-state capitalism; (c) state socialism with a command economy;[33] (d) property-owning democracy; (e) liberal (democratic) [market] socialism."[34] Consider three different similarity orderings of these systems:

> Alf: a–**b**–d–e–c
> Betty: a–d–**b**–e–c
> Charlie: e–a–d–c–**b**

I assume we are at world *b* (noted in bold above), a capitalist welfare state. Alf's ordering is an intuitive continuum of economic structures.[35] At one end is the classical system of economic freedom (*a*), embracing a strong system of private property and markets. Next to the classical system is the welfare state (*b*), keeping both these institutions and leaving property largely unregulated, with the proviso for state provision of basic welfare; property-owning democracy (*d*) might be seen as a development of welfare state egalitarian capitalism; market socialism (*e*) a step further away, as it gets rid of private property, while state socialism (*c*) continues on in this direction, rejecting both markets and property. Now we can imagine that Betty sees, and evaluates, the worlds in the exact same way, but has a somewhat different ordering. As in Alf's, property-owning democracy is next to our current world, but Betty's perspective emphasizes its deep reliance on markets and property and thus sees it as neighboring *a*, the classical world. Moving to market socialism (*e*) would thus be moving *away* from private property, thus going in the opposite direction. While the differing orderings of Alf's and Betty's perspectives can, I think, be plausibly construed as seeing economic systems in the same way, but with some slight difference in which features are emphasized in making similarity judgments, Charlie's ordering seems to be picking up on very different features. As Charlie sees it, our welfare state is next to state socialism, which, in turn, is next to property-owning democracy.

Physiocrats. It is unfortunate that, despite the efforts of historians of political economy, this confusion is still common. See Robbins, *The Theory of Economic Policy in English Classical Political Economy*. See also my "Mill's Normative Economics."

[33] What Wiles calls a "Soviet-type" system. *Economic Institutions Compared*, esp. chaps. 4, 11.

[34] Rawls, *Justice as Fairness*, p. 136.

[35] It is suggested by Chapman, "Justice, Freedom and Property."

To explain this, it seems plausible to conjecture that Charlie's similarity ordering is so different because he fundamentally differs in the features of the economic systems he is picking out. But this means that this difference in similarity must be linked to differences in the evaluative core of the perspective (relevant world features, WF). But if the features to be evaluated differ, then we must suppose that the overall evaluation will as well. Again, the assumption of the independence of the ordering from the core of the evaluative features is most dubious.

Because of its importance and power, it is useful to reflect on what changes in our model would accommodate Page's understanding of perspectives. If those accommodations are plausible, then perhaps we should alter our initial model (§II.1) rather than dismissing the relevance of the Hong-Page theorem to ideal theory. To clear the way for application of the theorem it is necessary to, as it were, cut loose the similarity ordering from the core evaluative elements. Recall again our initial example of searching for the best rights-protecting state (§III.1.2). The states were ordered along a dimension that did not identify properties that were directly evaluated by the evaluative standards, but by some additional property that the perspectives hypothesized is correlated with a state's overall justice. Thus one perspective identifies GDP, another economic liberty, and the third political functioning as the basis of similarity judgments, but none apply the evaluative standards to these features: the perspectives all evaluate the same justice-relevant features of states directly relating to personal autonomy and individual rights.[36] So, in terms of our model, they do agree on the evaluative standards, mapping functions, and relevant features, but they do not rely on these relevant features when deriving similarity, employing instead some entirely different feature that, they suppose, is correlated with the overall judgments of justice.[37] It is in

---

[36] These features are: "Do citizens enjoy freedom of travel or choice of residence, employment, or institution of higher education? Do citizens have the right to own property and establish private businesses? Is private business activity unduly influenced by government officials, the security forces, political parties/organizations, or organized crime? Are there personal social freedoms, including gender equality, choice of marriage partners, and size of family? Is there equality of opportunity and the absence of economic exploitation?" *Freedom House Freedom in the World Report,* 2014.

[37] It would not significantly alter what is said here if the perspectives agreed on the

this way that the similarity ordering floats free from the judgments of the evaluative core.

This is a puzzlingly roundabout way of orienting the quest for justice, the distinctive feature of ideal theory. If a perspective has identified the features of a social world that are relevant to evaluating its justice, the best way to orient the quest for justice surely is by focusing directly on these relevant features, rather than selecting some proxy dimension that is not itself to be evaluated for its justice, but is supposed to be correlated with justice. Page's conception of a perspective makes sense when we are confronted by a different sort of problem: when we have a reliable way of evaluating the overall score of an option, but are uncertain of the features that give rise to the score. Suppose, for example, we are constructing a component for a computer system, and we know that the best product will be one that optimally combines modularity with other components, reliability, and low cost, but we are not certain what underlying features will result in high scores on these dimensions.[38] Here a perspective would plausibly postulate some dimension that, it believes, tracks increasingly better solutions, but this would not be a direct function of the underlying features.

Page's model of a perspective then makes most sense when the investigators agree on how to score a solution, but not on the features on which the scores depend. Thus there is no need to include the relevant features in Page's notion of a perspective, for, in a fundamental way, those are what we are uncertain of. The diverse perspectives can employ different understandings of the salient features of each member of the domain because they have, as it were, a common test for judging the overall value of each element. As Landemore and Page put it in a recent essay, it is as if all the perspectives assume that there is an oracle who gives the correct answer, which all accept. "A problem-solving task consists then of generating potential solutions and identifying the best from among them. In this pure problem-solving context, we implicitly assume the existence of an oracle, namely a machine, person, or internal intuition, that can reveal the correct ranking of any

---

set of world features and then each picked one feature from that set as the sole basis of its similarity ordering.

[38] See D'Agostino, "From the Organization to the Division of Cognitive Labor."

proposed solutions."[39] So perspectives endorse the same elements to be evaluated and the same oracle but can disagree about the relevant features that give rise to the oracle's judgment.

Let us consider how the Utopia Is at Hand Theorem (§III.2.3) looks assuming Landemore and Page's understanding of a perspective, but allowing our basic Neighborhood Constraint. Recall that the crux of the Utopia Is at Hand Theorem is that there is some utopian perspective according to which the ideal, which seems far away from our present world on our current perspective is, as it were, next door on the utopian version. Let us call the utopian version *Ulysses's perspective* and the current version *Betty's*. Figure 3-5 makes this concrete with an example of a six-world domain, with three-world neighborhoods. Notice first that Betty's and Ulysses's perspectives concur on the justice score of each world in the set (column 2), as accepting the same oracle requires. Betty identifies certain fundamental features {*f g*}, of *a*, our current social world, as critical; she then draws on some dimension that yields similarity judgments for other possible worlds (in this case *b* and *c*) that form her current neighborhood. Thus on Betty's perspective, the local optimum is *b*, with a justice of 15. Ulysses sees things differently. He identifies *a*'s fundamental features as {*m n*}, and given his similarity judgments, the most similar worlds are *e* and *u*. And, of course, *u* is both the local and the global optimum. So on Ulysses's perspective the ideal is within the current neighborhood.

But why would they think they are actually talking about the same social worlds, at least when they are not talking about the current one? Given that they do not ascribe the same features to the social worlds, it seems doubtful that they could even communicate to each other *which worlds they are describing*. Recall figure 3-5 and the world designated as "*b*." If Betty's perspective is analyzing a world composed of {*f h*} while Ulysses sees the structure as based on {*n q*}, in what sense are they talking about the same possible social world at all? In our earlier example of states protecting individual rights, we had independent identification of the elements of the domain (existing countries

---

[39] Landemore and Page, "Deliberation and Disagreement," p. 6. "The oracle assumption requires only that if alternative *y* is better than *x*, then each individual's model must also rank alternative *y* above alternative *x*. Individuals need not know the exact values, they need only to be close enough." Ibid., pp. 7–8.

World	Justice	The features Betty sees and orders on her similarity dimension	The neighborhood Betty sees	The features Ulysses sees and orders on his similarity dimension	The neighborhood Ulysses sees
a	10	{f, g}	✓	{m, n}	✓
b	15	{f, h}	✓	{n, q}	
c	5	{f, i}	✓	{n, p}	
d	15	{i, j}		{n, o}	
e	20	{i, k}		{m, o}	✓
u	30	{i, l}		{m, p}	✓

Figure 3-5. Two perspectives that agree only about justice scores

with names); in Landemore's example there was also a domain (French cities) with names attached. As Page stresses, if there are artifacts that can be independently identified, then we can deeply disagree about their properties while agreeing what we are talking about.[40] Although figure 3-5 designated this world as "*b*," that begs the question in describing possible social worlds—we do not have names designating each world. A possible social world is designated by its features, and it is precisely about these that Betty and Ulysses disagree. Deep perspectival disagreement, in other words, will prevent them from characterizing certain social worlds in terms that others are capable of understanding as the same "thing." Betty and Ulysses thus do not agree on the domain, $\{X\}$, to be evaluated.

Suppose that this problem could be overcome, and Ulysses and Betty could agree on a way to identify social worlds, say by their causal histories (such as "the world that would be produced by pulling the red lever.") Nevertheless Betty would be perplexed by Ulysses's claim to have identified the ideal. His perspective radically disagrees with hers about the relevant features of the social world yet somewhat miraculously concurs on their justice. Why should worlds of $\{i, l\}$ and of $\{m, p\}$ have the same justice score? There is no test through which they can run these worlds to determine their overall justice; all they

---

[40] Page, *The Difference*, pp. 172–73. I consider in more detail the sense in which we might still agree in §IV.1.3.1.

can do is apply their predictive models to these features, and evaluate them according to their evaluative standards and mapping relations. If different features are being evaluated by the same evaluative criteria, then we would expect variance in their justice. Of course there may be cases where the justice of worlds with different features happen to be identical, but it seems a bit fantastical to expect (let alone assume) that this could be true for every social world. Surely Betty's most reasonable conjectures are either that Ulysses's perspective is simply erroneous, or that it he is using a different set of evaluative standards too, and, thus, Ulysses does not in fact share Betty's evaluative standards or weighing system. If, however, Ulysses is confused, or has very different evaluative standards, it is not clear that Betty has much to learn from him. This is different from saying that Ulysses's perspective does not make sense to Betty; but it is to maintain that she would have a very difficult time making sense that there could be so much difference in what is being evaluated (what the relevant features of the social world are), yet this does not affect their overall justice scores, only the terrain on the x-axis.

2.5 The Fundamental Diversity Dilemma

We can thus see why the Hong-Page theorem, based on their specific notion of a perspective, is inappropriate to ideal theory (but see §III.3.2). A theory of the ideal needs to fix on the justice-relevant features of possible worlds to identify them, and, on the basis of these features, construct a similarity ordering. And so the impressive formal Hong-Page results are not of central relevance to us after all. A more fundamental lesson from the forgoing, though, is that as perspectives become more deeply diverse their ability to communicate with one another is hampered.[41] Perspectives that are similar, but see things in somewhat different ways, obviously can help each other to overcome the Neighborhood Constraint. Alf's perspective may alter the neighborhood or call attention to justice-relevant features that Betty's overlooks. At some point, however, as the perspectives diverge they simply see things in what will seem to each puzzlingly different ways. Per-

---

[41] Page is aware of this. *The Difference*, p. 49.

haps as with Betty and Ulysses they radically disagree about what constitutes the neighborhood and the features of the world that are relevant. In one way, as Hong and Page show, this should be a great resource, helping perspectives to overcome their own limitations by confronting those who understand the optimization problem differently. However, although embracing deeper diversity improves the odds of identifying the global optimum and/or bringing it into our neighborhood, at the same time it reduces our ability to meaningfully share this information. Betty and Ulysses may disagree about so much that she cannot understand how his purported discoveries are relevant to the ideal that she is trying to find. Empirical analysis tends to confirm this, indicating that those with very different outlooks have difficulty communicating and coordinating with one another.[42] Overall, we are apt to disagree about the value of alternative social worlds, the identification of those worlds, and what the reports of other perspectives actually mean. As with the Tower of Babel, our collective effort to reach heaven can collapse into mutual incomprehension.

We thus have arrived at:

The Fundamental Diversity Dilemma: As we increase diversity of perspectives we can bring the ideal closer to our world, but as diversity increases we disagree about the justice of alternative social worlds, including that of the ideal.

A community drawing on multiple perspectives has the potential to increase the effective size of its neighborhood, as well as to bring the ideal closer to it. But perspectives on the ideal are integrated. A perspective has a certain similarity ordering because it sees certain institutional and other features as relevant to justice; these features are the basis of its evaluation of the overall justice of a social world.[43] When a perspective applies its mapping relation (including its predictive mod-

---

[42] Weber and Camerer, "Cultural Conflict and Merger Failure: An Experimental Approach." For a model showing that meaningful propositions emerge from shared overall perspectives, see Hazelhurst and Hutchins, "The Emergence of Propositions from the Co-ordination of Talk and Action in a Shared World."

[43] Page observes this interaction as well: "We bias our interpretations [the categories employed by WF] towards what we believe most important [our evaluative standards.] If Tom cares about energy conservation, he may ask to see the heating bills before buying a house. If Bonnie cares about internal light, she may count the number

els) and its evaluative standards to these features it arrives at an over-all justice score. Small variance in any of these may not make much of a difference, but substantial diversity in one element reverberates throughout the perspectives. We might call this *diversity contagion*: diversity is introduced into one element of a perspective, it induces diversity in another, and this in turn produces more diversity. We have seen that the sort of robust independence of elements of a perspective (ordering, features, overall evaluation) supposed by Page's insightful model of perspectives largely (though not entirely) avoids this contagion;[44] however, it is an inappropriate conception of a perspec-tive for the pursuit of the ideal. On the more appropriate model we have developed, if two perspectives on utopia differ much in one re-spect they substantially differ in others as well. When substantial and systematic differences set in, perspectives end up searching "different landscapes."[45] Thus, instead of seeing themselves as diverse teams ex-ploring the same evaluative core, diverse philosophers create deeply different perspectives and so different landscapes of justice.

The upshot of our analysis is that it is very difficult to "manage" evaluative diversity,[46] if this means allowing "just the right" amount of diversity to solve an optimization problem (say, by admitting views that orient the search for justice in helpfully different ways) without introducing deeper diversity (as, for example, about what worlds are the most just). These differences fracture the optimization landscape into multiple landscapes with people searching for divergent ideals, and so our searches often have little interest to others. Ensuring that large groups are diverse enough to effectively find new solutions to shared problems is difficult indeed. Authoritarian regimes have often learned this lesson the hard way. Stuck in the mire of approaching problems of reform in the same orthodox way (employing the ortho-dox perspective), such regimes have often sought to allow diversity of

---

of windows and their sizes. Because their preferences [ES] differ, so do their interpre-tations." Page, *The Difference*, p. 292.

[44] Even in Page's analysis they are not fully independent: "sometimes one type of diversity creates another and... the contexts to which they apply overlap, and their effects intertwine." Ibid., p. 285.

[45] Ibid., p. 289.

[46] Cf. Santos-Lang, "Our Responsibility to Manage Evaluative Diversity."

perspectives within in the limits of the orthodox ideology. Glasnost and Perestroika were the shining examples of the late twentieth century. In the twenty-first century Chinese communistic capitalism is another attempt—its efforts to manage diversity include the Tiananmen Square Massacre. Of course none of this is to say that such efforts cannot succeed, but they seem inevitably to rely on force, intimidation, and oppression.

3 THE BENEFITS OF DIVERSITY

3.1 The Fundamental Diversity Insight

I have been canvassing some of the problems arising from diverse perspectives, problems that I believe pose insurmountable obstacles to effective use of the Hong-Page theorem in a theory of ideal justice. But that this formal approach is not as helpful as it initially appeared by no means implies that diverse perspectives are not a great boon for a society that seeks greater justice, or better pursuit of the common good. The companion to the Fundamental Diversity Dilemma is

> *The Fundamental Diversity Insight*: Any given perspective Σ on justice that meets the Social Realizations and Orientation Conditions is apt to get caught at poor local optima; other perspectives can help by reinterpreting the problem or applying different predictive models, showing better alternatives in Σ's neighborhood.

The Fundamental Diversity Insight is the positive lesson to be learned from our examination of Page's pathbreaking work. While we must be skeptical that the formal Hong-Page theorem is of direct relevance to our problem, an underlying lesson remains. Yes, different perspectives can have great difficulty communicating, especially in ideal theory, where it may be very hard to know whether we are talking about the same social worlds at all. And yes, as perspectives differ, normative disagreement arises, so that in the end the perspectives are exploring different landscapes (optimization problems). *A society that embraces deep perspectival diversity will be one of deep normative diversity.* But none of this shows, as Fred D'Agostino puts it, that the different perspectives cannot ever "get it together."[47] It shows, rather, that getting it together is the really difficult task; diversity's benefits are by no means automatic, but neither are they always beyond our reach.

Of course we learn in multitudinous ways from each other. Other perspectives uncover features that our way of looking at the world neglected. In the last generation feminist perspectives certainly have played a fundamental role in alerting almost all theories of justice to features of the social world that were all-but-invisible to them. Feminists explored features of the social world, such as the family and language, that simply did not register as critically important to most traditional political theories. Here, Landemore and Page are certainly correct that the force of the better argument can produce convergence on parts of perspectives.[48] Some claims of feminist perspectives have been accepted by liberal, conservative, and other perspectives, while others could not be integrated, and the perspectives remain distinct, pointing to different views of justice. All of this is as important as it is familiar—I shall not seek to rehearse these considerations. Let us focus on those benefits highlighted by our model.

3.2 The Deep Insight of Hong and Page's Analysis

Recall Popper's and Elster's fundamental insight that a reasonable utopian theory must admit that its ideal is constantly revisable (§II.3.4). However, we cannot suppose—as perhaps Wilde did—that once "humanity" lands at Σ's utopia, Σ adherents will be able to see from there the "better country" for which they should now set sail. After all, Σ supposed that it was landing at an island with the highest peak. It may be so lucky as to constantly see further and higher, but there is no reason to expect so. The critical feature of Hong and Page's pass-the-baton dynamic is that, when Σ has done as well as it hoped, some other perspective *may share enough while also differing enough* with Σ that it can, as we put it, see a way upward (§II.1.1.2). Suppose a traditional

[47] D'Agostino, *Naturalizing Epistemology*, p. 1.

[48] Recall: "This assumption can be equated with Habermas' claim that the 'unforced force of the better argument' will triumph in an ideal speech situation (that is, the superiority of the 'right answer' will appear as such to all)." Landemore and Page, "Deliberation and Disagreement," p. 6.

socialist perspective saw socialism as the abolition of "capitalism," understood as "markets-with-private property." And suppose that socialism thus understood was secured (as it was in much of the world in the early and middle twentieth century). Now enter another perspective, which sees "private property-with-markets" as not a single feature (or two that always march hand-in-hand), but two quite different features, and so "state socialism" could be improved by "market socialism." In a stylized history of ideas, we might understand this as a claim of the perspective of Tito's Yugoslavia.[49] It shared enough with Soviet state socialism to make intelligible to the Soviets the claim that "according to our understanding, 'socialism' should distinguish much more sharply markets and private property, and the improved socialist ideal lies in accepting the former but not the latter."

A perspective does not need to "land" at its utopia to understand this. What can be done after arrival can be done before—deliberating with allied perspectives to see what properties it has overlooked, or what properties it has mistakenly bundled. And what holds for the highest peak also holds for all peaks from which it cannot really see the "next destination." It is other, differing but related perspectives, that are most likely to see overlooked superior alternatives—ones that the original perspective can appreciate it has overlooked. This is the great insight of the handing-off-the-baton dynamic, even when the conditions for the formal proof are not met. It is a deep and important idea that we must not overlook, though remaining skeptical of more ambitious attempts to use the Hong-Page model.

3.3 Modular Problems

This is another case where we tend to learn the most from those whose perspectives have more in common with ours. D'Agostino, though, has fruitfully analyzed the social epistemology of more radical forms of perspectival disagreement. Even perspectives that differ on all five of our elements can, perhaps with modification, adopt solutions from other perspectives to help solve problems. To borrow an idea from

[49] See Wiles, *Economic Institutions Compared*, pp. 85ff., chap. 6; Ward, *The Ideal World of Economics*, pp. 246–53.

D'Agostino, when a problem is of a modular nature, its solution by one perspective can be fitted into that of others.[50] One of the noteworthy features of social democratic perspectives in Western Europe and the United States in the 1990s and the first decade of this century was concern about improving the quality of delivery of social services. While traditionally many social democratic perspectives saw the relation between providers and recipients in resolutely antimarket terms, a number of social democratic governments and parties adopted efficiency criteria from more traditionally liberal or libertarian perspectives to improve delivery of public services, such as health care and education. Although these social democratic perspectives did not simply adopt the evaluations of health care and education arrangements of more free market–friendly perspectives, they did see that for some particular problems central to the social democracy, features stressed by free market perspectives (such as aligning agent incentives closer to those of principals) were also features relevant to justice as understood by the social democratic perspective.

As I have stressed earlier, institutions can have important interdependencies (§II.2.1), and so what we take as a "modular" solution may be more embedded in other commitments than we first realized, leading to much more radical changes than initially contemplated. Whether a problem is modular is something we discover. Consider, for example, the evolution of the Labour Party in the United Kingdom, from its early twentieth-century founding to, say, its perspective at the turn of the twentieth-first century. By taking over efficiency and market considerations as part of its perspective, it came to the point of explicitly rejecting what was a fundamental commitment—"the common ownership of the means of production"—as one of its official aims.[51] Learning from other perspectives and revising one's own perspective are deeply intertwined activities. Of course this sort of dynamic is to be expected if we accept Popper's (and my) basic point—that we learn what our ideal is as we seek it (§II.3.4).

---

[50] D'Agostino, *Naturalizing Epistemology*, pp. 128–32.

[51] The famous "Clause IV" of the Labour Party constitution, written by Sidney Webb, which called for "the common ownership of the means of production," was dropped in 1995.

3.4 Recombination

Different perspectives can recombine to form new perspectives. At times this process is carried out radically and quickly, when diverse political perspectives recombine into a new one. One remarkable instance of this was the emergence in 1950s America of "fusion" conservatism, fusing conservative traditionalism with classical liberalism, most notably in the work of Frank S. Meyer.[52] Meyer insisted that traditional conservatism "was far too cavalier to the claims of freedom, far too ready to subordinate the individual person to the authority of the state."[53] Whereas traditional American conservatives such as Russell Kirk upheld James Fitzjames Stephen's critique of Mill's defense of liberty, Meyer defends Mill: "The only alternative to the moral rule of liberty is to enthrone the sad tendency of human history as right, to glorify with James Stephen 'the man of genius who rules by persuading an efficient minority to coerce an indifferent and self-indulgent majority.' ... Liberty is the political end of man's existence because liberty is the condition of his being. It is for this reason that conservatism, which in preserving the tradition of this truth, is only consistent with itself when it is libertarian."[54] It was not only Mill—Meyer insisted that Adam Smith and the Austrian economists such as Carl Menger, Ludwig von Mises, and Hayek must be integrated into an adequate American conservatism for the twentieth century.[55] "Fusion conservatism" had a profound effect on American conservatism in the latter part of the twentieth century and continues to this day. "Extremism in the defense of liberty is no vice.... Moderation in the pursuit of justice is no virtue!"[56] is not the rallying cry of a traditional conservative.

---

[52] See Schneider, *The Conservative Century*, pp. 54–60.

[53] Meyer, "Freedom, Tradition, and Conservatism," p. 22.

[54] Meyer, "In Defense of John Stuart Mill," p. 168. Compare Kirk, *The Conservative Mind*, pp. 265–75.

[55] Meyer, "Freedom, Tradition, and Conservatism," pp. 26–27.

[56] These words, of course, are from Barry Goldwater's acceptance address at the 1964 Republican convention. "Extremism in the Defense of Liberty," p. 245. In *The Conscience of a Conservative* (p. 13), Goldwater insists: "the Conservative's first concern will always be: Are we maximizing freedom?" Meyer agrees: the principles of political right require "a state capable of maintaining order while at the same time guaranteeing to each person in its area of government the maximum liberty possible

This is but one example. Liberalism has recombined with versions of socialism, producing an egalitarian liberalism, distinctly ambivalent about private property and the market. In the first part of the twentieth century, this "new liberalism" sought to merge the socialist ideas of the United Kingdom labor movement with traditional liberal concerns to produce a "Liberal Socialism."[57] To L. T. Hobhouse, one of its chief architects, liberal "individualism, when it grapples with the facts, is driven no small distance along Socialist lines."[58] In the United States, John Dewey pursued a similar recombination project, more Marxist than Hobhouse's.[59] Recently we have witnessed fusions of feminism or environmentalism with various liberal, socialist, and conservative worldviews. And, as our example of "bleeding heart libertarianism" in §II.2.1 indicates, products of recombination such as egalitarian liberalism themselves can be combined with doctrines such as libertarianism.[60] The diversity of perspectives has led to yet more new perspectives, each with their own distinctive understanding of the ideal—ones which, at least to their proponents, are more adequate than the perspectives out of which they arose.

3.5 Improving Predictions

Throughout the last two chapters I have stressed the heavy reliance of ideal theories on predictive models. To evaluate possible social worlds we rely on predictive models as to how their institutions operate—when the worlds are far off, I have argued, we must rely on these predictive models and very little else (§II.3). When the concern is the

---

to him short of his interference with the liberty of other persons." *In Defense of Freedom*, p. 98.

[57] Hobhouse, *Liberalism*, p. 87.

[58] Ibid., p. 54.

[59] See Dewey, *Individualism, Old and New*, esp. chap. 6, "Capitalist or Public Socialism?" The fusion of liberalism and Marxism is an ongoing project; note how Cohen, whose early work was firmly in the Marxist tradition, entered mainstream liberal political philosophy by the end of his life, though the mix in this particular fusion is not clear. See his *Rescuing Justice and Equality*, esp. pp. 186ff.

[60] This is an especially interesting case. It seems that libertarianism arose partly as a reaction to the fusion of liberal and socialist ideals in "the new liberalism"—bleeding heart libertarianism pretty explicitly seeks to fuse a classical liberal view with that earlier fusion. See Tomasi's *Free Market Fairness*. The possibilities are endless.

interaction of the institutions in social worlds very dissimilar from our own, the accuracy of these models is, to be generous, not high. We have already seen how predictive diversity is critical in improving our predictive models (§II.4.2, appendix B). As Page notes, diversity contagion, which led to the breaking up of perspectives—producing different classifications of the relevant features of the world, different understandings of similarity, and so different optimization problems—also encourages perspectives to employ different tools for understanding their (differing) social worlds, with their different problems.[61] As our perspectives differ, we develop new tools for modeling and predicting, and diversity of the tools is itself an important force in helping all perspectives better model their landscapes. As has been discussed (§III.2.2), whereas some features of Page's analysis depend on agreement in perspectives, diversity of predictive models helps everyone better search their own justice landscapes.

4 ESCAPING THE TYRANNY OF THE IDEAL

4.1 The Tyranny of The Choice

Let us pause to take stock of some of our conclusions thus far. Recall first that an interesting ideal theory must meet the

> *Social Realizations Condition*: T must evaluate a set (or domain) of social worlds $\{X\}$. For each social world i, which is a member of $\{X\}$, T evaluates i in terms of its realization of justice (or, more broadly, relevant evaluative standards). This must yield a consistent comparative ranking of the members of $\{X\}$, which must include the present social world and the ideal, in terms of their justice.

I claim that this is a condition for an "interesting" ideal theory in the sense that only an ideal theory that meets it identifies an ideal social world that allows us to compare its justice to our world and to intermediate social worlds. It is certainly conceptually possible to have a theory of the ideal that is like a dream (§I.1.4), from which, when we

---

[61] Page, *The Difference*, p. 286.

awake, we are uncertain how this dream world compares to our world, or whether there might be other worlds that fall short of the dream world but still are admirably just. But we have set dreaming aside. The Social Realizations Condition also requires that an interesting theory of the ideal be able to give us a prediction of how different worlds, structured by certain institutions and practices, will work out in terms of their overall justice. And that is because we wish to aim at the ideal—even if we cannot actually achieve the ideal "down to the least detail,"[62] we can achieve approximations of it (§I.1.5). Recall Rawls's conviction that "by showing how the social world may realize the features of a realistic Utopia, political philosophy provides a long-term goal of political endeavor, and in working toward it gives meaning to what we can do today."[63] But if we are to actually seek out the ideal—if it is to guide our quest for justice—we must know how this set of social and political institutions will work out under whatever constraints the theory deems morally relevant and fundamental to the human condition.

I added to this:

> *The Orientation Condition*: T's overall evaluation of nonideal members of $\{X\}$ must necessarily refer to their "proximity" to the ideal social world, u, which is a member of $\{X\}$. This proximity measure cannot be simply reduced to an ordering of the members of $\{X\}$ in terms of their inherent justice.

If the Orientation Condition does not hold, the ideal is unnecessary to orient our search for greater justice—when it is not met the pursuit of justice can be understood in terms of Sen's climbing model (§I.1.3). If we could just climb up the Social Realizations ordering we would not need to orient ourselves by locating the global optimum. When the Orientation Condition is fulfilled we cannot simply move up the ordering to more just social states, eventually arriving at (or at least near) the global optimum in $\{X\}$. Increase in inherent justice and proximity to the ideal are distinct dimensions. On the model I have advanced, "proximity" is understood in terms of basic structures of the

---

[62] Plato, *The Republic*, p. 178 [v. 473].
[63] Rawls, *The Law of Peoples*, p. 128.

worlds; we have seen that the much-discussed idea of feasibility is unsuitable for the orientation function (§II.1.3).

In addition to these two conditions I have insisted that any ideal theory confronts the Neighborhood Constraint (§II.3): we have better knowledge of the social realizations of near worlds than of faraway worlds. Remember, the Orientation Condition requires that there be a dimension of similarity (the x-axis) that tells us something about the difference in the underlying structures of social worlds; the Neighborhood Constraint insists that our knowledge of justice is not uniform across this structure, but is, in general, a decreasing function of the distance a social world is from our current one. Now, to be sure, many ideal theorists will reject much of the rest of my analysis by simply denying this constraint: they will claim that we have as firm knowledge of the social realizations of institutions in worlds radically different from our own as of those that are very similar to the world we live in. One can *say* this, but since the Social Realizations Condition requires that we employ predictive models to judge how an interacting set of institutions will function, and since these models are very imperfect, predictions that rely on them alone will be of dubious accuracy. Roughly, in our neighborhood the justice of our current world is correlated with those that are close to it, and so small changes in the basic structure of our social world can be expected to have modest effects on justice within this vicinity. Outside of this area we are relying solely on predictive models that have a marked tendency to decrease in accuracy as we move away from observed conditions. Because any perspective's understanding of the ideal is based on incomplete information and predictive models of uncertain reliability, its location of the ideal and the estimation of its justice are always subject to revisions, perhaps quite radical ones (§II.3.4). Popper was absolutely correct: "*it is not reasonable to assume that a complete reconstruction of our social world would lead all at once to a workable system*"[64]—much less the ideal system—because we simply do not know enough about the ways such a completely different social world would work. If a theory of utopia denies this then, as Popper says, it replaces inspiration for sound social science: as has often been the case, it is more of an exer-

---

[64] Popper, *The Open Society and Its Enemies*, vol. 1, p. 167. Emphasis in original.

cise in fiction and imagination than an analysis that should seriously inform our recommendations about how to make our world more just.

If we take the Social Realizations and Orientation Conditions together with the Neighborhood Constraint, we have seen that an ideal theory is almost certain to be confronted with

> *The Choice*: In cases where there is a clear social optimum within our neighborhood that requires movement away from our understanding of the ideal, we must choose between relatively certain (perhaps large) local improvements in justice and pursuit of a considerably less certain ideal.

We considered various ways to mitigate The Choice; diversity of perspectives can expand our neighborhood and move high optima into it. But we have seen in this chapter that anything but modest forms of diversity result in deep disagreement about the justice of social realizations and the ideal; if we keep anything near the normalized evaluative perspective supposed by any given ideal theory T, the Neighborhood Constraint can, at best, be modestly mitigated, and so The Choice will still confront T.

If the ideal theorist always refuses to choose the ideal over local improvement the ideal is not necessary for recommendations; it may still be an interesting intellectual exercise, but such an ideal political philosophy will fail to provide "a long-term goal of political endeavor, and in working toward it [give] meaning to what we can do today."[65] If the ideal is to be such a long-term goal, the ideal theorist must sometimes—one would think often—stress that we should pursue the ideal and so forgo possibilities to create a more just social world by moving away from the ideal to some near social arrangements. It is critical to stress that this *must* be the case: if the ideal theorist denies that such choices need ever be made, then Sen is right and we can do very well without knowing anything about the Mount Everest of justice, and should simply climb the hills that confront us. But if we really do need the ideal, then we must press: why should we forgo opportunities to create a more just social world so that we can pursue an uncertain ideal? Those who bear the cost of this pursuit will live in a less just

[65] Rawls, *The Law of Peoples*, p. 138.

world—their pleas must be discounted. The ideal theorist is convinced that we can give meaning to our political lives by pursuing an inherently uncertain ideal, turning our backs on the pursuit of mundane justice in our own neighborhoods. A tyrant rules in a manifestly unjust way; for us to be under the sway of an ideal theory is for us to ignore relatively clear improvements in justice for the sake of a grander vision for the future. And yet this grand vision is ultimately a mirage, for as we move closer to it, we will see that it was not what we thought it was, and in all probability we can now see that a better alternative lies elsewhere.[66]

Ideal theorists in the academy today are good democrats who would never think of taking political power in their own hands[67] to pursue their visions of the ideal. But for those who remember their twentieth-century political history, the position that such theorists have talked themselves into is far too reminiscent of less democratic idealists. Recall that Lenin explicitly argued that his Marxian socialism "subordinates the struggle for reforms... to the revolutionary struggle for liberty and for Socialism." He admonished those who advocated climbing models of "stages" from current injustice to socialism; "by coming out at this moment, when the revolutionary movement is on the upgrade, with an alleged special 'task' of fighting for reforms,... [they are] dragging the Party *backwards* and... playing into the hands of both 'economic' and liberal opportunism."[68]

Even in democratic settings, we must seriously question an approach to political life that inherently encourages its adherents to neglect what, on their own view, are clear improvements in justice for the sake of pursuing an ideal, the pursuit of which gives meaning to their political lives or fulfills their dreams. When The Choice is made to pursue the ideal, the opportunity cost is the persistence of a less just condition, one that we can have higher confidence would be alleviated by moving to near social worlds. Surely, though, normative political

---

[66] Cf. Simmons, "Ideal and Nonideal Theory," p. 24.

[67] Well, perhaps they would *think* of it; recall Cohen's remark that his "own inclinations are more liberal" (*Rescuing Justice*, p. 186), and so he rejects the Stalinist approach to assigning occupations; he wrestles with freedom v. Stalinism in *Rescuing Justice and Equality*, chap. 5.

[68] Lenin, *What Is to Be Done?*, p. 269. Emphasis added.

philosophy should provide a reasoned response to deficits in justice, not a justification for ignoring them so we can seek "Paradise Island." Political philosophers have not paid sufficient heed to Sen's fundamental insight: what moves most of us, "reasonably enough, is not the realization that the world falls short of being completely just—which few of us expect—but that there are clearly remediable injustices around us which we want to eliminate."[69] To be moved by the former to the disregard of the latter is an all-too-common vice of the grand theorist, who demands too much from political philosophy—a firm orientation in understanding where our world stands in the conceptual space of justice, meaning in political life, a reassurance that humans are not too corrupt for justice, to feel at home in the political world, or to seek a social world where, finally, all is as it should be within the limits of human nature.[70] These are noble aims, and certainly, all things equal, most of us would value securing them. However, under the very conditions that render ideal theory a distinctive and alluring project, pursuit of these noble aims often "subordinates the fight for reforms" to the pursuit of utopia. As I have been stressing, Sen would be entirely right, and the ideal would be unnecessary to the pursuit of justice, if our road to the global optimum did not confront us with The Choice.

4.2 From Normalization to Deep Diversity

The tyranny of The Choice derives from the assumption—which Rawls says is fundamental to the social contract (§II.1.1)—of supposing that we approach political philosophy through a normalized, or common, perspective on justice. As Page stresses, even really insightful perspectives on a problem (for example, the third perspective in our search for the best rights-protecting state, §III.1.2) can get stuck short of the global optimum, and, as I have argued, even insightful perspectives must confront the Neighborhood Constraint. Thus in this chapter I

---

[69] Sen, *The Idea of Justice*, p. vii.

[70] See Rawls, *Justice as Fairness*, p. 104. For an insightful and sympathetic treatment of Rawls's political philosophy as a "naturalistic theodicy," see Weithman, *Why Political Liberalism?*, chap. 1. See also chapter V of the present work.

have focused on a collective pursuit of the ideal, drawing on diverse perspectives.

The problem, we saw, is that an evaluation-normalized perspective on the ideal, Σ^V, which is necessary for effective collective pursuit of a common evaluative core (with shared evaluative standards, world features, and mapping relations) combined with robust disagreement on similarity and distance metrics is, in the end, an illusion. The parts of a perspective on the ideal are interconnected—as we introduce substantial differences in one element, other elements are affected. Disagreement about one element of a perspective typically supposes, or leads to, disagreement on yet deeper elements of the evaluative perspective. As Benjamin Ward once remarked in the context of economics, "almost every attempt to communicate across world views is an attempt to alter value systems."[71] Unless diversity is "managed"—unless there are institutionalized means for ensuring that some sort of disagreements do not arise, or that if they do, they are suppressed—we cannot expect such a common ideal of justice to arise via diversity. Absent institutions to manage diversity, what we should expect in a free society is that individuals will understand justice in deeply different ways, differing on all the elements of a perspective. Such a society will not agree about the ideal; in effect, different groups will be searching different justice landscapes. But, we might ask, having abandoned a collective search for a common conception of the best, does this mean that deep moral diversity is not an engine of moral improvement?

4.3 A Liberal Order of Republican Communities?

Recall D'Agostino's distinction between "liberal" and "republican" communities of inquiry (§III.4.2). In a diverse liberal community, each "research team" explores the landscape generated by its perspective, using the heuristics and predictive models it finds most appropriate. "Each team will construct and traverse that region of the space which they find interesting."[72] This is consistent with maximum diversity, but, as we have seen in this chapter, it also encourages "justice teams"

---

[71] Ward, *The Ideal Worlds of Economics*, p. 468.
[72] D'Agostino, *Naturalizing Epistemology*, p. 138.

to develop views of the problem and solutions that may not be easily translatable into other perspectives. If the diverse perspectives are to put their findings together and so benefit from their diversity, they require something akin to D'Agostino's "republican approach," in which inquirers successfully communicate their results because they possess common standards of assessment.[73] Given that the interdependence of the elements of a perspective produces a diversity contagion—diversity in one element of a perspective produces diversity throughout the perspective—an open society will not itself form a common, giant, republican community: the very engine of diverse searching leads, at least in the context of justice that has been our concern, to deep diversity according to which different perspectives have disparate views of the nature of an ideally just society.

However, the "liberal" and "republican" approaches are not inconsistent: an overall liberal, open society may contain numerous republican communities which, because they are similar enough, some version of the Hong-Page dynamic can get traction, and so they can reap the benefits of diverse (but not too diverse) searches. They are able to share their results within their communities and so improve their collective understandings of justice. Moreover given the modularity of many problems, the links between different "republican" communities may crisscross the entire community. This can be formalized in the idea of a "small-world network,"[74] as in figure 3-6.

We often suppose that the diverse ideological groups are arrayed along a single left-right dimension (say, from left-justice inquirers to libertarian justice); but this leads to familiar perplexities. Consider the relation between orthodox libertarianism (L), "left-libertarianism" (LL), socialism (S), and conservatism (C). Calling L "right libertarianism" suggests an affinity to conservatism; but to an orthodox libertarian, LL is more statist than is orthodox libertarianism, and so the orthodox libertarian may view LL on the path to statism, in its socialist (S) version, which has affinities with conservative statism (C).[75] An

---

[73] Ibid., pp. 138–41.

[74] The classic analysis is Watts and Strogatz, "Collective Dynamics of 'Small-World' Networks."

[75] For some of these perplexities, see Mack and Gaus, "Classical Liberalism and Libertarianism."

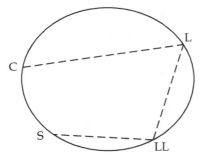

Figure 3-6. The small world of an open society

alternative to the left-right spectrum is to array the positions in a ring, as in figure 3-6, in which L is in one way next to C, yet it also allows that S is next to C, despite LL being next to S and far from C. Now as Ryan Muldoon, Michael Borgida, and Michael Cuffaro point out, when we model sociopolitical relations with a ring model, we can depict "small-world" networks by communication links between points along the ring.[76] For example, L shares problems with C (recall "fusion conservatism," §III.3.4) as well as with LL (e.g., the nature of Lockean natural rights); in turn LL can work on some problems with S (e.g., understanding equality of welfare). Thus despite the very different justice landscapes of S and L, they are linked via others to a common problem-solving network. The point here is that great diversity of problem-solving communities need not imply sectarian research programs in which the discoveries of very different groups have no benefit outside of one's own sectarian community. The liberal, open society can form a small-world network, in which the various communities of inquiry are linked in complex ways.

Such an Open Society will not be characterized by a shared ideal. Through the interactions of its constituent "republican" communities it will be a forum of contestation, disagreement, and, sometimes, mutual incomprehension. That it will not share an ideal or even a rough roadmap to an approximate utopia does not, however, mean that its communities cannot come to agree on moral improvement, and point the way to more just social relations. When networks connect diverse

[76] Muldoon, Borgida, and Cuffaro, "The Conditions of Tolerance."

perspectives, ideologies that seem entirely at odds can provide important inputs into each other's searches, leading to common recognition of more just social worlds.

This may all appear a Pollyanna perspective on diversity. Why should various perspectives on justice, each committed to its own ideal of the just society, endorse the structure of the Open Society, which by its very nature precludes complete attainment of what each treasures—a collective life based on *its* ideal? Perhaps if we still shared the Enlightenment's conviction that free inquiry in morality, as well as in science, will eventually lead to consensus on the truth, all perspectives might concur on the liberal framework of free inquiry. "Enlightenment philosophers," John Passmore observed, were convinced that "mankind had in the seventeenth century lit upon a method of discovery [the scientific method], a method which would guarantee future progress."[77] Each field was awaiting its Newton: "in the eighteenth century there was a fairly wide consensus that what Newton had achieved in the region of physics could surely also be applied to the regions of ethics and politics."[78] And so, as Alasdair MacIntyre noted:

> It was a central aspiration of the Enlightenment, an aspiration the formulation of which was its great achievement, to provide for debate in the public realm standards and methods of rational justification by which courses of action in every sphere of life could be adjudged just or unjust, rational or irrational, enlightened or unenlightened. So, it was hoped, reason would replace authority and tradition. Rational justification was to appeal to principles undeniable by any rational person and therefore independent of all those social and cultural peculiarities which the Enlightenment thinkers took to be mere accidental clothing of reason in particular times and places.[79]

Some cling to this Enlightenment faith that free inquiry will lead to moral consensus, but the history of morality in open societies exhibits a far more complex pattern: there has been both remarkable agree-

---

[77] Passmore, *The Perfectability of Man*, p. 200.
[78] Berlin, *The Roots of Romanticism*, p. 23.
[79] MacIntyre, *Whose Justice? Which Rationality?*, p. 6.

ment about some improvements (e.g., the wrongness of racial and gender discrimination), together with ever-deepening disputes about the place of humans in the universe, the roles and natures of the sexes, the role of the state, the relative importance of liberty and equality, and indeed the very nature of morality itself. "Western Judeo-Christian society" has not been transformed into a new secular order, but has dissolved into a complex, global pattern of Christian, Islamic, Jewish, and secular orientations—and each of these refracts into a spectrum of versions. Thus Rawls's core insight: the exercise of human reason under free institutions leads to disagreement. An Open Society, in which each is free to pursue his or her own inquiry into justice, exploring the terrain of justice as he or she sees it, using the methods he or she thinks most fit, will be characterized by continued, deep diversity, with no shared ideal. Given this, can a diverse, open society faced with "intractable struggles" and "irreconcilable" conflicts of "absolute depth" share a common moral existence on terms that are acceptable to all perspectives?[80] Can there be a moral, liberal framework for the Open Society, which itself abjures the pursuit of the ideal while providing a framework for diverse individual perspectives on justice? It is to this question that I now turn.

[80] Rawls, *Political Liberalism*, pp. xxvi, 4.

CHAPTER IV

The Nonideal

The Open Society

It takes all sorts to make a world.
—ENGLISH PROVERB

1 JUSTICE WITHOUT NORMALIZATION?

1.1 Normalization and Determinate Justice

CHAPTER II EXPLORED THE DEEP DILEMMA AT THE HEART OF THE "NOR-malized" approach to ideal justice: the very normalization that defines the "correct" perspective in political philosophy leads to the conclusion that this correct perspective on justice cannot effectively identify its own ideal. Chapter III analyzed ways to ease this tension—abandoning a fully normalized perspective in favor of various partial normalizations. We saw that when a partial normalization generated enough diversity to drive effective searching it ultimately engendered disagreement on the ideal itself. It would seem—at least on first inspection—that we must choose between full normalization, which yields a definite theory of justice but makes it most unlikely that we can find the ideal, and relaxing normalization, which improves the chances that many will find better alternatives, but which yields disagreement about what ideal justice is.

This "first look" conclusion resonates with the trajectory of Rawls's work. Throughout most of his career Rawls supposed that a theory based on a shared (or, which comes to much the same thing, a single) evaluative point of view will generate a determinate social contract. From the 1960s through the 1980s, philosophical inquiry into justice was largely dominated by the pursuit of such an "Archimedean point": a description of an impartial, normalized chooser such that his choice would identify *the* correct principles of justice. As David Gauthier pointed out, "Archimedes supposed that given a sufficiently long lever and a place to stand, he could move the earth. We may then think of an Archimedean point as one from which a single individual may exert the force required to move or affect some object. In moral theory, the Archimedean point is that position one must occupy, if one's own decisions are to possess the moral force to govern the moral realm. From the Archimedean point one has the moral capacity to shape society."[1] This normalized chooser was to identify a single, determinate ranking of social states. Rawls explicitly justifies the introduction of the veil of ignorance and maximin reasoning as a way to overcome what he saw as a gross deficiency in his 1958 "Justice as Fairness." In that first version of his social contract, the second principle of justice was simply a Pareto condition that required inequalities to fall on the Pareto frontier of mutual benefit.[2] The principle, however, did not say anything about *where* on the Pareto frontier society must settle. By the time Rawls wrote "Distributive Justice" he was convinced that this indeterminacy was a serious problem. "There are," he wrote, "many such [Pareto-optimal] distributions, since there are many ways of allocating commodities so that no further mutually beneficial exchange is possible. Hence the Pareto criterion, as important as it is, admittedly does not identify the best distribution, but rather a class of optimal, or

[1] Gauthier, *Morals by Agreement*, p. 233. Compare Rawls, *A Theory of Justice*, p. 511. John Thrasher and I consider this matter in far more depth in "Rational Choice and the Original Position." See also the insightful analysis of Wolff, *Understanding Rawls*, part 2.

[2] The standard Pareto condition is that a given allocation of goods is Pareto efficient when no one can gain more without someone else having less. Presently (§IV.1.2.1) I shall have recourse to a Pareto criterion for collective decisions: if everyone in some group holds that x is better than y, then by this Pareto rule the collective decision must be that x is better than y. While these two criteria may appear very different, both stem from the aim of being able to say that one social state is unambiguously better than another in a way that does not require trade-offs between gains for some and losses for others. In the allocation rule, if we can move from state S_1 to state S_2 and some gain and no one is worse off, then the Pareto criterion recommends it. We should keep on making such moves until the distribution is Pareto efficient in the sense described above—at that point changes can only be made by weighing gains for some against losses for others. In the collective choice context, if some people prefer x to y and others y to x, we need to weigh the two sets of preferences to arrive at an outcome; if, however, everyone agrees that x is better than y, we have a clear case of improvement without weighing preferences (or counting votes).

efficient distributions.... The criterion is at best an incomplete principle for ordering distributions."[3] Rawls's work leading up to *Theory*,
which shaped much of contemporary political philosophy, was to
identify a normalized choice perspective that provided a theory of justice ("justice as fairness"), specific enough to give authoritative, determinate rankings of social states and/or institutions. By *Political Liberalism* this project is abandoned:

> The view I have called "justice as fairness" is but one example of a
> liberal political conception; its specific content is not definitive of
> such a view.... The point of the ideal of public reason is that citizens
> are to conduct their fundamental discussions within the framework
> of what each regards as a political conception of justice based on
> values that the others can reasonably be expected to endorse and
> each is, in good faith, prepared to defend that conception so under-
> stood. This means that each of us must have, and be ready to ex-
> plain, a criterion of what principles and guidelines we think other
> citizens (who are also free and equal) may reasonably be expected
> to endorse along with us. We must have some test we are ready to
> state as to when this condition is met. I have elsewhere suggested
> as a criterion the values expressed by the principles and guidelines
> that would be agreed to in the original position. *Many will prefer
> another criterion.*[4]

At this point, then, the argument from the original position is one test
as to what reasonable people may be expected to endorse: it yields
what Rawls calls "justice as fairness." But "many will prefer" a different test; perhaps a differently described original position, yielding a
different conception of justice. Those who wish to minimize the fundamental importance of this shift content themselves with saying that
in Rawls's later work a "family" of liberal views is still justified, one
member of which is "justice as fairness." Two observations are in order.

(*i*) In 1958's "Justice as Fairness" a "family" of distributive views
was also justified, and Rawls saw this as a core weakness in a theory
of justice, which aimed at a well-ordered society that could agree on a

---

[3] Rawls, "Distributive Justice," p. 135. Compare *Theory of Justice*, p. 121.

[4] Rawls, *Political Liberalism*, pp. 226–27. Emphasis added, paragraph break
deleted.

determinate ranking of claims. On the original version of the contract we would have no shared conception of justice to resolve distributive disputes. In *Theory* Rawls searched for a well-ordered society: that is, "a society in which (1) everyone accepts and knows that the others accept *the same principles of justice*, and (2) the basic social institutions generally satisfy and are generally known to satisfy these principles."[5] As Samuel Freeman notes, it is anything but clear that this ideal of a well-ordered society survives the last developments of political liberalism.[6] This surely is a fundamental change.

(*ii*) It is not as if Rawls identifies a single original position with a single normalized perspective that yields a "family" (i.e., set) of conceptions as its conclusion.[7] Rather, Rawls suggests that different "tests"—say versions of the original position, employing different plausible normalizations of the choosers—will arrive at different conceptions of justice. So at the end we seem to be left with multiple reasonable original positions, or we might say, a set of arguments that, together, presuppose *partial normalizations*: choosers are not fully normalized across all original positions, since they differ in various reasonable original position set ups. In an interesting yet somewhat puzzling way, we are confronted with a family of liberal *theories* of justice—a variety of reasonable perspectives on liberal justice. Rather than *a theory* that gives rise to *a family*, it seems more apt to say that we have a family of theories.

One has to be an especially devout disciple of Rawls not to conclude that by the close of his political liberalism project the theory of justice was in disarray.[8] Rawls insisted that a theory of justice was charac-

---

[5] Rawls, *A Theory of Justice*, p. 4. Emphasis added.

[6] Freeman, *Justice and the Social Contract*, pp. 255–56.

[7] As we shall see later in this chapter, to do this would require fundamental changes in the nature of argument from the original position, as it would introduce basic disagreement about justice into the choice situation. For an attempt to model such an original position see Muldoon et al., "Disagreement behind the Veil of Ignorance."

[8] Some might argue that political liberalism is concerned with legitimacy, not justice. Even if so, this would not show that a coherent *theory of justice* remains. A theory of legitimacy is supposed to analyze a citizen's attitudes and obligations toward a state that is not fully just; but that very idea supposes that citizens have a coherent view of what social justice is in a society in which reasonable citizens disagree, as well as supposing that they have some grounds to seek to legislate their favored view over

terized by choice from a certain normalized perspective, but his later view allows multiple partially normalized perspectives that yield different conceptions of justice. However, if one acknowledges that there are other reasonable normalizations that yield inconsistent conceptions, in what sense can one plausibly claim that one has identified *the* principles of justice for the definitive ordering of social claims in a well-ordered society, based on one's preferred normalization? To be sure, one can conjecture that, say, justice as fairness is the most reasonable,[9] but in all our reasonable disputes one believes that one's views are the most reasonable—that is, after all, why one holds them over competing views. But if "citizens will of course differ as to which conceptions of political justice they think the most reasonable,"[10] on what grounds can I insist that others, who uphold differing reasonable conceptions, must conform to mine? Of course I can hope that "an orderly contest between them over time is a reliable way to find which one, if any, is most reasonable,"[11] but that does not tell me what to do, here and now, when faced with reasonable disputes about justice. "Go ahead and impose your own preferred theory" does not seem especially attractive for a public reason view, even if one employs majoritarian methods or the Supreme Court to do so.

1.2 Sen's Partial Normalization Theory

1.2.1 A Social Choice among Multiple Spectators. Although many philosophers have been dismissive, if not downright contemptuous, of Amartya Sen's analysis in *The Idea of Justice*, it is one of the most important advances in the post-Rawlsian public reason project. It seeks to reconcile the idea of *a* definite theory of justice with the recognition that there is no single, normalized perspective from which to reason about justice. This latter point is one of the lessons to be derived from

the reasonable objections of others. "It's only about legitimacy" is not a magic phrase that can make these issues disappear. What *is* the liberal theory of justice?

[9] Rawls, *Political Liberalism*, p. 381.

[10] Rawls, "The Idea of Public Reason Revisited," p. 578.

[11] Rawls, *Political Liberalism*, p. 227. Notice the echoes of the Enlightenment View (§III.4.3). Given Rawls's account of reasonable pluralism and its inevitability under free institutions, appealing to convergence of reasoning here looks, ad hoc, indeed desperate.

Sen's parable of three children and the flute.[12] Three children are quar-
relling about who is to get a flute. If we consider only claims based on
who can best use the flute, it goes to Anne, who alone can play it; if we
consider only claims of need, it goes to Bob, who is so impoverished
that he has no other toys;[13] if we consider only claims to desert and
self-ownership, it goes to Carla, who made the flute. We can construct
a choice situation in which all will agree with any of the three distributions if we filter out information about the other relevant distributional criteria—that is, if we normalize the evaluative perspective (to a
common evaluative standard) such that only one criterion matters. But
all three qualify as reasonable impartial principles of justice, and there
is no uniquely correct way to weigh them.[14] "At the heart of the particular problem of a unique impartial resolution of the perfectly just
society is the possible *sustainability of plural and competing reasons of
justice, all of which have claims to impartiality and which nevertheless
differ from—and rival—each other.*"[15] Unless we invoke a highly controversial normalization procedure (for example, simply excluding information relating to desert), rational and impartial free and equal
persons will rank the alternatives differently, disagreeing on the optimal element.

Even after we have done our best to identify impartial spectators
(i.e., eligible partially normalized perspectives) who base their judgments on considerations acceptable to all, and who are free from bias
and parochialism, Sen holds that we are left with multiple impartial
spectators.[16] *We have multiple partially normalized perspectives.* Even
if we suppose that each impartial spectator could give a complete
justice-based ranking of feasible alternatives,[17] their rankings will

[12] Sen, *The Idea of Justice*, pp. 12–15.
[13] Though what he will do with a flute he cannot play isn't obvious. Sen says the
flute "will give him something to play with" (ibid., p. 13), rather suggesting that he
will use it as fancy stick or like a party favor that can make a loud noise. If he learns
to play it, then Anne's case is weakened. If he does not learn to play it, it is unlikely
to satisfy his needs for long.
[14] That is, we do not share a mapping function (§II.1.1).
[15] Sen, *The Idea of Justice*, p. 12. Emphasis added.
[16] Adam Smith also suggests a plurality of impartial spectators. See *Theory of Moral
Sentiments*, e.g., pp. 78, 82.
[17] This is a simplification; Sen's solution does not require that each spectator can

Spectator Alf	Spectator Betty	Spectator Charlie
a	c	d
b	a	a
c	d	b
e	b	e
d	e	c

Figure 4-1. Orderings of partially normalized impartial spectators

only partially overlap. "There will, of course, be considerable divergence between different impartial views… [and] this would yield an incomplete social ranking, based on congruently ranked pairs, and this incomplete ranking could be seen as being shared by all."[18] Figure 4-1 provides a drastically simplified, stylized example of three impartial spectators ranking five alternatives. Here the ordering shared by our three impartial spectators (or, in the terms of our model, partially normalized perspectives) is $a \succ b$,[19] $b \succ e$ (so, by transitivity, $a \succ e$). Notice that this is to apply a Paretian rule over impartial spectators: if for all spectators $a \succ b$, then according to *the* full (comprehensive) theory of justice, a is more just than b. Notice that while each impartial spectator can rank c and d, we might say that "reasonable conceptions of justice" disagree (for Spectators Alf and Betty, $c \succ d$, but for Charlie, $d \succ c$). On Sen's view the (full) theory of justice cannot order c and d (or the pairs [c, e], [d, e]) as there is reasonable disagreement about their relative justice.

Much of Sen's most innovative work has been on rational choice from incomplete orderings.[20] He thus points a way out of Rawls's conundrum. Even though we have multiple, inconsistent, partially normalized perspectives, if we allow our theory of justice to be incomplete, we can acknowledge that different perspectives will have some-

---

give a complete ordering. Drawing on Sen, I have shown how such incompleteness can be addressed in *The Order of Public Reason*, pp. 303–10.

[18] Sen, *The Idea of Justice*, p. 135.

[19] Read "a is preferred to (or ranked as more just than) b."

[20] See, for example, Sen, "Maximization and the Act of Choice."

times conflicting unequivocal pairwise judgments of justice, and yet we still can generate rational choice based on consensus about justice in a wide range of situations. We can achieve definiteness (though not completeness of definite judgments) with only partial normalization.

1.2.2 Severely Constrained Evaluative Diversity. If, employing Sen's idea of impartial spectators, we end up with a small group of eligible normalized perspectives, it seems plausible that the Pareto rule will generate an interestingly large class of pairwise comparisons, so that our (full) theory of justice, while incomplete, will not be empty. But as we increase the set of possible normalized perspectives so that the number of impartial spectators becomes large, the Pareto rule is apt to be of little help. As soon as a single spectator deems $b \succ a$, the full theory cannot conclude that according to (overall, or complete) justice $a \succ b$. Is this a problem? The reply by a proponent of Sen's view appears straightforward: plausible normalized perspectives about justice can disagree about a lot, but so too must they agree about a lot. Any normalization, a defender of Sen might say, partial though it might be, necessarily restricts the domain of possible orderings of the worlds to be evaluated. Worlds characterized by severe human rights violations and famine are not admissibly preferable to those that score very high on protection of rights and have sufficient food for all, on any plausible perspective on justice.[21]

While all this is true as far as it goes, it leads us right back to the core of Rawls's worry concerning the diversity of reasonable views about the right or just: how deep and wide are these differences? Rawls insisted that the partially normalized views that resulted were all versions of egalitarian liberalism,[22] but there is no sustained argument for this conclusion; if there are many political values that can be weighed in many ways, we have prima facie grounds for thinking that the set of eligible perspectives on justice may be rather larger than either Rawls or Sen intimated. And if we are confronted with a large set of diverse eligible perspectives on justice, then Sen's Paretian rule is apt, after all, to be radically incomplete. It thus seems that Sen's approach

---

[21] See here David Estlund's list of "primary bads," *Democratic Authority*, p. 163.

[22] Rawls, *Political Liberalism*, pp. 6, 7n.

works well for the sort of limited diversity of eligible perspectives that Rawls sometimes seemed to have in mind but falters if we cannot make considerable progress in identifying a rather small set of appropriately partially normalized perspectives.

1.2.3 Complete Normalization of Social Worlds. But that is not the truly deep worry about Sen's approach. Sen makes much of the fact that his account is based on a "social choice perspective," which directly evaluates societies, states of affairs, or, we might say, social worlds, rather than focusing on rules or institutions. Drawing on Indian thought, Sen emphasizes the contrast between *niti*—which seems a severe, rule-based approach to justice related to deontology, and *nyaya*, according to which "justice is not just a matter of judging institutions and rules, but of judging societies themselves."[23] *Nyaya* is a broadly consequentialist idea—the focus of evaluation should be the state of affairs that constitutes a society, not simply its rules and institutions. "Justice is ultimately connected with the way people's lives go, and not *merely* with the nature of the institutions surrounding them."[24] Thus, Sen insists, we must focus on evaluating the justice of entire states of affairs. "Even though the possibility of describing any state of affairs 'in its entirety' is not credible (we can always add some more detail) the basic idea of a state of affairs can be informationally rich, *and take note of all the features that we see as important.*"[25]

This raises a subtle but fundamental problem: Sen's account supposes a full normalization in how the eligible perspectives characterize the elements in the domain {X} of alternative social worlds.[26] Although Sen would appear to allow differences in evaluative standards (ES) such as desert, need, and so on, and the mapping relation (MP), in the form of different judgments by impartial spectators, the domain of social worlds in {X} and the relevant properties of these social worlds is fixed and fully normalized among the partially normalized perspectives (§II.1). If their exercise is to make any sense, the impartial spectators must order the *same domain of social worlds,* where the spectators

---

[23] Sen, *The Idea of Justice,* pp. 20–21, 210.
[24] Ibid., p. x. Emphasis added. See also p. 410.
[25] Ibid., p. 214. Emphasis added.
[26] Of course, for Sen {X} need not include the ideal.

agree on the options to be ordered (what social choice theorists often call "the feasible set"). Consider again figure 4-1. Our impartial spectators must agree on the identity conditions of a and b if we are to make sense of the conclusion that *they agree* that $a \succ b$. Now as we saw earlier (§III.2.4) states of affairs are not like artifacts or cities where we can identify the thing (perhaps via a name) but disagree about almost all its properties. The state of affairs simply *is* its relevant properties. So in this case to agree on the identity of any given option, a, is to agree on its relevant properties. If the spectators do not agree on its properties, they do not agree on *what* they are ordering, and so they cannot agree *in* their orderings. That all agree that $a \succ b$ would not tell us much if they did not agree on what a and b are. If Alf's "a" is really a' and his "b" is really b',[27] then he is not really agreeing with Betty's ranking that $a \succ b$.

It might seem that this problem could be overcome by partitioning these differently described social worlds (a and a') into smaller social worlds about which they do agree. Suppose the impartial spectators come to realize that Spectator Alf has in mind by a' the set of features $\{f, g\}$, while Spectator Betty identifies $\{f, j\}$ as the relevant features of her a. Alf and Betty do agree on feature $\{f\}$, so we might think that they could agree to focus on the "small common world" defined by the intersection of a and a'—characterized by $\{f\}$—and rank *that* world in relation to others. But our spectators will not think this small world defined by $\{f\}$ is very important, as it is divorced from other relevant features, which, when considered (recall the interdependencies of features [§II.2] may make all the difference when evaluating the justice of the "larger" social world). Given that the evaluation of a social world arises out of the evaluative standards (ES) as applied to the relevant features (WF), Alf's and Betty's judgments about a social world will change when they consider it as, say, possessing only relevant feature $\{f\}$ and as possessing features $\{f, g\}$, so an evaluation based only on the shared, common, feature $\{f\}$ will not be of much interest to either.

Another alternative—let us call this *the common projection criterion*—is that Alf and Betty use $\{f\}$, as it were, merely to *identify* a common social world, but Alf continues to see the world as composed of

---

[27] Where, of course $a \neq a'$ and $b \neq b'$.

$\{f, g\}$ and Betty $\{f, j\}$. We might say that Alf's perspective cannot "see" feature $\{j\}$ while Betty's cannot see $\{g\}$ as properties relevant to justice. But they do concur that "world a" is that world which they both see as possessing $\{f\}$.[28] On this alternative each evaluates the full (large) social world as he or she sees it, but they individuate social worlds by the shared feature they both see, in this case $\{f\}$. This clearly avoids the problem of the "small-worlds" approach, as each evaluates the full set of relevant properties as he or she understands them. But recall that in our model social worlds are individuated by their full set of relevant features (§II.1.2). This was not arbitrary, for many worlds with vastly different justice will share many common features. Consider another world (let us assume that it makes sense to call it b), that Alf's perspective identifies as $\{f, x\}$ and Betty's as $\{f, z\}$. If we use our common feature as the common identification criterion, both Alf's a world, $\{f, g\}$, and his b world, $\{f, x\}$, will be publicly identified as the same social world—that world characterized by feature $\{f\}$. And of course the same will be true for Betty's quite different social worlds, $\{f, j\}$ and $\{f, z\}$. Worlds a and b are the same world as identified by common features, but Alf and Betty each see these as quite distinct, with different justice scores. Alf might well be confused by Betty, who sometimes when evaluating the $\{f\}$ world gives it one score (that is, when it is a world she sees as $\{f, j\}$) and sometimes another score (when she sees it as $\{f, z\}$). As Alf sees it, she gives differing justice scores to the same common world. And the same will be true of Betty in relation to Alf's evaluations. Each will see the other as inconsistent when each is, in fact, entirely consistent in their full world evaluations.[29]

[28] As we shall later put it, $\{f\}$ is the common projection of their different perspectives on this social world. See §IV.1.3.1.

[29] It might seem that another alternative would be for them to characterize their joint (interperspectival) social worlds by the unions of the properties they each see. For world "a," this would be Alf's $\{f, g\}$ and Betty's $\{f, j\}$, so the interperspectival identity of world a is the world with properties $\{f, g, j\}$; in this case neither Alf nor Betty sees the world as having all three properties. This raises a number of deep puzzles. For one, Alf is committed to employing a criterion of individuation that relies on properties that he does not think world a possesses. Suppose his is a Marxist perspective: he may be committed to the interperspectival world a being characterized by property rights, exploitation (two features he sees), and the violation of God's commands (a feature Betty "sees" that he thinks bizarre)! Leaving that puzzle aside, the union procedure still will not give a unique account of individuation. Sup-

The upshot is that the social choice approach to diversity requires normalization of the features of states of affairs. This is no mere formal point. Recall that, referring to the "intractable" struggles in our history of religious conflict, Rawls proclaims that "political liberalism starts by taking to heart *the absolute depth of that irreconcilable latent conflict.*"[30] A fundamental reason why these struggles are so deep and wide is not simply (perhaps in some cases not at all) because various religious perspectives and secular worldviews have radically different understandings of the principles of justice (ES), but because they have fundamentally different understandings of the social world that principles of justice are intended to regulate (WF).[31] An Evangelical Christian has a very different understanding of the social world—its real, underlying features—than does, say, a secular Darwinist philosopher. The social world of the Evangelical perspective is one where sin and sanctity are features of states of affairs; they are not merely values or preferences, but basic aspects of the ontology of the world that determine the circumstances of social life. These features simply do not exist in the social world of the secular Darwinist—as he sees it, they are illusions or fantasies. He has no categories that correspond to them; in his understanding of social worlds (WF) that are within the domain to be taken seriously, none has such properties. If he is being generous and "liberal-minded," he may admit that Evangelicals have "preferences" to continue with their religious practices, and since preferences are indeed real, they at least count, but the underlying social world simply does not have the fantastic entities the Evangelical assumes. There is only one world, and it is the secular world revealed by science. This is

---

pose Betty continues to see a world with simply $\{f, j\}$, but Alf sees two worlds, one with $\{f, g\}$ and one with $\{f, g, j\}$. On the union account, given Betty's perspective, both of Alf's worlds have the same interperspectival identity of $\{f, g, j\}$, but this fails to distinguish Alf's $\{f, g\}$ and $\{f, g, j\}$ worlds, which he is apt to evaluate differently. Most puzzling of all, the union account "creates" a multitude of "new worlds" simply by combining the properties of the worlds identified by different perspectives. Because the perspectives see radically different features in these worlds, they will evaluate the union of their properties very differently, thus leading to almost unlimited diversity in the orderings of our impartial spectators, and so undermining the use of Sen's Paretian rule.

[30] Rawls, *Political Liberalism*, p. xxvi, 4. Emphasis added.

[31] Ibid., p. 17.

the normalized world that all theories of justice, says the secular Darwinist, must presuppose.

This seems to be Sen's view. It is revealing that nowhere in *The Idea of Justice* do we confront a serious discussion of religious perspectives, and the nature of a religious person's social world—a critical issue in many, perhaps most, societies today. Sen defends freedom of religion as a sort of liberty to participate in one's ancestral culture,[32] but it is clearly supposed that any eligible impartial spectator will have a normalized secular, naturalistic, social ontology. The impartial spectators have different evaluations, but they categorize social worlds in the same way. However, we do not even begin to understand the problem of reasonable pluralism about justice if we translate the Evangelical's claim of a duty to obey the word of God as a claim to a right to engage in a cultural practice. We see no hint in Sen's writings of the worry that consumed Rawls's later work—whether liberal justice can be endorsed from a variety of comprehensive views that interpret the world and the universe in fundamentally different ways. And that is not because of any oversight by Sen. Unless he strictly normalizes what constitutes the social worlds to be evaluated, his Paretian social choice–based solution to the problem of diversity of views about justice cannot possibly work.

It is important to stress that disagreements about the nature of the social worlds in which we live are neither peripheral nor can they be redescribed as value or preferential disputes (i.e., pushed into the evaluative standards element of a perspective). Some of our deepest and most intractable disputes are not about values or principles of justice, but about the world to which these principles apply. The most obvious instance is the long-standing and persistent struggle concerning abortion rights. Advocates of such rights see the case as decisively about fundamental rights of personal autonomy; opponents of abortion rights are depicted as having little sensitivity to a woman's claim to control her own body.[33] But this by no means follows, and often is simply not the case; opponents of abortion can be deeply devoted to such autonomy, but not in cases where it entails overriding another's

---

[32] Sen, *The Idea of Justice*, p. 237.
[33] See Rawls, *Political Liberalism*, pp. 243–44n.

right to life. And, of course, in the abstract, most advocates of abortion rights would also draw back in such situations. The dispute is centrally about the social world to which the principles of autonomy and the right to life apply: the two social worlds do not have the same set of persons, and so even perfect agreement about abstract principles of justice would not resolve the dispute. It is only because so many moral philosophers agree with Sen that there is only a single, fully normalized, secular social world that the dispute has to be misdescribed as one simply about values or abstract principles of justice.

A similar problem has plagued discussions of the harm principle. Recall a classic objection by Robert Paul Wolff, who notes that according to Mill's harm principle,

> I am liable to others when I affect their "interests." Society may interfere only in those areas of my life in which it has, or takes, an interest. Now this distinction between those aspects of my life which affect the interest of others, and those aspects in which they do not take an interest, is extremely tenuous, not to say unreal, and Mill does nothing to strengthen it. Mill takes it as beyond dispute that when Smith hits Jones, or steals his purse, or accuses him in court, or sells him a horse, he is in some way affecting Jones' interests. But Mill also seems to think it is obvious that when Smith practices the Roman faith, or reads philosophy, or eats meat, or engages in homosexual practices, he is not affecting Jones' interests. Now suppose that Jones is a devout Calvinist or a principled vegetarian. The very presence in his community of a Catholic or a meat-eater may cause him fully as much pain as a blow in the face or the theft of his purse. Indeed, to a truly devout Christian a physical blow counts for much less than the blasphemy of heretic. After all, a physical blow affects my interests by causing me pain or stopping me from doing something I want to do. If the existence of ungodly persons in my community tortures my soul and destroys my sleep, who is to say that my interests are not affected?[34]

Proponents of the harm principle, if they are interested at all in accommodating such "harms," typically seek to depict them as psychological

---

[34] Wolff, *The Poverty of Liberalism*, pp. 23–24.

harms or offensive actions.[35] No one *truly* has a basic interest in living in a society without homosexuality, or one free of ungodly rituals, since such religious worldviews are inadmissible in the normalized world of the secular harm principle. However, if people get really upset, *that* at least is real, and perhaps something can be done about that. This may be enough for the secular, normalized view, but it misses the point of the religious complaint.[36] The complaint is not that one is getting upset; whether or not one knew about it, one's interests would be set back by such behavior.[37] Perhaps one of the most striking ways in which debates involving religious categorizations have been normalized (and in Foucault's more sinister sense)[38] in much contemporary liberal discourse is the redescription of religious-based disapproval of homosexuality as a disease, "homophobia"—a manifest effort to control a deviant categorization by labeling it as illness.[39]

Many of the same points apply to environmentalism and various forms of support for animal rights. Again, some of the claims of environmentalists and animal rights advocates can be translated into, say, a standard Western normalized world, where humans are the sole persons, but pain to all sentient creatures is bad.[40] But many cannot. Those who see nature as an entity to be respected, or who hold that ecosystems have basic rights, do not live in this normalized world.

---

[35] I am criticizing myself here. See my *Social Philosophy*, chap. 8.

[36] Note that even Wolff appeals to both torturing the soul, which certainly depends on a religious categorization, and destroying sleep, which does not.

[37] For a fascinating analysis of harms that presuppose controversial views of the social world, see Muldoon, "Perspective-Dependent Harm."

[38] Foucault, *Discipline and Punish*, pp. 177ff.

[39] Similarly, those who reject feminist claims, or, more generally, feminist perspectives, are very often labeled "misogynistic," normalizing feminism such that only a pathological emotional state could explain opposition. Normalization of one's political position by depicting opposing perspectives as pathological is becoming something of a fashion; witness John Tomasi's (idiosyncratic) labeling of classical libertarians, who believe social justice is normatively objectionable, or presupposes an erroneous view of the social world, as suffering from "Social Justicitis" (by which he means, oddly, "Social Justice–phobia"). *Free Market Fairness*, chap. 5. The very thesis of the present work has been described as a sort of illness; see Estlund's "Utopophobia."

[40] The morality of this normalized world is what some call WEIRD—Western, Educated, Industrialized, Rich Democratic—morality. See Haidt, *The Righteous Mind*, chap. 5.

Other examples abound. Even those who embrace almost all the details of the Rawlsian analysis of justice fundamentally disagree on its application to international or global justice, and surely one of the important reasons for this is a fundamental dispute whether "peoples" are entities with moral status.[41] Here we have a stark reminder that agreeing on a theory of justice, without agreeing about the social world to which it applies, by no means guarantees agreement in judging social realizations.

None of this is to say that in a society where there is great disagreement about the social world we inhabit any perspective may legitimately insist that its social world be imposed on others. That in your social world ecosystems are persons, that God forbids homosexuality, or that jokes about sex are not funny[42] does not itself tell me anything about what I am to do, or how I am to live with you. It is to insist however, that, unless our thinking about diversity takes seriously these extraordinarily deep disagreements about the nature of the social world (the categories used to characterize it), we will fail to understand what is required to live in a free and open society.

1.3 Muldoon's Nonnormalized Contract

1.3.1 When Worlds Overlap. The most innovative and sophisticated work rethinking political philosophy in light of deep perspectival differences is that of Ryan Muldoon, who proposes a social contract free of normalization assumptions. Muldoon's key insight is that, even if your and my social worlds do not categorize objects in the same way, we may still have common social "objects," or, we might say, partial projections of objects, about which we can negotiate. Taking our cue from Muldoon, let us start with a simple case,[43] as in figure 4-2. Alf, Betty, and Charlie have three perspectives on the same object; all can

---

[41] "Liberal peoples have three basic features: a reasonably just constitutional democratic government that serves their fundamental interests; citizens united by what Mill called 'common sympathies'; and finally, a moral nature." Rawls, *The Law of Peoples*, p. 23.

[42] They are not aptly categorized as jokes at all; they are not jokes in that social world, but forms of domination.

[43] Muldoon, *Beyond Tolerance*, chap. 3.

see the world in three-dimensional space. On Alf's perspective the object is a two-dimensional circle, as it is on Charlie's, though on Charlie's perspective it is a different circle (it does not share the same spatial location as the one Alf sees). Betty sees the shape as a cylinder, but not as a closed one. Compare: to a research scientist, a fetus may be a source of stem cells; to a Catholic, a person with a soul; to a natural rights philosopher, a fetus may be a trespasser violating the rights of the mother-owner. That there is no normalized characterization of the real object that all must endorse does not imply that these non-normalized perspectives share nothing; they share partial characterizations of the object (or, we might say, they see different projections of the object). That, after all, is why the three can argue about the proper treatment of "the fetus" even though they ascribe very different properties to it—and so in a fundamental sense do not have the same object in mind at all. Notice that, in contrast to Sen's social choice approach, which founders on disagreements as to the objects being evaluated, Muldoon makes such disagreement the center of his analysis.[44]

The core of Muldoon's insightful—indeed revolutionary—proposal is that we can model social contracts as bargains about who has rights over an "object" while simultaneously acknowledging that the parties do not agree precisely about the nature of the object over which they are bargaining. Writes Muldoon:

> If two agents have different categorizations, this means that they will not divide state space up in the same way. This is simply because they categorize the world differently, and so they have different conceptions of salience.... They are seeing the same thing, but just interpret it differently. As there is no neutral [or normalized] representation of the state space, we cannot take one partition as better than another, and so we cannot just pick one and require

---

[44] This is not to say that some of the problems with the *common projection criterion* that we explored in §IV.1.2.3 do not appear in Muldoon's contract. It is possible that Alf will distinguish two different bargains that, as far as Betty is concerned, have the same projection. In terms of our shape example, Alf may sometimes see an oval and sometimes a cylinder, but if these always have the same projection for Betty—in both cases Betty sees a cylinder—she will think his valuations inconsistent, for she will not be able to see why he values (what looks to her as) the same cylinder differently at different times. His individuation of the bargain differs from hers.

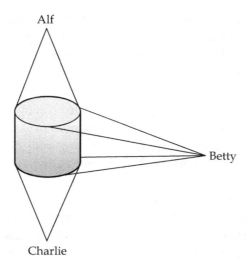

Figure 4-2. Common projections of different perspectives

everyone to use it. This much is clear. But we also cannot just take the union of everyone's partition sets and expect everyone to share this larger partition set. This is because there is no assurance that people can *see* the distinctions that are in other perspectives if they do not themselves hold them. So just as we do not have the same accounts of value (and hence utility functions), we do not have the same partition sets. But even though we cannot expect that individuals can adopt this union of all partition sets, we can describe the overall bargain by making reference to this union set, so long as we do not assume that the agents in the bargain themselves are aware of it.[45]

The overall bargain really concerns the *union* of Alf's, Betty's, and Charlie's perspectives, for depending on how the bargain comes out, it will affect, as it were, the way the entire cylinder is used; but none of them see a closed cylinder, so none will think the bargain is about that (it will, from their individual perspectives, be a bargain about who has rights over which circle, or who has rights over an open cylinder).

[45] Muldoon, "Justice without Agreement."

Muldoon's nonnormalized social contract, then, is an n-person bargain over the allocation of rights that, in one respect, is about rights over overlapping bits of the world, yet determines rights over the "full objects" in each perspective (when these full objects include the bits that are jointly seen). Note that this contract does not require that we share a normalized, or even partially normalized, perspective on the social world. Yet the allocation of rights applies to each nonnormalized social world and—if we accept the Nash bargaining solution on which Muldoon relies—each perspective can endorse the overall social distribution of rights.[46]

Muldoon's contract yields public justification without normalization. The ultimate terms of association are justified to all relevant evaluative perspectives insofar as each perspective deems the terms ones that advance its concerns as far as reasonably can be expected, given the perspectives of others.[47] Although Muldoon often sees his proposal as an alternative to public reason political theories, that is only because the dominant public reason views have been committed to strong normalization: public reason has typically been identified with the reason of the normalized public perspective—the liberal perspective.[48] Muldoon, though, is correct that such traditional public reason views, rather than helping us devise a theory of justice for all, valorize one perspective and its understanding of justice. In response, those

---

[46] There is considerable debate about the appropriateness of the Nash bargaining solution to moral justification. Ken Binmore defends it in *Natural Justice*. For a period David Gauthier endorsed the Nash solution, before abandoning the idea that moral contractarianism should be modeled on bargains. See his "Twenty-Five On." For Rawls's criticism, see "Justice as Fairness," p. 58n. Rawls, as have many others, worried about the way that the Nash bargaining solution is sensitive to threat advantage: "To each according to his threat advantage is hardly the principle of fairness." Although Muldoon relies on the Nash solution he is not adverse to alternative solutions so long as the equality of participants is respected. Muldoon, *Beyond Tolerance*, chap. 6. For a defense of a modified Nash bargaining solution that mitigates some fairness concerns, see Moehler, "The (Stabilized) Nash Bargaining Solution as a Principle of Distributive Justice."

[47] We can understand the idea of what can be "reasonably expected" as articulated by the relevant bargaining axioms—especially symmetry. See Thrasher, "Uniqueness and Symmetry in Bargaining Theories of Justice."

[48] As in Quong, *Liberalism without Perfection*, esp. chap. 1, part 2. See my "Sectarianism without Perfection? Quong's Political Liberalism."

excluded either oppose public reason liberalism as a sectarian project, or draw back, alienated, into their own perspectives. The promise of public reason as providing a justified conception of justice in the midst of diversity goes unfulfilled. More than that: it becomes a screen for the dominance of a controversial secular social world.[49] In the end, such public reason views are very similar to traditional moral theories, which are based on a normalized perspective claiming to be the uniquely correct way to identify the morally relevant properties of social worlds.[50] Muldoon's project promises to revive public reason as a doctrine that truly responds to our deep and enduring differences.

1.3.2 Dynamism and the Open Society. Muldoon insists that his understanding of the social contract is dynamic, stressing constant adaptation. As new perspectives enter and old ones die away, the social contract must adjust.[51] Not surprisingly, he endorses John Stuart Mill's stress on experiments in living, and the ongoing discovery of better ways to live together;[52] conversely, he is especially critical of Rawls's claim that in modeling a social contract, we should suppose the parties will be bound through an unpredictable future, and cannot renegotiate as they proceed.[53] Constant changes in the perspectives of the population (for example, the immigration of Muslim groups), changes in environmental conditions, and discovery of better ways of living together all require that we conceive of the social contract as a set of dynamic, evolving bargains for mutual benefit, not a set of principles fixed "once and for all." Because there is no normalized, fixed perspective from which to reason about fixed principles, the social contract is necessarily tightly coupled to the perspectives presently populating a society.

[49] See Haidt, *The Righteous Mind*, chap. 5.

[50] On this point see Van Schoelandt's analysis in "Justification, Coercion, and the Place of Public Reason."

[51] Muldoon, *Beyond Tolerance*, chap. 6.

[52] Muldoon, "Expanding the Justificatory Framework of Mill's Experiments in Living."

[53] See Rawls, "Justice as Fairness," where uncertainty about the future is fundamental to the choice of the principles. Rawls insists that modeling the agreement as non-revisable is fundamental to the contractual nature of the project. See his "Reply to Alexander and Musgrave," p. 249.

In a fundamental sense Muldoon is absolutely right: an adequate social contract (or theory of justice that can be justified to diverse perspectives) must have the resources to adapt to drastically changed conditions, both internally and externally. We must incorporate the Millian-Hayekean-Popperian insight that we are always refining our ideas about justice and our analysis of the conditions for its social realization.[54] The notion of ideal justice as a fixed point not subject to revision is perhaps the most implausible assumption of what Popper called "utopian" theory (§II.3.4). On all this, we should follow Muldoon. However, Rawls's supposition that we should conceive of the parties as choosing principles "once and for all" need not be interpreted as a statement of the fixed point view but, rather, as reminding us about two important facts about the very idea of rules of justice as a basis for social cooperation.

First, to endorse a rule of justice requires that the endorsement is "reversible": if rule R specifies the way that roles 1 and 2 must relate to each other, for Alf, basing his judgments on perspective Σ, to truly endorse a rule requires that Alf endorses it whether he occupies position 1 or 2.[55] If Alf endorses a rule because he believes he will solely occupy position 1 (say, he knows that he is only an employer and never an employee), in an important sense he does not endorse it as a requirement of justice (but as, say, a rule of self-interest). Even though our goal in a nonnormalized social contract is to uncover rules of justice that do not presuppose a normalized perspective (or small groups of such perspectives), we still seek terms of association that conform to some ideal of impartiality in the sense of reversibility. To say that a rule is not open to continual renegotiation is to stress that parties are *bound* by it, even on those occasions when it does not promote what their perspective deems important (including their interests). More pragmatically, if Alf's endorsement of the rule presupposes that he will never occupy role 2, expected changes in circumstances (i.e., he becomes an employee) will lead him to abandon the rule, showing his endorsement of it to be unstable. In his early versions of his social

---

[54] For Hayek, see *The Constitution of Liberty*, pp. 23–24.

[55] I consider this requirement more fully in *The Order of Public Reason*, pp. 299–301.

contract theory, Rawls thus argued that the parties must suppose the agreement cannot be renegotiated should it turn out that they did not occupy the more advantaged positions. "They each understand further that the principles proposed and acknowledged on this occasion are binding on all future occasions. Thus each will be wary of proposing a principle that would give him peculiar advantage, in the present circumstances, supposing it is accepted. Each person knows that he will be bound by it in future circumstances the peculiarities of which cannot be known, and which might well be such that the principles are to his disadvantage."[56] Because one is bound by the choice of the principles over an extended period of time regulating circumstances that one cannot predict, a rational person will not seek to tailor the principles so that he gains advantages given his present circumstances, since these may unpredictably change, and he may end up on the losing end of rigged principles.[57] In *this* case resisting calls for renegotiation because the facts have changed is fundamental to the very idea of what it means to endorse rules of justice.

Second, as Hayek so effectively argued, *just because* we want a society that is dynamic and constantly adjusting to new conditions, we need *relatively* stable social and moral rules.[58] A deep source of uncertainty in social life concerns the actions and expectations of our fellows; binding us to common rules allows us to reduce this uncertainty and so engage in fruitful cooperation. Unless we are bound to relatively stable rules we cannot reduce this uncertainty. The basic moral rules of society, and the basic moral norms governing the political, provide the background for social and economic experimentation. Unless this background sets relatively fixed parameters as to, say, what claims of property are to be respected and what personal rights are to be guaranteed, innovators have insufficient settled points from which to plan. Innovation is not typically a planless, random activity; it is

[56] Rawls, "Justice as Fairness," p. 53. Buchanan and Tullock also proposed such a veil of uncertainty in *The Calculus of Consent*, pp. 77ff.

[57] Note that this argument seeks to secure some of the results that the veil of ignorance achieves in the later formulations. See Kohlberg, *The Philosophy of Moral Development*, pp. 190–201.

[58] See Hayek, *Law, Legislation, and Liberty*, vol. 1, *Rules and Order*, esp. chaps. 2 and 3.

based on decentralized individual plans, and these plans and their co-ordination require important fixed parameters.[59]

To be somewhat less abstract, contrast two views of a dynamic society, in the sense of one that readily and continually admits new perspectives—say, immigration from ethnic or religious groups not presently represented or simply internal processes (such as recombination, §III.3.4) that regularly create new perspectives. On Muldoon's proposal, such a society will acknowledge that the social contract will require continual revision, so the basic allocation of rights is being revised as new groups (with new perspectives) enter.[60] But note that this can entail a high cost for current perspectives. While Muldoon rightly stresses that through the division of labor I can benefit from new groups and perspectives (see §IV.3.3), it also is the case that on his dynamic bargaining model I do not know the rules on which I shall interact with them, as the social contract will be renegotiated as they enter. So it will be harder to anticipate the costs and benefits. Supposing also, as seems to be the case, that most people are conventionalists and so endorse most of the rules they live under, they will certainly see one clear and significant cost in allowing immigration of culturally different groups: it is apt to significantly revise the current system of moral rules. Perhaps a worry about the nature of religious accommodation as it was negotiated in some Western European countries is that it was rather close to Muldoon's model, being based on a bargain between different Christian sects, who all received their share of state influence and funding. Enter Muslim populations, and this basic bargain has to be renegotiated, and now with groups whose perspectives are less familiar. The result is apt to be great reluctance to accommodate Muslim groups: the costs are upfront and clear, the potential benefits in the future, and, given that we are unclear about the new allocation of rights, far less certain. In contrast, if our rules

[59] On the importance of individual planning, see Hayek, "The Use of Knowledge in Society."

[60] Muldoon, *Beyond Tolerance*, chap. 6. Muldoon recognizes that the challenge to his approach is that we have far fewer fixed points, and thus we are without stable principles of justice. He hopes, however, that his account provides for periods of stability.

are able to secure significant stability in the face of new perspectives, although current residents will anticipate new interactions (some welcomed, some not) the basic allocation of rights and duties will not constantly change. And because the rules of the game will be relatively stable, there will be both a greater ability to plan how to interact with the newly arrived groups and far less cost—new arrivals do not mean new social contracts.

1.4 Not All Liberal Justice Is Fit for the Open Society

Let us draw together some of the lessons we have learned from our analyses of Rawls, Sen, and Muldoon. Under full normalization, the relation of a perspective Σ to judgments of justice is manifest; Σ draws on the five elements of its perspective[61] to determine the justice of any social world. When we allow a theory of justice that itself seeks to accommodate multiple partially normalized perspectives on justice, so that we have fundamental disagreements about justice, we immediately confront the question of the relation of any given partially normalized perspective to the theory's overall judgment of justice. As I argued (§IV.1.1), Rawls never really solved this problem: he allowed for a set of eligible perspectives based on different principles of justice (the family of liberal views), but he was never clear how the diverse set of "reasonable" perspectives could all be encompassed in overall, consistent judgments of justice in his theory. His political liberalism project understood some perils of normalization but did not see how we might arrive at way to relate each of the eligible perspectives to the interperspectival judgments of justice.

In §IV.1.2 we saw that Sen provides a method to integrate diverse evaluative standards into a theory of justice; each partially normalized view of justice (modeled as an impartial spectator) takes its evaluative standards and applies them to a common, normalized set of social worlds. If all impartial spectators agree that social world a is more just than b, then according to the full or complete theory of justice a is

---

[61] Evaluative standards, the features of social worlds, a mapping relation, a similarity ordering, and a distance metric.

more just than *b*. As we saw (§IV.1.2.3), Sen's procedure requires full normalization of the properties of the set of social worlds in the domain {*X*}; while Sen clearly makes progress in thinking about justice without full normalization, his social choice approach cannot accommodate significant differences about the justice-relevant features of the social worlds. This suppresses a great deal of perspectival diversity about the nature of the social world. But it also suppresses diversity of evaluative standards; some evaluative standards—such as religiously informed ones—make sense only if the world has certain features. If souls and knowledge of God's will are not features of the social world, there is not much to say for a Divine Command theory (or, perhaps, even for a liberal egalitarian theory).[62]

Muldoon's analysis overcomes this limit. It is useful to think of his account as making justice a vector of all the eligible perspectives.[63] For any given array of perspectives, interperspectival justice is the result or upshot of the combined effects of the perspectives in the array. To use more philosophically familiar language, justice is "constructed" out of the entire set of eligible perspectives. The worry is that this ties interperspectival justice too closely to the set of current eligible perspectives, and so Muldoon's proposal, insightful as it is, leaves something to be desired as a framework for a diverse and open society.

Recall that our problem is creating an overarching "liberal" framework for "republican" communities of moral inquiry and experimentation (§III.4.3). The liberal theory of justice can provide a framework for diverse moral perspectives only to the extent that those communities endorse the liberal framework as a bona fide just way to relate; the aim is to uncover a theory of justice that diverse perspectives can, to paraphrase Rawls, see as something they can live with.[64] Now an open, liberal framework seeks to accommodate two realms of diversity. *First*, it seeks to accommodate the array of existing eligible perspectives in

---

[62] See Waldron, *God, Locke and Equality*, esp. chap. 3.

[63] I say "eligible" because a theory will restrict the set as views of justice that should be taken seriously. What is important at present is that the set of eligible perspectives is assumed to be quite large. I turn in §IV.3 to the limits of what can be considered eligible.

[64] Rawls, "Kantian Constructivism," p. 306.

a society so that all of them can, in some way, endorse the claims of overall, interperspectival justice. In Sen's impartial spectator model this is achieved via the Paretian rule: if all the eligible spectators hold that a is more just than b, then that is the conclusion of interperspectival justice. Note that in this case the interperspectival claim is necessarily endorsed by all perspectives. In Muldoon's account, interperspectival justice is a rational bargain or compromise among all the relevant perspectives; it would normally not be the precise view of any one of them, but all presumably could endorse the compromise as rational from its own perspective. *Second*, however, a liberal framework accommodative to diversity seeks to be open to new perspectives, ones generated either internally or through immigration. It seeks to accommodate and harness the diversity not only of existing perspectives, but of new and yet unthought-of ones. It is the accommodation of this diversity that is the basis of a liberal society's openness to inquiry and change—its accommodation of diversity is not tied to a specific array of diversity.

An open and just liberal society would simultaneously like to maximize its accommodation to both types of diversity, being respectful of current perspectives while being open to new ones. If a liberal order was concerned only with the first sort of diversity, Muldoon's social contract would be a compelling solution: under a broad range of circumstances, each member of the social order can engage in bargains with all others, producing a contract which, in our terms, each perspective can endorse. But if a liberal order accommodates the diversity of existing perspectives by tying interperspectival justice very closely to the existing array of perspectives, it will be able to accommodate new perspectives only by altering the basic liberal framework of interperspectival justice. If the current framework is, as it were, constructed out of the specific materials present in the current array of perspectives—if it is responsive to *that specific diversity configuration*—it seems doubtful that new perspectives will generally fit in without significant, perhaps major, shifts in the liberal framework. Thus we might have a diverse society with a justified liberal framework that would nevertheless not be an especially open society, for innovation and immigration may well pose fundamental threats to its conception of justice. It may prefer to be what Rawls calls a "closed system."[65] This, I would venture, is no mere theoretical possibility, but a feature of many current liberal societies, whose very framework of shared life is threatened by inclusion of new perspectives not part of the current settlement.

However, another possibility presents itself. A liberal framework might be good at accommodating the existing array of perspectives because it is good at accommodating diversity per se. The framework's success is not so much in accommodating its current set of diverse perspectives, but in accommodating diversity itself. Having developed an interperspectival conception of justice that does well at achieving the endorsement of diverse perspectives, additional diverse perspectives can be relatively easily accommodated. It is so good at working with difference that new and more difference is not a great challenge. On this view, a society can reach a point where, having developed a diversity-accommodative understanding of interperspectival justice, it has no difficulty being open to further perspectives. Here the liberal society is also an open society.

We are now in a position to refine our inquiry into a justified liberal framework: under what conditions can we live under a shared moral framework that is diversity accommodative because it is accommodative to diversity per se, and so is an open society? I shall argue (§2 of this chapter) that such a framework of liberal diversity seems most likely when our public social world is shaped by a set of characteristic features of the Open Society. I believe that we now have had sufficient experience of life in diverse societies that we can at least draw some tentative conclusions about the sorts of institutional structures and principles that are friendly to diversity per se. Of course, like any claims about social realizations these may prove wrong, but that, I take it, is a benefit of, not a worry about, the analysis. However, I shall argue in §3 of this chapter that even these diversity-friendly arrangements cannot make room for all perspectives; I try there to make some progress in identifying the limits of liberal diversity, and why these limits make sense in the context of defending the Open Society.

---

[65] Rawls, *A Theory of Justice*, p. 7. Rawls sees this as a simplifying assumption that could be relaxed later; here we see that it may not be easy to relax given some methods of accommodating diversity.

2 An Artificial, Open, Public Social World

2.1 On Creating a Public Social World

2.1.1 The Idea of a Public Moral Constitution. Although it is seldom noted, Rawls's later works are rife with references to the idea of social worlds. He employs the idea in various ways, two of which are of importance for our current discussion. On the one hand, Rawls refers to social worlds in a manner that suggests that they are broadly sectarian: when we are alienated, Rawls, says, "we grow distant from political society and retreat into our social world."[66] On the other hand, Rawls stresses that from the perspective of the original position "the parties in effect try to fashion a certain kind of social world; they regard the social world not as given by history, but, at least in part, as up to them."[67] Or, as he says in *Political Liberalism*, "insofar as we are reasonable, we are ready to work out the framework for the *public* social world."[68]

Let us interpret this distinction as one between the social world that characterizes one's "comprehensive perspective" and the "public social world" of rules and institutions that is collectively created by members of a society. In this latter sense, but not in the former, a public moral framework and basic institutions *are* a public social world—they compose it.[69] We can think of the public social world of rules and institutions as an artificial social world, one whose existence is a feature of the coordinated mental states of its members.[70] The critical point is that in a diverse, liberal society, this shared social world does not reflect a basic choice between the competing social worlds of the different perspectives. It does not have significant ontological commitments: it is our social world because these are the rules and institutions that we, collectively, conceive of and act on. As Rawls says, we can

---

[66] Rawls, *Justice as Fairness*, p. 128.

[67] Ibid., p. 118.

[68] Rawls, *Political Liberalism*, p. 53. Emphasis added.

[69] Ibid., pp. 41, 77.

[70] There are a number of different ways of theorizing about these coordinated mental states; different accounts can underwrite the claims made in the text. For various approaches, see the essays in Lagerspatz, Ihäheimo, and Kotkavirta, eds., *On the Nature of Social and Institutional Reality*.

"fashion a certain kind of social world" through our joint choices and beliefs. The aspiration is for the various perspectives, each committed to its understanding of the nature of the social world and ideal justice, to find the public social world endorsable. If each perspective can make sense of the categories of the artificial social world and endorse their use (an issue that I put aside until §IV.3), we can have a shared artificial world without normalization. None of the perspectives that can relate to and endorse the artificial social world would find themselves normalized away, for each would be related to the public artificial world in a way that makes sense *to* that perspective.

Although I have employed the idea of social worlds extensively throughout this book, we can put much the same point in terms of developing a "public moral constitution" for our society.[71] Our shared public social world simply is a stable, shared, moral, and political framework for living together. Its institutional structure provides common categories, and common sources of interpreting those categories, which allow us to share cooperative ventures characterized by what all perceived to be just social relations.[72] Nevertheless, it is an institutional structure of our own collective creation.[73] This is not to say that each perspective literally participates in its beginnings, but that it is continually maintained as a public perspective by the diverse perspectives that relate to and endorse it; for each participating perspective, the artificial public world is sustained by the way its categories can be related to the underlying social world the perspective identifies.

Such a public social world is required for a truly open society, for it provides relatively settled public categories, rules, and interpretations, which provide the necessary fixed points to allow for individual planning and dynamic changes. Just as markets are dynamic only because the rules of property and contract are not constantly being renegoti-

[71] Rawls, "Kantian Constructivism in Moral Theory," p. 326. See further my essay "Moral Constitutions."

[72] This is why it was deeply mistaken for Sen to accuse Rawls of "institutional fundamentalism" (*The Idea of Justice*, p. 82). It is only through institutions that those with deeply divergent perspectives can share a common, public social world. See further my "Social Contract and Social Choice."

[73] For a careful and insightful analysis of the importance of institutional structures, see Van Schoelandt, "Rawlsian Functionalism and the Problem of Coordination."

ated, a dynamic and open society has a relatively stable public social world. But this is not a normalized social world, on which we base our theory of public reason. It is a common world that arises *out of* public reason: it is our collective creation.

This basic social moral framework for our common social world—our moral constitution—is not to be equated with any specific moral perspective, with its particular understanding of values, rightness, and the morally relevant nature of the social world. Rather, the core of this morality is a set of public, shared rules that provide the basis of shared normative and empirical expectations as to what others will demand of one, and how competing claims will be adjudicated. Such a system of shared expectations is critical in allowing groups of diverse agents to overcome many of the collective problems we face, such as helping us cooperate in "social dilemmas"—situations in which we will all do better if we cooperate than if we all act on what we take as best from our own perspective, but each can do even better by defecting on cooperation and do what is best from one's own point of view.[74] To use Rawls's phrase, solving these sorts of collective problems is the sort of thing our public framework must do if it is to play its "expected role in human life."[75] Without shared normative expectations (what I expect other people ought to do, and what they think I ought to do) and empirical expectations (what I expect other people will actually do, and what they expect I will do), cooperation is impaired and social conflict aggravated.

An analysis of what I have called a moral constitution has obvious affinities with constitutional political economy, as developed by James Buchanan. Like the constitutional political economy project, my concern here is how highly diverse agents may converge on a set of rules to regulate their cooperative activities. And like Buchanan, I shall consider what sorts of rules might receive near-unanimous consent in a highly diverse society. On the face of it, one might think that a fundamental difference is that Buchanan's project supposes selfish agents, concerned only about their own costs and benefits, whereas our con-

---

[74] The importance of shared rules for overcoming such dilemmas is confirmed not only by theoretical investigation, but by practical fieldwork. See, for example, Bicchieri, *Norms in the Wild*; Ostrom, "Collective Action and the Evolution of Social Norms."

[75] Rawls, "The Independence of Moral Theory," p. 286.

cern is a diversity of perspectives on justice. While Buchanan at times does suggest a selfishness postulate, this is not essential to his core analysis, which is critically about our concern: agents who differ deeply in how they order the possible outcomes.[76] Nevertheless, it is true that we are concerned here with a far deeper diversity, which goes beyond diversity of preferences to diversity in perspectives. The main difference, however, is that while Buchanan's constitutional political economy tends to focus on the formal rules of the state—especially second-order rules about how to make and change rules—my concern is the informal moral framework that provides the foundation for state institutions. There is, of course, no sharp break between these; as we shall see, the informal moral framework often calls for legal rules to complete its tasks, and legal rules are typically ineffective without a basis in the moral constitution. Still, differences in emphases are important, and our emphasis is not so much the state but the moral framework that provides the foundation for an effective liberal state in the Open Society.

2.1.2 A Practice of Accountability. These common social rules, coordinating our empirical and normative expectations, are the warp and woof of our common existence, but unless we hold each other to them, individuals may give in to the temptation to go their own way—acting as they think best, given their point of view. This is not to say that they are selfish; defection from the set of shared rules occurs whenever one acts as one's perspective deems best, putting aside the shared rules of social life. Consequently, maintenance of this shared set of rules requires a practice of public responsibility: a practice in which we hold each other responsible for failing to abide by our common rules. Maintaining a public moral framework requires maintaining shared expectations—rebuking people who do not act on the shared rules (their actions undermine empirical expectations) and those who make mistakes about what the rules require (and so undermine shared normative expectations). Recent empirical studies have proven overwhelm-

---

[76] This project commences with Buchanan and Tullock, *The Calculus of Consent.* On the assumptions necessary to that analysis, see Thrasher and Gaus, "The Calculus of Consent." Cf. my essay "The Limits of *Homo Economicus.*"

ingly that cooperative individuals do care about policing these rules, often using their own resources to punish offenders.[77] And societies where such public responsibility is lacking have sought methods to establish it, as a foundation for enhancing cooperation.[78]

Not only is the public moral constitution sustained by a practice of mutual responsibility, but, critically, it provides the necessary foundation for the very practice that sustains it. As Peter Strawson famously showed us, our social moral practices are inescapably about our reactions to what we perceive to be the goodwill or ill will of those with whom we interact. We make demands on them, and they on us; and we hold them (and ourselves) responsible for failure to meet these demands.[79] The reactive attitudes—resentment, indignation, guilt, and so on—are fundamental to these relations of responsibility; we experience resentment because those who fail to meet our demands manifest an ill will toward us; we are indignant when, as a third party, we view others as the objects of such ill will. Strawson stressed that we do not really have the option of deciding whether or not we should care about the attitudes of others toward us in these practices: we cannot help but react to the ill will of those with whom we interact.[80] Thus understood, the moral constitution is not centrally about objective judgments of the rightness or wrongness of the actions of others (and ourselves): it is a system of expectations embedded in our attitudes toward others, and our judgments of their intentions and attitudes toward us. When I hold another responsible I do not simply judge his action against some standard; I react to his ill will, his lack of respect or consideration.

---

[77] The experimental literature confirming this is extensive. Much of the critical work has been done by Ernst Fehr and his colleagues; see, for example, Fehr and Fischbacher, "Third Party Punishment and Social Norms." For an excellent overview, see Bowles and Gintis, *A Cooperative Species*, chap. 3. See also my "Retributive Justice and Social Cooperation."

[78] The most famous "fieldwork" in a large urban setting is that of Antanas Mockus in Bogotá, who, as mayor, devised a variety of methods to instill a sense of public responsibility for social rule violations. For a short overview, see "Building Citizenship Culture in Bogotá." See further §IV.2.6.

[79] Strawson, "Freedom and Resentment."

[80] Ibid., p. 197.

However, if the other does not share my perspective on justice, the reactive attitudes are easily undermined.[81] Even supposing that I have the correct perspective, so that I know what justice truly requires, if I live in a social milieu of reasonable diversity of perspectives—I acknowledge that others, entirely reasonably, have different perspectives on justice—I am thwarted in ascribing ill will to others. I demanded that they conform to a rule because it is part of a more just social world, but I acknowledge that on their perspective this is not so. Unless I think their perspective is manifestly unreasonable (and so we are on our way back to normalization), I must admit that their lack of uptake of my appeal to the rule does not manifest ill will. They just do not see that justice calls for conformity to it. And because they do not manifest ill will, the reactive attitudes, and so the practice of responsibility, do not get a grip. Thus simple appeal to my perspective on justice is not sufficient to sustain a practice of responsibility. However, a shared justified[82] moral constitution, which articulates our shared normative expectations of each other, provides just this: when we possess such a constitution we endorse these shared expectations, and so violators are prime targets of the reactive attitudes. You knew that our moral constitution, which you endorse, requires conformity to the rule, and yet you failed to conform. Now *that* does typically manifest an ill will, a lack of due regard.

This relation of mutual support between the reactive attitudes and a public moral constitution is fundamental to a moralized social life. We require a public moral constitution to live cooperatively given our diverse moral perspectives; we maintain it through a practice of mutual responsibility. Following Strawson we can call this an analysis from the objective perspective on our constitution and the attendant practice of moral responsibility. But, as Strawson stressed, as participants in moral relations—when taking up the transactional or interpersonal view—we cannot help but make demands on them for consideration, and react when these demands go unheeded. From this view a public moral constitution endorsed by the diverse members of the

---

[81] See further Bringhurst and Gaus, "Positive Freedom and the General Will"; and my *The Order of Public Reason*, chap. 4.

[82] On justification, see §IV.3 below.

social order grounds the very reactive attitudes it requires for its (objective) success.

2.1.3 Functionalism. From the objective (but not from the transactional) perspective the rules of the public moral constitution can be understood as serving a function. As I have just said, we can analyze the conditions that the constitution requires to successfully do its job. Again, it must be stressed that this functional character of the public constitution is not a general claim about morality, or admissible perspectives on justice, per se. Many perspectives on justice embrace an *antitechnology conviction,* namely that justice is not a technology to enable human cooperative social life—justice does not have functions or roles. A framework for the Open Society does not affirm or deny this conviction—it is a matter that is internal to a perspective on justice. Our concern here is not to identify the correct perspective on justice (which would simply add one more perspective into the mix), but to reflect on the public social world that we create *in order to* productively and cooperatively live together and to search our disparate understandings of justice. And that is a matter of creating what might be called a social technology of cooperative life.

The public moral constitution's fundamental task of providing the framework for social life and cooperation can be achieved only when we coordinate on a common set of moral rules. Because the public moral constitution has the job of coordinating our normative and empirical expectations, it is to no avail for each to have a unique, idiosyncratic view of it. I can have a terrific theory as to what the ideal public moral constitution would be, but for me alone to act on it cannot do the job. Indeed, even if we all happened to share the same view of it (say, *R* was a rule of justice on all our perspectives) but we did not know this fact (i.e., there was not public knowledge of it), we would not have coordinated normative and empirical expectations about acting on *R*. What is required is that people actually share, and know that they share, common normative and empirical expectations about each other.[83] Because of the *functional requirement,* a social morality thus has an *existence requirement:* only if a set of rules in a society is sufficiently

---

[83] See Chwe, *Rational Ritual.*

widely shared among its members (they have the relevant shared beliefs, intentions, attitudes, and behaviors), and it is sufficiently widely
known that they share these, can it be the public moral constitution of
the society. The public moral constitution is partly constituted by the
coordinated beliefs, intentions, and attitudes of the members of society. It is public not simply in the sense that it pertains to common matters (any morality can have public matters as its content), but it is also
public in its constitutive conditions. Thus, a set of rules is the public
moral constitution only if a social fact holds: only if the set of rules
satisfies the existence requirement is it the "positive morality" of that
society, and only if the set of rules is the positive morality of the society can it be its public moral constitution—its normatively justified
social morality. That is why a public social world is not simply a matter
of what can be justified, but what has been created.[84]

2.2 Polycentrism

Although for simplicity's sake it is useful to analyze the idea of *a* public moral constitution for a society, the moral constitution of the Open
Society is actually characterized by a variety of sets of rules, regulating different areas of social life, different types of problems, over different areas. And often the same society will be characterized by competing sets of rules, followed by different parts of the population (see
further §IV.4.2). As I have emphasized, the rules of our shared social
life are tools to address a variety of shared problems; different problems require different tools, and their effective solutions require that
they range over groups of varying sizes. The group that shares a problem, and so requires a rule to assist in its solution, will vary from
problem to problem. The important work of Elinor and Vincent Ostrom, drawing on decades of research in a wide variety of social contexts, has shown how often informal social rules with an attendant
practice of responsibility can be effective for a particular population to
address its specific problems.[85]

---

[84] Contrary to what some have alleged, this claim does not involve a naturalistic
fallacy. The social fact is necessary, not sufficient, for a normative public moral constitution. See my "On Dissing Public Reason."

[85] For excellent analyses of the overall project of the Ostroms and its relation to

Understanding a society as composed of a wide variety of social networks, addressing different problems at different levels in different networks, yields two insights into the institutions of the Open Society. *First*, as different people come together to solve their particular problems (say, about the use of a certain water supply or safety in their neighborhood), their shared concerns in solving *this* problem provide a robust basis for wide agreement on *these* particular rules or institutions. Even though their perspectives may be deeply diverse, they forge common small public worlds and common classifications when, as an interacting group, they confront problems that all participants appreciate. An atheist and an Evangelical may share neighborhood watch duties. In cases such as these, the very nature of the local problem helps produce convergence on common ways to contend with it. Those who would say that our differences are so great we cannot share any commonly endorsed rules conceive of the problem too abstractly. When we face commonly perceived problems that require coordinated action, those with deeply diverse outlooks are apt to devise and abide by common rules.

Second, for many matters within the same society, different social networks may gravitate to competing rules: witness the social networks of vegetarians, religious citizens, feminists, and libertarians. As we live among each other, we simultaneously live in different, and often competing, small public worlds: the common classifications of feminist social networks are distinctly different than the small worlds of libertarian networks (even though some may be members of both).[86] Each cluster of perspectives forges its own common world—which is inherently richer and deeper than our general public world—while also offering to the public at large competing small social worlds, often seeking to attract other perspectives into its networks. In this way, the competition between the networks can be seen as ways to search for thicker, more substantive rules that might, from the bottom up, be taken up by larger numbers in the society. Recall the difficulties with

---

diversity of perspectives, see Aligica's insightful *Institutional Diversity and Political Economy*. For a general overview, see Aligica and Boettke, *Challenging Institutional Development*.

[86] On the importance of "reference networks" to actual rules, see Bicchieri, *Norms in the Wild*, chap. 2.

the idea of small-scale social experiments (§II.4.1). Given the small number of such experiments on any specific problem, it is always difficult to determine the causes of the experiment's outcome, and so whether its lessons can be transferred to other contexts. In contrast, in a polycentric system, competing networks can explore, in the same social circumstances, different rules; innovations can spread throughout a population as different perspectives take up what they see as a better social rule, perhaps displacing ones that are less suited to the group's participant perspectives.[87] This points to a model of normative change—and from the perspective of the group, normative improvement—in the Open Society.

Like most insights—that the moral constitution of a society may be transformed by gradual switching to a better, competing social rule—this one can enlighten us about much, but we must also recognize its limits. Many parts of the moral constitution have been changed by this process: the astounding changes that have occurred in Western countries over the last fifty years regarding rules regulating sexual relations is a striking example. However, other social rules require something like a simultaneous change of belief and/or attitudes among members of a social network. If a rule is held in place by a network of beliefs about what others expect one to do (for example, a norm among prison guards that all guards expect other guards to beat inmates and will ostracize one who does not), individuals will be reluctant to depart from what they see as firm social expectations. Here collective reasoning and/or some sort of legal intervention may well be critical (see §IV.2.6).[88] There is no single analysis that accounts for all the dynamics of rule change in the Open Society. Moreover, we should not forget that, as the Ostroms' analyses of polycentrism stressed, these diverse networks of organization must be united under global common rules when their small worlds collide.[89] Still, the polycentric insight is that we should not make the mistake of equating the

[87] For a model of such a process see Boyd and Richerson, *The Origin and Evolution of Cultures*, chap. 12.

[88] See Bicchieri, *Norms in the Wild*, chaps. 1–2; Bicchieri and Mercier, "Norms and Beliefs."

[89] See Aligica, *Institutional Diversity and Political Economy*, pp. 58ff.

entire moral constitution with this overarching framework that applies to all.

2.3 Liberty, Prohibitions, and Searching

2.3.1 The Principle of Natural Liberty. It is a platitude that liberty is fundamental to the moral constitution of the Open Society: after the work of Mill, Popper, and Hayek, what more can be said? As Mill in particular so decisively demonstrated, an open, dynamic society must be based on freedom of thought and speech. If different perspectives are to communicate their insights, and hopefully enrich each other, an open society must secure the conditions for freedom of thought and ensure that the channels of communication are kept open. The Open Society is not a mere standoff or compromise between opposing perspectives, but a forum in which, while ignoring or even disparaging some, a perspective can gain from others. And just which others have something to teach one—which of their discoveries are discoveries one can make use of—is itself always a matter of discovery.

All this is as familiar as it is fundamental. There is no point in once again rehearsing these important insights. I believe, however, that we can say something rather less familiar yet enlightening about the place of freedom in the Open Society.

Rawls notes that although there are, in principle, an indefinite or infinite number of possible moral (or legal) rules, a moral (or legal) conception that seeks to guide behavior supposes a *principle of closure*: given such a closure rule, the system of rules can be complete and provide a full guide to behavior.[90] Drawing on this idea, John Mikhail identifies one closure rule as:

> *The Principle of Natural Liberty:* Whatever is not prohibited (and this includes the non-performance of specific acts) is permitted.[91]

On this closure rule, Alf consults the system of rules and determines whether his ϕ-ing is prohibited by some rule in the system; if it is not,

---

[90] Rawls, *A Theory of Justice*, pp. 300–301.
[91] Mikhail, *The Elements of Moral Cognition*, §6.3.1.

then he is free to φ. This closure rule is intimately related to the standard formulations of the Principle of Natural Liberty that are to be found in liberal writings.[92] For example, Stanley Benn's grounding principle of morality is that those who are simply acting as they see fit are under no standing obligation to justify their actions to others (while those who interfere with others' actions are under an obligation to justify their interference).[93] As Benn says, "justifications and excuses presume at least prima facie fault, a charge to be rebutted."[94] If Alf has no justificatory burden he is permitted to act without justification—Alf has no charge to rebut, no case to answer. Thus on Benn's view Alf is free to act until, as it were, he runs into a moral rule that regulates what he is doing. The moral code does not having a standing requirement that Alf be able to identify a permission to φ; it only requires that he not φ when so doing is prohibited (a requirement to φ can be understood as a prohibition on failing to φ). Thus, in the interpersonal context, Betty is not warranted, as it were, to call him out for φ-ing unless she can point to a prohibition that he has flouted. Benn's point is that merely acting does not itself invoke the context of justification, because, according to the Principle of Natural Liberty, Alf need not, as a matter of course, cite a permission to act before acting; the context of prima facie fault arises only when Betty can point to a prohibition that his φ-ing appears to flout.

The Principle of Natural Liberty implies a basic asymmetry between action and objection to action.[95] It is clearly unnecessary that, as a matter of course, Alf possesses a justification for φ-ing in the sense of showing that morality allows it; however, the claim that he should be stopped from φ-ing because it runs afoul of morality implies that there is a prohibition such that φ-ing is prohibited, and so the rule must be identified. Thus we can get from the closure principle to a moral objection principle:

---

[92] See, for example, Feinberg, *Harm to Others*, p. 9; Rawls, *Justice as Fairness*, p. 44; Mill, *The Subjection of Women*, p. 262. See also Mill, *On Liberty*, p. 299.

[93] Benn, *A Theory of Freedom*, p. 87.

[94] Ibid.

[95] A feature to which some object. See Wall, "On Justificatory Liberalism"; Hillinger and Lapham, "The Impossibility of a Paretian Liberal." As Sen notes, to deny this asymmetry implies that "everyone's right to do anything whatsoever is made conditional on non-opposition by others." "Liberty, Unanimity and Rights," p. 227.

The Interpersonal Principle of Natural Liberty: Alf need not possess a moral justification for φ-ing, unless φ-ing appears to run afoul of a prohibition. A morality-based objection to Alf's φ-ing thus must be based on a justification of the form "Rule *R* prohibits φ-ing."

This, I am convinced, was Benn's basic point: it is Betty, the moral objector, not Alf, the actor, who has the onus, as a first move in the conversation, to cite a morally relevant reason for her stance. It is in this sense that in a system of natural liberty there is indeed a basic moral asymmetry in favor of voluntary action over moral objections to it.

Thus understood, the core of Natural Liberty is a closure principle. Now logically, a closure principle is not required for a system of rules. If all action types were specified, then theoretically each type could be binned into the prohibited or the permitted. Depending on the number of action types and the capacity of the learner, this list could be internalized by rote. In the case of human moral rule systems, however, it seems that the list of action types is vast and cognitive resources limited.[96] Real human reasoners can learn only a relatively modest set of the moral rules, and they do not possess the cognitive resources to infer all the possible applications of the set of rules. Without a closure rule, humans deliberating whether to φ may simply be unable to determine the status of φ-ing. Such a system would lack *decisiveness*. A decisive system of rules, for any action φ, always allows, requires, or prohibits φ (with the "or" being exclusive). Formally, decisiveness is a consistency condition—for any action φ, the moral system is single functioned, providing one and only one answer.[97] If the moral system is not single functioned in this way, it is in principle impossible that a person can always comply with it. This is obvious if the system fails to be single functioned because, for some action φ, it declares that in the same circumstances φ is both prohibited and required. Of course the system may yield "prima facie" or "pro tanto" contradictory judgments, which need to be weighed, and, as a practical matter, it may be

---

[96] As Gilbert Harman argues, the ideal of a belief system that is deductively closed, or complete under logical implication, is neither required by rationality nor realistic for humans. *Reasoning, Meaning and Mind*, pp. 21–23.

[97] See May, "A Set of Independent Necessary and Sufficient Conditions for Simple Majority Decision," p. 681.

very difficult to do the weighing. But these complexities are all consistent with the requirement that the system is not, in principle and all things considered, "overcomplete":[98] that is, inherently inconsistent. Another failure of decisiveness, undercompleteness, may seem less worrying. Here, in a context in which ϕ is a feasible option, the system does not generate any of the judgments: ϕ is required, ϕ is prohibited, or ϕ is permitted. Such undercompleteness also makes it impossible to comply with the system: if the system is undercomplete among "ϕ is permitted, ϕ is required, ϕ is prohibited," one cannot always act in accordance with these rules, for the rules do not entail *any* instructions. One cannot go ahead and ϕ in this case, for that would be to suppose that ϕ is permitted, and that is what the system is incomplete about. And one cannot simply refrain from ϕ-ing, for the system is incomplete about whether ϕ is required.

As we have seen, a critical task of the moral constitution is to secure shared empirical and normative expectations within a group that allows coordination of behavior. To achieve coordination in cooperative contexts the rules must guide our expectations, so that one can anticipate whether a person must, must not, or may ϕ, and there is also a shared understanding of when one may demand that another ϕs (or refrain) and when one appropriately blames others for what they have done. A moral constitution that lacks decisiveness will thus to some extent fail to perform the very job that we require of it. Of course, every set of rules falls short of decisiveness in important ways: in some contexts the rules may by unclear, and perhaps multiple rules that imply inconsistent directives may apply to a single case. We shall see in §IV.4 that such imperfections can actually help make a system of rules more flexible. Nevertheless, the system of rules that makes up the moral constitution must generally be decisive if it is to play its expected role in coordinating the moral life of a diverse society. Note that decisiveness and closure rules are supposed by plausible systems deontic logic: "ϕ is not prohibited & ϕ is not required" imply "ϕ is permitted."

2.3.2 The Residue Prohibition Principle. So (*i*) the presumption in favor of Natural Liberty can be interpreted as a closure principle, and (*ii*) a

[98] For a discussion, see Sen, *On Ethics and Economics*, pp. 66ff.

decisive social morality requires a closure principle. But it is not the only closure principle. Many appear to reject the Principle of Natural Liberty. Ranier Forst, for one, explicitly does so, insisting that only plausible "presumption" in favor of liberty is one of "equally *justifiable* liberty."[99] Contrasting to the Principle of Natural Liberty is:

> *All Liberal Liberties Are Specifically Justified*: In a liberal society Alf only has a liberty to φ if he can provide a justification to all other persons.

This would capture Forst's insistence that a person has a liberty only when this is an equally justifiable liberty. The All Liberal Liberties Are Specifically Justified Principle has a weak and a strong reading. On the weak reading this principle is very close to the Principle of Natural Liberty supposing we add a proviso: the Principle of Natural Liberty, as a closure rule, is itself a justified part of the moral system. The Principle of Natural Liberty would then be a justified closure rule, and Alf's φ-ing is justified, as it is an action of his falling under this blanket justification. On this interpretation we might say "one is always justified in doing something that is not prohibited." This, as it were, mimics the Principle of Natural Liberty, but it is not equivalent to Benn's Interpersonal Principle of Natural Liberty, since Betty can indeed always challenge Alf, but he would always have an answer on the tip-of-his-tongue, that he has a justified presumption in favor of his action.

The stronger, and I think more interesting, interpretation is that Alf must always be able to show that φ-ing comes under some specific rule or principle that accords him a liberty to φ. Some have argued that a liberal society is not based on a general commitment to liberty, but to a justification of specific liberties that have value to us.[100] We could,

---

[99] Forst, "Political Liberty," p. 242. Emphasis in original.

[100] Dworkin, "Liberalism," pp. 124–25. According to Macedo, "an account of basic liberties is itself a product of the justificatory enterprise.... No general presumption of liberty as non-interference forms a prior baseline." "Why Public Reason?," p. 13. Macedo's reference to "basic" liberties makes it difficult to interpret his view, which he takes as constituting a rejection of natural liberty. A system of morality that accepts a principle of natural liberty can insist that important, *basic* liberties such as freedom of speech are specially justified, and that is why they are morally protected (a view that, indeed, Rawls seems to take). In relation to, say freedom of speech, one possesses not only a blameless liberty to speak in public, but a *claim right* to do so. Macedo's deep worry, like Forst's, seems to be that the Minimal Principle of Natural

perhaps, have a liberal society that strongly values freedom in the form of a public moral constitution comprising an extensive list of permissions—a system of moral rules according to which one is *permitted* to act on one's perspective, is *permitted* to do with one's property as one pleases, is *permitted* to deliberate with others about superior answers to common questions, and so on. If this were our liberal public constitution one would be free to act if and only if one could cite a liberty (i.e., permission) to do so. Now as Mikhail notes, this would imply an alternative closure rule:

> *Residual Prohibition Principle*: Whatever is not permitted is prohibited.

If this is the closure rule, a person is prohibited from φ-ing unless the system of rules permits φ-ing. Here we would see the opposite of the interpersonal dynamic that Benn points to: Alf is going to φ, and so Betty could quite intelligibly claim that he must be able to cite a permission to if he is not to act wrongfully. In an obvious sense there is always an onus on a rule-following actor to cite a permission before acting, to show that the Residual Prohibition Principle does not apply.

2.3.3 Moral Learning and the Two Closure Principles. Do people actually employ such closure rules when they act on deontic systems? Under what conditions do learners employ one or the other? Do they have to be taught, as one of the rules in a system, or do rule learners close the system themselves? In a recent series of experiments Shaun Nichols and I have explored these questions and have found that learners do indeed infer closure rules.[101] In one experiment, for example, participants were told:

> There is a Farm with squeaky mice, and all the mice are supposed to follow The Rules of Mice, written in a book. The Farm has four barns: Red, Blue, Yellow and Green.[102]

Liberty attributes to Alf a blameless liberty to φ that is itself exempt from the need to be morally justified, and that unacceptably biases the moral system toward liberty rather than, say, equality or claims of justice, which do face the burdens of justification. Quong has similar worries. See his "Three Disputes about Public Reason."

[101] Gaus and Nichols, "Moral Learning in the Open Society."

[102] This experiment was partly inspired by the work of Cummins, "Evidence for the

Some participants were given two prohibition rules:

The Rules of Mice Book has only two rules:

1. Squeaky mice are not allowed to be in the Red Barn
2. Squeaky mice are not allowed to be in the Yellow Barn.

Other participants were given two permission rules:

The Rules of Mice Book has only two rules:

1. Squeaky mice are allowed to be in the Red Barn
2. Squeaky mice are allowed to be in the Yellow Barn.

We had a third, mixed condition with these rules (counterbalanced for order):

1. Squeaky mice are not allowed to be in the Red Barn
2. Squeaky mice are allowed to be in the Yellow Barn.

All subjects were then asked whether mice were allowed in the green barn. Because rules typically call for action and so a rule follower must make a decision, in this experiment subjects were forced to take sides, requiring them to answer on a six-point scale,[103] from "Mice are not allowed in the green barn" to "Mice are allowed in the green barn."

Our hypothesis was that subjects trained on prohibition rules would infer the Principle of Natural Liberty as a closure rule, while those trained on permissions would infer a Residual Prohibition Principle. This was based on the supposition that learners suppose that their teachers are seeking to be efficient; the cases that are called to their attention are critical for understanding how to, as Wittgensteinians would say, "go on from here." Thus, if the closure principle is Natural Liberty, the teacher should provide examples of prohibitions, for those are what you need to have pointed out to you. If the closure rule is the Residual Prohibition Principle, the teacher should point to permis-

---

Innateness of Deontic Reasoning," and "Evidence of Deontic Reasoning in 3- and 4-Year-Olds."

[103] In other treatments, with compatible results, subjects were given a seven-point scale, which allowed them to sit on the fence by choosing the middle. Interestingly, subjects trained on permissions seemed far more likely to sit on the fence (not knowing what to do) than those trained on prohibitions.

sions. Note in this experiment subjects cannot be understood as guessing what a missing rule might be; they know that this is the complete set of rules, so they are being induced to directly postulate a closure rule for the system. Interestingly, this means that a closure rule cannot be part of the system. The Rules of Mice contain only two rules, and a closure rule is not among them. They are thus not being taught a closure rule, or even instructed that there is one. Nevertheless, as we predicted, subjects did indeed tend to infer closure rules in the expected way: those trained on prohibition rules tended to infer that the mice are allowed in the green barn (as implied by the Principle of Natural Liberty) while those trained on permission rules tended to infer that they are not (as is implied by the Residual Prohibition Principle). In this task, responses in the mixed condition also differed from chance, with participants being significantly more likely to think that the new action was allowed when given an example of one prohibition rule and one permission rule.

Both closure rules can thus be taught. That subjects inferred the Principle of Natural Liberty even when they were told that the rules were complete (and the rules stated did not contain a closure rule) suggests that, *pace* the weak interpretation of the All Liberal Liberties Are Specifically Justified Principle, they did not see Natural Liberty as one of the rules of the system. Rather, they tended to see closure rules as operating on a complete system of rules that renders the system decisive. So far from being taught, they have grounds for concluding that it cannot be part of the Rules of Mice, yet they employ it.

2.3.3 Moral Decision Making in the Open Society. Both closure rules can be taught. If a morality is largely taught in terms of prohibitions people tend to infer the Principle of Natural Liberty, while teaching through permissions inclines them to the Principle of Residual Prohibitions. There is some tendency to infer Natural Liberty in the face of mixed teaching. Now there is a decisive advantage to teaching a public constitution focused on prohibitions and, so, the Principle of Natural Liberty. The very essence of an open society is that new perspectives are arising, which categorize actions and the world in new ways. As new act-types arise (i.e., those that are not categories in the original set of rules), a Residual Prohibition morality will sort them into prohi-

bitions: act-types that are not on the list of the permitted are prohibited. Thus new ways of acting are morally prohibited. To be sure, eventually the system might be revised so that these new act-types are
specifically sorted into, say, the permitted category, but that process of
explicit revision will be relatively slow and will never comprehen-
sively categorize all the new act-types that arise in dynamic societies.
A residual prohibition system is thus conservative even if it enumer-
ates extensive liberties: it will have great difficulty adapting to new
environments, in which the social or individual value of engaging in
certain action types fluctuates. Such a public moral constitution may
be suited to a closed liberal society, but not an open one (§IV.1.4).

It might be thought that a residual prohibition system could cope
with the emergence of new act-types through analogy or similarity.
This is, indeed, a way in which change occurs in rule systems: a new
type of action is reinterpreted as akin to some familiar one that is covered by an existing rule. In 2015, for example, the United States Federal
Communications Commission categorized some activities of cable
companies as public utilities,[104] thus drawing cable companies' provision of Internet services under rules originally designed for telephone
providers. In similar ways, "blogging" can be categorized as publishing, "cyber-terrorism" as violence. And therein lies the problem. In all
these cases the extensions of current categorizations are uncertain and
controversial. There is real disagreement about these matters, and that
is why centralized authoritative bodies such as the Federal Communications Commission make authoritative (and often highly controversial) rulings. In the informal system of social regulation that is the
heart of our public moral constitution, when the Residual Prohibition
Principle is operative new act-types are thus either simply prohibited
(and so the morality is conservative) or are reinterpreted by individuals, thus rendering the scope of the rules highly uncertain, and so undermining their decisiveness.

In contrast, a public morality of natural liberty will sort new act-
types as permissible; one is free to engage in a new type of action that
is not covered by existing prohibitions. To be sure, systems of natural

---

[104] Federal Communications Commission, *Report and Order on Remand, Declaratory
Ruling, and Order,* http://transition.fcc.gov/Daily_Releases/Daily_Business/2015/
db0312/FCC-15-24A1.pdf.

liberty are not immune to disputes about how to categorize new actions. Consider a rule that was clear in, say, 1980: one has the right to control information about (legal) activities that occur in one's own home. Others are thus prohibited from obtaining and using this information for commercial purposes without one's consent.[105] As the new action type of web browsing arose, and Google can use information about one's browsing history (that in one way is) "on one's home computer" to select ads for future viewing, some argue that this new act-type should be included in the older prohibition against "commercial spying," while others resist this analogy.

There is, however, a critical difference between the two systems, even in the face of uncertainty and dispute. In a natural liberty system, if a moral innovator does not conclude that the analogy holds, he will conclude that morality allows his innovative activity; in a residual prohibition system, unless the innovator concludes that a relevant analogy holds—that the new action type is analogous to a permitted type—he will desist. It is in this sense that a natural liberty system encourages experimentation and discovery. Moral experimenters—those who are exploring a new perspective on justice—need not first convince themselves that a new action type falls under a previous permission; they proceed as long as they do not conclude that the new type falls under a current prohibition. Given that in many circumstances any analogy to previous types of action will be very imperfect and so uncertain, this asymmetry is of great significance, freeing innovators from proving (to themselves) their freedom to discover.

It may seem that a public moral constitution rejecting the Principle of Natural Liberty could avoid the conservatism implicit in a residual prohibition system by appealing to:

> *The Proceed with Justification Principle*: If one is engaging in some new action type γ for which there is no current permission in the system of moral rules, one may γ if and only if one can justify γ-ing to others.

For some, this may be a Kantian public reason principle, in which one justifies γ-ing to all free and equal persons; to a utilitarian it could be

---

[105] See Benn, *A Theory of Freedom*, pp. 289–91.

a principle that allows new activity to be justified by appeal to the general welfare. In environmental thinking, this could be a version of the "precautionary principle," which allows new action when a clear case can be made that its benefits exceed the costs. All such views might insist that, by including this general principle within the system of rules, a residual prohibition system can be dynamic, allowing those new act-types that are justifiable, useful, and so on.

The Proceed with Justification Principle clearly lacks a sort of epistemic decisiveness; it is often extraordinarily unclear how these calculations are to be made. While, perhaps, in theory Proceed with Justification might have a definitive answer, it is most unlikely that people will be able to coordinate on it. At least from the perspective of our public moral constitution, and its aim to coordinate normative and empirical expectations, inclusion of such a principle scores badly on the functional desideratum (§IV.2.1.3). And in some cases, given our current information there may be no determinate answer we can reach, and so an even deeper idea of determinacy is violated.

Still, it might be thought that the costs in determinacy entailed by accepting the Proceed with Justification Principle are exceeded by the benefits. The benefits, however, are not great—even with the addition of this principle, moralities of residual prohibition remain hostile to the Open Society. As we saw earlier (§IV.1.3.2) much innovation depends on planning, but often enough innovators cannot justify their innovative activity, not only because they have little idea of its consequences, but because they have little idea of just what they are doing. A classic example is Alexander Fleming's discovery of penicillin; when he noticed a "blob of mold" when cleaning out his Petri dishes, he did not know that he was about to discover penicillin.[106] As Fleming remarked, "One sometimes finds what one is not looking for."[107] Fleming may well have been unable to justify his experiments that led to discovery of penicillin, because he did not know that was what he was doing, and no one could have known. There is no logic of discovery; some innovators seek a result and achieve something in the neighbor-

---

[106] See Royal Society of Chemistry and American Chemical Society, *The Discovery and Development of Penicillin, 1928–1945.*

[107] Ibid.

hood, others find something entirely different, and others are not quite sure what they are doing or why they are doing it. If, before proceeding with their innovative activity the innovators must justify it, very often the justification will not be forthcoming, as they have no clear idea of what it is that they are trying to justify. And, if so, the Residual Prohibition Principle will once again come into play, with its conservative implications.

The public moral constitution of the Open Society, then, is largely a morality of prohibitions and requirements, for such a morality allows individuals maximal opportunity to explore novelty and diversity, and so explore their perspectives while still possessing a shared moral constitution—a common public world—via which they can coordinate their activities and advance claims against each other employing public rules and categories. This is not to say that permissive rules have no place, much less that all schemes of prohibitory rules provide adequate moral constitutions for an Open Society. It *is* to say, however, that the formal features of moral constitutions matter much more than many contemporary liberals have realized: some formal structures are much more hospitable to diversity per se than others.[108]

2.4 Reducing Complexity through Jurisdictions

A diverse society is, by definition, composed of heterogeneous agents— agents with different understandings of the social world, their options,

---

[108] The analysis presented here concerns the distinction between, on the one hand, prohibitions/requirements and, on the other, permissions. This should not be confused with Hayek's case for prohibitory rules over requirements. Hayek stressed that it was a fundamental mistake to follow Hobbes and J. L. Austin in seeing laws as commands. Although he recognized a continuum, Hayek emphasized that at one end is a quintessential command, which seeks to drastically reduce the feasible options open to the agent (at a limit to simply one act), and a prohibition that does not seek to prescribe specific actions in specific circumstances (and so reduce the feasible set to a singleton) but rather prohibits certain specific conduct, allowing complying individuals to choose their course of action from a slightly pruned set of options. For Hayek, the crucial difference between the two extremes is that prohibitory rules allow individuals to use their information to form plans and respond to novel situations while requirements do not. There is more to this point than most philosophers think, but developing it would take us too far afield. See Hayek, *The Constitution of Liberty*, p. 150. Compare Adam Smith, *Theory of Moral Sentiments*, pp. 78–82.

and their values. On what I dubbed the "vector" account of justice under diversity, the moral constitution of a society is a resultant of the specific set of perspectives in that society (§IV.1.4). Because a moral constitution is tightly coupled with a specific set of perspectives, changes in that set have a strong tendency to produce changes in the public moral constitution. Consider, for example, a moral constitution that is the product of a bargain between all members of a society; each member bargains with the $N - 1$ other members, with the result being a specific moral constitution. This combination of heterogeneity of participants and holism of the bargain (everyone has some claims on everyone else) renders the system highly complex; a change in any perspective is apt to reverberate throughout, at a limit, changing all bargains and surely the public moral constitution as well. Complex systems exist between order and randomness.[109] While they operate on general principles and some system states are possible while others are not, complex systems are exceedingly difficult to predict, and over-all system states can be extremely sensitive to changes in the constituent heterogeneous elements.

Although we cannot eliminate complexity from networks of hetero-geneous interactions, we have powerful reasons to seek to reduce complexity and secure a social order that provides relatively stable frameworks for interactions. As I have argued, this is necessary for an open society (§§IV.1.3–4). Confronted by diverse evaluative standards (or, more generally, perspectives), we could seek to commensurate them by a Sen-like aggregation system or via some sort of bargain; both methods commensurate, but they do so in a way that tends to tightly couple the social outcome to the existing sets of perspectives. The opposite approach is to decouple the perspectives, and so lessen the complexity of the system, so that changes in one do not automati-cally induce changes throughout. What I have elsewhere called "juris-dictional rights" serve this function.[110] Rather than seeking to con-struct "a system of assessment that enables diverse interests to be brought together in a field of calculation," this method aims "to keep them apart, in order to simplify the basis for decision making."[111]

[109] See Page, *Diversity and Complexity*, chap. 1; Waldrop, *Complexity.* See also §II.2.2.
[110] *The Order of Public Reason*, §18. See also my *Justificatory Liberalism*, pp. 199ff.
[111] D'Agostino, *Incommensurability and Commensuration*, p. 104.

In effect, we say that in a society with *n* individual members, there are *n* separate spheres in which an answer... may be sought, each of which is, in theory, inviolable and particular to the individual who occupies it. A decides for himself what he should believe; B decides for herself; and so on.... In other words, we don't approach the matter of "basic belief" as one which... requires that individuals' judgments about this matter be aggregated (perhaps after normalization), with some one (collectively best) option binding on all. We see it, rather, as one which is devolved to individuals whose rights to decide the matter for themselves are scrupulously protected.[112]

Jurisdictional rights reduce complexity by decoupling the public moral constitution from changes in perspectives, allowing high levels of change in some perspectives without affecting the shared public world.

Consider again the example of religious accommodation (§IV.1.3.2). On one understanding of effective religious accommodation, a society is confronted with a set of religious perspectives (in Europe, traditionally Christian ones), and in many countries the accommodation took the form of a bargain—each religion ran its own schools, got a share of public funds, had representation on various national councils, and so on. We have here an example of what D'Agostino calls bringing the disputants into the "same field"; the result is to radically increase the complexity of the moral constitution. As the constituent perspectives recombine and fade away, and as new perspectives enter, continued application of the aggregation method will generate a constantly changing constitution (or else, more likely, the constitution will freeze the settlement at some past configuration of perspectives until the pressures for change overwhelm it). In contrast, jurisdictional rights to religious practice, teaching, and inquiry will be far more robust in the face of change just because, via separation, they weaken the linkages between the constituent perspectives and the common public world. And because of this, a moral constitution employing them is open to a wide range of new perspectives.

---

[112] Ibid., p. 105. Paragraph break deleted.

As D'Agostino points out, property rights and markets function in essentially this way.[113] John Gray once noted, "The importance of several [i.e., private] property for civil society is that it acts as an enabling device whereby rival and possibly incommensurable conceptions of the good may be implemented and realized without any recourse to any collective decision-procedure."[114] Private property rights are quintessentially jurisdictional. To own property is to have a sphere in which one is free to act on, and explore, one's perspective. Property allows us to create small social worlds in which a perspective, or at least elements of it, can be instituted without negotiation with others, and to a large extent without taking other perspectives into account.

Socialism has been understood either in terms of all property being held by the state or, more attractively, the doctrine that "ownership is or ought to be in the hands of the people, not the state."[115] But in either case socialism is manifestly unsuited to the Open Society. The attempt to genuinely respond to diverse perspectives in making innumerable allocation decisions puts tremendous—and unsupportable—weight on social aggregation mechanisms. Given that allocation decisions require complex value trade-offs, nothing less than a comprehensive, implementable social welfare function is required: some way to produce either a social ordering or an interpersonally comparable social utility scale.[116] Given diversity of perspectives, a social welfare function that did not normalize the world features element of a perspective could not suppose canonical descriptions of the state of affairs being evaluated (§IV.1.2.3). Not surprisingly, then, efforts to implement socialism have been accompanied by public ideologies that strongly normalize the admissible evaluative perspectives.

The importance of property rights does not entail that distributional questions (concerning opportunities, income, and wealth) have no place in the political life of the Open Society. The justification of property rights and questions of distribution go hand in hand: one cannot maintain the importance of the institution of property rights while denying that their distribution is a matter of political competence.

---

[113] Ibid. See also *The Order of Public Reason*, pp. 374–80.
[114] Gray, *Post-Enlightenment Liberalism*, p. 314.
[115] Wiles, *Economic Institutions Compared*, p. 40.
[116] For an excellent analysis, see Mueller, *Public Choice III*, chaps. 23–24.

However, we must recognize that ideals of distributive justice are part of particular perspectives on justice, and in the Open Society no perspective has a special claim to have its ideals legally instituted.[117] Questions of distribution, like so much, are matters of democratic politics. A democratic polity in the Open Society must beware of undermining the moral constitution that renders a shared public life among diverse perspectives possible, but it has many tasks that go beyond maintaining this general framework.

2.5 Markets

Although D'Agostino is surely correct that markets employ "separation," their place in the Open Society is rather deeper. They are not simply one more jurisdictional device. To be sure, agents in the market pursue their evaluative standards as each understands them, but markets also are a fundamental way in which different perspectives can interact without normalization. Consider again Muldoon's insightful analysis of the way in which different perspectives can bargain about some social object, without agreeing about the object's features, and so in a fundamental sense, without truly agreeing what they are bargaining over (§IV.1.3.1). While I do not believe the moral constitution should itself be conceived as such a bargain, in market transactions this is precisely what constantly occurs. Alf wishes to sell his 1998 Subaru Outback; he sees it as a worn-out symbol of sensible middle-class attitudes and seeks something new, flashy, and more fun to drive. Betty is an environmentalist, who recognizes that driving used but reasonably fuel-efficient cars decreases her carbon footprint; and as an untenured assistant professor in a college of humanities, she sees it as showing her colleagues that she is not captured by American car culture and takes only the most utilitarian view toward automotive transport. But despite this, Alf can sell the 1998 Subaru to Betty, and they can agree on the terms of the exchange—though they do not agree about what Alf is selling and Betty is buying, they do, as Muldoon

---

[117] For a more thorough analysis of this question, see Van Schoelandt and Gaus, "Political and Distributive Justice." I have also considered these matters in *The Order of Public Reason*, pp. 509–29.

wonderfully demonstrates, have overlapping projections, which make their dealing possible.

Markets thus provide bridges between different perspectives; each sees the object in different ways (indeed, as different objects), but participants typically share enough so that, from the perspective of each, they can agree on what is being traded, and that each is better-off. It is thus not at all surprising that those who would have the moral constitution establish the supremacy of their perspective often disparage markets. Consider the artist who bemoans that gallery owners view his art as an investment, the environmentalist who insists that forests are not to be viewed as productive resources, the feminist who is adamant that it is degrading for women to sell their sexual favors, the conservative who insists that American flags must be revered and never used as a patch for jeans, or the Catholic who demands that stem cells not be sold for scientific research. Of course most perspectives claim that their characterization of the features of the social world (WF) is the correct characterization, and so other perspectives, which do not view the objects as possessing the same properties, are misrepresenting them. However, when, on the basis of their perspective, some insist that the characterizations of others are illicit, and so trades based on them should be prohibited, they are then insisting that incompatible perspectives be normalized away (i.e., deemed illegitimate). Such views often take the form of criticizing markets, and the deep assumption that what is traded is up to buyers and sellers.

To be sure, in any given community perspectives may converge on their conception of some objects and their properties, and so a moral constitution could prohibit some trades. More importantly, it may be impossible to allow some trades without deleterious effects on third parties, and there is no practical way to include them in the bargain.[118] But as the moral framework increases the class of "taboo trades"[119]— trades that are conceived of as not respecting the "true character" of the objects—it is normalizing the public perspective, assuming a correct understanding of the social object and its value. To the extent it

---

[118] See Satz, *Why Some Things Should Not Be for Sale.*

[119] For a study of people's different understandings of "taboo trades" and their relation to ideology, see Tetlock, "Coping with Trade-Offs."

does so, the moral constitution impairs the ability of markets to perform their critical role in facilitating exchange and cooperation between those who understand their worlds very differently.

The Open Society arose in the great commercial cities of Western Europe. The widespread extent of their markets facilitated cooperation among those with deeply diverse religious and cultural backgrounds, who saw the world in very different ways. Without great reliance on markets, diverse perspectives will be unable to work out the terms of their myriad interactions—in which they do not fully agree on how to characterize their exchanges or the benefits obtained from them. No set of social rules could ever itself define the rational bargains for the daily interactions of a large, diverse society.

None of this, however, is to say that the rules of the market are beyond the ken of the moral constitution. There is good evidence that concern with fair, nonexploitative transactions is something approaching a universal feature of diverse societies.[120] An especially important finding concerns play in the widely replicated Ultimatum Game. An Ultimatum Game is a single-play game between two anonymous subjects, Proposer and Responder, who have X amount of some good (say, money) to distribute between them. In the simplest version of the game, Proposer makes the first move and gives an offer of the form, "I will take n percent of X, leaving you with $100-n$ percent," where n is not greater than 100 percent. If Responder accepts, each gets what Proposer offers; if Responder rejects, each receives nothing. If players cared only about the amount of X that they received, it would be rational for Proposer to, say, take 99 percent, offering Responder 1 percent. Responder would be faced with a choice between 1 percent of X and nothing; if the Responder cares only about maximizing the amount of X to be received, she will accept the offer. Since Proposer knows this, and since Proposer also will not choose less over more, Proposer will make the "selfish" 99:1 offer. This is not the observed outcome. In the United States and many other countries, one-shot ultimatum games result in median offers of Proposers to Responders of between 50 percent and 40 percent with mean offers being 30 percent to 40 percent.

---

[120] For a discussion of this matter, see my essay "The Egalitarian Species."

	UCLA	Ariz	Pitt	Hebrew	Gadjah	Machi-guenga	Mapuche
Mean offer	.48	.44	.45	.36	.44	.26	.34
Modal offer	.50	.50	.50	.50	.40	.15	.50/.33
Rejection rate	0	—	.22	.33	.19	.048	.065
Rejection offers <20%	0/0	—	0/1	5/7	9/16	1/10	2/12

Figure 4-3. Comparison of Ultimatum Game results

Responders refuse offers of less than 20 percent about half the time.[121] Strikingly, while those in market societies throughout the world play Ultimatum Games in these ways, there is much *more* variance in small-scale, nonmarket, societies. Indeed, in some small-scale societies (the Machiguenga of the Peruvian Amazon and the Mapuche of southern Chile) the game is played in the relentlessly "selfish" way, as figure 4-3 indicates.[122] The Machiguenga are essentially without markets; the Mapuche have limited acquaintance with markets. Note that fair play in the Ultimatum Game seems characteristic of market, but not non-market, societies. A plausible hypothesis is that market societies have developed moral rules—parts of their basic frameworks—for fair terms of interaction with strangers. The Machiguenga, for example, do not seem to have social rules regulating anonymous transactions with strangers and thus do not see anything unfair about "selfish" Proposer offers. Machiguengan Responders seem to simply view it as bad luck that they were not chosen as Proposers. The Mapuche do see "selfish" offers as unfair but do not seem to think there is a basic moral rule to which they can hold others accountable.

---

[121] Bicchieri, *The Grammar of Society*, p. 105. For a helpful overview see Güth and Tietz, "Ultimatum Bargaining Behavior." See also van Damme et al., "How Werner Güth's Ultimatum Game Shaped Our Understanding of Social Behavior."

[122] Henrich and Smith, "Comparative Evidence from Machiguenga, Mapuche, and American Populations." The Machiguenga and the Mapuche are small-scale societies; the other results are from urban university students in the United States, Israel, and Indonesia. The Ultimatum Game does not show significant variance in play on the basis of age or gender.

2.6 The Moral and Political Constitutions

I have been stressing the moral constitution of the Open Society, rather than the political constitution and the legal framework. Political philosophy has typically focused on the state and the law, often ignoring—indeed denying the existence of—the moral constitution. This has led to a state-legal-centric view of the regulation of the Open Society. A typical view in political philosophy is to take it as axiomatic that if there is an injustice the state should enact a law that prohibits it; if people have a human right to perform an act, or to a performance on the part of others, the law should make it so. The truth about morality dictates what justice demands, and the law must enforce it. Gerry Mackie has recently argued that this is an error. As he points out, there are hundreds of critical cases around the world in which deeply unjust practices—among them female genital cutting, caste discrimination, child marriage—have been widely criminalized yet continue to be practiced. Laws that depart from the basic moral and social norms of a society mostly likely will be ignored, often engendering contempt for the law. As Mackie, following Iris Marion Young,[123] concludes, "Criminalization is an appropriate response to a criminal injustice, a deviation from accepted norms, its harmful consequences intended, knowingly committed by identifiable individuals, whose wrongdoing should be punished. It is not an appropriate response to a structural injustice, in compliance with accepted norms, its harmful consequences unintended byproducts, and caused by everyone and no one. The proper remedy for a harmful social norm is organized social change, not fault, blame, punishment."[124]

In recent years students of social change have come to something of a consensus that effective legal regulation cannot stray too far from the underlying informal social rules.[125] One of the most striking "social

---

[123] Young, *Responsibility for Justice.*

[124] See Mackie, "Effective Rule of Law Requires Construction of a Social Norm of Legal Obedience." My thanks to Gerry Mackie for discussions about this matter.

[125] In addition to ibid., see Bicchieri, *Norms in the Wild*; Bicchieri and Mercier, "Norm and Beliefs"; Platteau, *Institutions, Social Norms and Economic Development*; Stuntz, "Self-Defeating Crimes."

experiments" based on this insight was that of Antanas Mockus, mayor of Bogotá in the late 1990s and early 2000s.[126] In terms of the present analysis, Mockus's aim was to harmonize the moral constitution and legislation; he recognized that unless supported by the underlying informal moral and social framework, attempts to induce change though the law would not succeed. For example, Bogotá was characterized by a very high rate of traffic fatalities in the mid-1990s, with widespread disregard for traffic regulations. Mockus distributed 350,000 "Thumbs Up/Thumbs Down" cards that drivers could display in response to dangerous driving by others, to drive home the message that such behavior not only was illegal but violated the informal normative judgments of other drivers. Along with related programs, Bogotá witnessed a 63 percent decrease in traffic fatalities between 1995 and 2003. Similar programs based on harmonizing the law with informal social normative expectations led to decreases in water usage and, critically, homicides.

Of course the law does have a fundamental place in the regulation of interactions in the Open Society. Gillian K. Hadfield and Barry R. Weingast have developed an enlightening model of legal coordination according to which the critical function of law is to provide shared classifications of prohibited behavior among those with, essentially, different perspectives.[127] In this sense law is absolutely critical in creating a shared social world. Nevertheless, the fundamental point of this section stands: political philosophers and policy experts have too often conceived of the legal system as an autonomous center of social regulation, failing to realize that its efficacy depends on harmonizing its requirements with the underlying moral constitution.

---

[126] For a short description of this experiment, see Mockus, "Building Citizenship Culture in Bogotá." For an in-depth treatment, see Mockus, "Bogotá's Capacity for Self-Transformation and Citizenship Building." See also http://www.corpovisionarios. org.

[127] Hadfield and Weingast, "What Is Law?" For an application of this model to broader themes concerning public reason, see Hadfield and Macedo, "Rational Reasonableness." Van Schoelandt demonstrates the superiority of an alternative application (to that proposed by Hadfield and Macedo) in "Rawlsian Functionalism and the Problem of Coordination."

3 RULES WE CAN LIVE WITH

3.1 On Choosing without Agreeing on the Best

In the previous section I sketched a set of institutions that are hospitable to diversity as such. We now turn to the critical question of justification: in what sense can we say that a perspective on justice could endorse the rules of the public moral constitution? That is, under what conditions can Alf, holding perspective Σ, endorse these rules and institutions in a way that allows him to see them as a practice of moral responsibility to which he holds others, and accepts that others appropriately hold him accountable? I first consider the conditions under which some single perspective can do this, and then extend the analysis to examine the range of perspectives that might accomplish it.

Recall the problem with which we began this chapter. Rawls seemed unable to build his insight about deep diversity of views about justice into his contractual model. One can see why he might have been reluctant to build diversity into a contract: it is easy to assume that a contractual model that yields no unique result may be one that simply ends in a deadlock, and a deadlock is of no help at all in deciding what is just. In *A Theory of Justice* Rawls modeled the parties in the original position as ranking the various competing conceptions of justice in pairwise comparisons.[128] But the choice depends on unanimity about what is ranked best in the set: if in your ranking you hold that x is preferred to y, and in my ranking y is preferred to x, we seem stuck. As Sen saw it, the social contract's unanimity requirement appears to be a "straightjacket" that leaves us unable to make any choice at all.[129] As Rawls came to recognize the diversity of reasonable conceptions of justice, he appeared to allow multiple original positions, which would yield multiple conclusions. But this leaves us without *a* conclusion about what justice is. At the end of a fifty-year quest, we have no coherent *theory* of justice. For some partially normalized perspectives we have one conception (say, "justice as fairness"), for another normalization, another theory. But what is *the* theory of justice?

---

[128] Rawls, *A Theory of Justice*, p. 106.
[129] Sen, *The Idea of Justice*, p. 135.

Let us commence with a version of this problem. Instead of a set of theories of justice $\{T_1 \ldots T_n\}$, let us substitute a set of alternative rules $\{R_1 \ldots R_n\}$, which are proposed as part of the moral constitution over some matter regulating the interactions of a set of perspectives $\{\Sigma_1 \ldots \Sigma_n\}$, which includes Alf's perspective. We suppose these are strict alternatives in the sense that for every such rule in the set, other members provide inconsistent deontic requirements or permissions over the core cases which R-type rules are intended to regulate.[130] I assume for simplicity's sake that all perspectives (or, alternatively, all representatives of a perspective) $\{\Sigma_1 \ldots \Sigma_n\}$ strictly rank all the rules in $\{R_1 \ldots R_n\}$ in terms of their justice, as that perspective judges it.

It might seem that we have simply recreated Sen's problem: in order for the choice situation to make sense, the different perspectives must be ranking the same thing, but it is precisely in their identification of the features of objects on which perspectives disagree (§IV.1.2.3). Recall, however, that a rule simply *is* a common public system of classification: it is a socially constructed artifact. The question for the perspectival "contractors" is how some artificial system of social classification relates to their perspective on justice: given their view of justice, they ask how well this system of social classification scores.[131] For now I assume that they have a very high level of agreement as to the characterization of a given rule R; I relax this assumption in §IV.4.2.

Granting for now, then, that the perspectives agree on how they understand any given proposed rule, and given that our concern is a contract among deeply diverse perspectives, we clearly see the dead

---

[130] The difficulty in further formalizing this idea is to distinguish R-type rules that are inconsistent with other R-type rules from other types of rules (Q-types) that may yield deontic prohibitions, requirements, or permissions that in some specific case are inconsistent with those yielded by the relevant R-type rule, and so are in that sense inconsistent with the R-type rule. It is, for example, the difference between assigning inconsistent property rights (a clash of alternative R-type rules) and property rights clashing with a right to assistance (a Q-type rule). If one holds that all rights must be compossible this problem will not arise, but then one must choose over entire schemes of rights (entire moral constitutions) rather than over individual rules. For a more thorough analysis of the idea of alternative social rules, see *The Order of Public Reason*, pp. 267ff.

[131] On a plausible contractarian account, the evaluation of proposed rules will be what Sen calls "comprehensive": the perspectival representatives will consider how well the rules do on both procedural- and outcome-justice. See §I.2.2.

end of what we might call optimizing (i.e., best in the set) unanimity: it is almost certain that the perspectives will not agree on the best rule in the set. Of course we can guarantee optimizing by full normalization—if Alf's perspective is the unique normalized perspective, then his choice necessarily identifies the best in the set; his choice defines the Archimedean perspective (§IV.1.1). At this point in our analysis the attractions of normalization have hopefully faded. Now ironically enough, it is Sen's pathbreaking work on choice sets, maximal sets, and choice under incompleteness that helps rescue the contractual project from the specter of optimizing deadlock. To simplify, suppose that there are three rules in the set $\{R_1, R_2, R_3\}$, which each perspective ranks from best to worse, and no single rule is ranked best by all perspectives. The perspectives disagree in their rankings of this set, yet, as Rawls so often stressed, they require a public moral constitution—a public social world. It will not do for some to insist that R_1 is the one and only correct rule; given that other equally eligible perspectives hold that $R_2 \succ R_1$, how can a proponent of R_1 claim that all must endorse it over R_2? As Sen recognized, it is ranked higher on one evaluative perspective, but, since we have supposed that it is not the only perspective that matters, its conclusions are not determinative for other perspectives. The parties need to devise a public social world, but they do not agree about what is best.

Our parties are in a position similar to "Buridan's ass," the donkey who was precisely midway between two haystacks and could not decide whether to turn right (x) to eat from one or left (y) to eat from other, and ended up dying of starvation (z). Sen writes:

> The less interesting, but more common, interpretation is that the ass was indifferent between the two haystacks, and could not find any reason to choose one haystack over the other. But since there is no possibility of a loss from choosing either haystack in the case of indifference, there is no deep dilemma here either from the point of view of maximization or that of optimization. The second—more interesting—interpretation is that the ass could not rank the two haystacks and had an incomplete preference over this pair. It did not, therefore, have any optimal alternative, but both x and y were maximal—neither known to be worse than any of the other alternatives.

In fact, since each was also decidedly better for the donkey than its dying of starvation z, the case for a maximal choice is strong.[132]

Our contract among diverse perspectives is in the same position. If z is $\{\neg R_1, \neg R_2, \neg R_3\}$, and all concur that $R_1 \succ z$, $R_2 \succ z$, and $R_3 \succ z$, all three rules are best elements in the set $\{R_1, R_2, R_3, z\}$; they are all ranked higher than z, but there is no unanimous ranking of any pair in $\{R_1, R_2, R_3\}$. However, if the parties do not choose from $\{R_1, R_2, R_3\}$ they know they will end up with z, which all deem their worst choice. Theirs is Buridan's ass's predicament: at this stage of their deliberation they cannot, via unanimity, select any of the three rules as the best, but if they do not choose they end up with z. And, as Sen suggests, only an ass would do that. Thus the contract among diverse perspectives may well have an outcome—a choice set (a set of best options) from which all the contractors have reason to endorse *a* choice. The important thing is not to get stuck with z.

3.2 The Socially Eligible Set

We can divide the set of the rules $\{R_1 \ldots R_n\}$ into three parts. The critical divide is between the rules in $\{R_1 \ldots R_n\}$ that all perspectives agree are better than "z," which we can define as no moral rule at all on this matter. If any of the perspective-contractors rank z above some proposed rule R_i that perspective deems it better to have the moral constitution silent on this matter than to include R_i. Another way of thinking of this is that Alf's perspective cannot acknowledge R_i as the basis of a practice of accountability; Alf is not willing to have others hold him responsible for failing to act on R_i, nor is he willing to hold others accountable. Thus, faced with a choice between conforming to R_i and simply acting as his own perspective deems best, Alf would choose to act as he thinks best. Let us, then, define the *socially eligible set of moral rules* as all those rules that all perspectives in the contract rank as better than z.

It is important to stress that stating that a society forgoes a *moral* rule on this matter is not to say that it has no rule whatsoever about it. It is common to distinguish injunctive from descriptive social rules

---

[132] Sen, "Maximization and the Act of Choice," p. 184.

(or norms).[133] On Cristina Bicchieri's influential analysis, a descriptive norm is solely focused on a group's empirical expectations of what others in the group will do. An example of such a norm is a pure convention, say of walking on the right side of a sidewalk or footpath. If one expects others to walk on the right side, then it is typically in one's interest to also walk on the right. In the case of walking on footpaths (unlike, say driving cars on a busy road), one may sometimes deviate from the norm (say one is going to a next-door shop, and it is easier to walk against the current), and others are unlikely to be significantly disadvantaged by one's deviation. Thus descriptive norms are not enforced; the sole motivation by Betty is to best promote her interests and goals by aligning with the actions of others. Still, overall, groups can achieve large-scale coordination simply by knowing what most others are likely to do. In contrast, injunctive social rules carry not simply empirical, but normative expectations: others expect one to follow them, and are apt to hold one responsible for violations. They can form a practice of mutual responsibility (§IV.2.1.2). Norms of fair division are such injunctive rules: subjects tend not only to follow fair division norms, but to blame and punish those who do not comply.[134]

While Alf's core concern is whether a practice of responsibility regulating some matter is justified given his perspective, he also recognizes that a practice of accountability requires that other perspectives have reasons to comply: thus his concern in justifying a moral rule is whether all have adequate reasons to endorse *injunctive rules*. This is a stronger claim than saying all have an interest in conforming to a social rule. When thinking about the "no moral rule" option we should not conceive of it as precluding a descriptive norm about this matter. This is important, for the question whether to endorse some rule R_i is not simply whether we seek to achieve some coordination in some area of social life (a mere convention can do that), but whether this area is of such a nature and of sufficient importance that we must regulate it via (justified) injunctive rules—a system of shared norma-

---

[133] See, for example, Cialdini, Kallgren, and Reno, "A Focus Theory of Normative Conduct"; Bicchieri, *The Grammar of Society*, chap. 1; Mackie, "Effective Rule of Law Requires Construction of a Social Norm of Legal Obedience." I am employing the idea of a "descriptive norm" widely here, to include conventions.

[134] See Fehr and Fischbacher, "Third Party Punishment and Social Norms."

tive expectations and demands, and quite possibly punishment. This is why a chaotic moral state of nature is an inappropriate benchmark for a contractualist theory, as if the absence of a moral constitution is no coordination at all. From the justificatory point of view, the absence of a justified injunctive rule about some type of social interaction may well be simply a descriptive norm or convention about it.

That said, injunctive moral rules often have great advantages over purely descriptive norms or conventions when social cooperation needs to be secured. Descriptive norms can be unstable: since they are sustained only by empirical expectations of general conformity, as soon as one begins to doubt whether others are actually conforming to the norm, one is apt to withdraw one's compliance.[135] Thus "trembling hands"—noncompliance with the norm caused by errors in applying it—may lead others to abandon the norm as they conclude that general conformity is breaking down ("Look at the people violating the rule; it isn't much of a convention!"). In contrast, injunctive social rules are upheld by a system of normative expectations and demands and thus are designed to respond to noncompliance. Consequently, while the absence of an injunctive rule about some matter does not imply the absence of social cooperation, it often does imply imperfect and fragile cooperation. The simple game of the Stag Hunt provides a good example (figure 4-4).[136]

The best for both parties is to hunt a stag, but for that they must cooperate. While Alf cannot catch a stag alone, he can capture a hare alone, though the meat is much less than half a stag. It would seem that, since cooperating on hunting a stag is best for both, a descriptive norm ("We hunt stag around here") would suffice. But note that if either Alf or Betty suspects that the other will not act according to the convention, he or she will be tempted to defect and hunt hare; in this sense the Hunt Stag/Hunt Stag equilibrium is fragile. An injunctive norm ("Hunt Stag!") could change the game, allowing players to *demand* that the other Hunt Stag, and punish those who fail to. A practice of responsibility for hunting stag may well be to the advantage of both, even on a matter of simple coordination. When Alf and Betty

---

[135] Bicchieri, *The Grammar of Society*, pp. 29–43. For a different analysis of how conventions become injunctive rules, see Sugden, "Spontaneous Order."

[136] See Bicchieri, *The Grammar of Society*, pp. 39–40.

Betty

		Hunt Stag	Hunt Hare
Alf	Hunt Stag	1st / 1st	2nd / 3rd
	Hunt Hare	3rd / 2nd	2nd / 2nd

Figure 4-4. A simple Stag Hunt game

seek to cooperate in situations with a Prisoner's Dilemma–like structure (where each does best under universal cooperation rather than universal defection, but one does yet better if others cooperate when one defects), the case for an injunctive rule is obviously even more compelling.[137]

Thus whether a perspective ranks an injunctive moral rule above no such rule is the critical distinction for our contractors: any rule injunctive R_i ranked below the "z" option by a perspective is not eligible for that perspective; the set of rules that are eligible for all perspectives constitutes the socially eligible set. Now within this socially eligible set, some rule injunctive R_x could be judged by all contractors (*i*) as better than "z" but (*ii*) as a worse option than some other member of the socially eligible set. In more technical language, this rule would be Pareto dominated by another member of the socially eligible set. The set of rules that are (*i*) in the socially eligible set and are (*ii*) not Pareto dominated by any rule in the socially eligible set is the *socially optimal eligible set*.[138] Clearly our contractors would prefer to select a rule from

[137] It is because injunctive rules can solve such problems that, as the Ostroms have shown, it simply does not follow that the state and law are necessary for solving "tragedy of the commons" problems—where resource use has Prisoner's Dilemma–like properties. See Ostrom, *Governing the Commons*.

[138] In Sen's terms, the optimal socially eligible set is the joint choice set for our contractors. In *The Order of Public Reason* the optimal eligible set was defined in a less demanding way, requiring only what Sen calls a "maximal set" rather than a choice set (the elements of the choice set are always part of the maximal set, but not vice versa). I employ the latter, more demanding idea here because the logic of choice is more manifest and the problem simpler. See Sen, *Collective Choice and Social Welfare*, pp. 1–20.

the socially optimal eligible set; to abide by an eligible rule that was, in the eyes of all, worse than another member of the socially eligible set would be unfortunate for all. They might feel a bit like asses—from everyone's perspective on justice, they could do better. However, for our purposes the critical issue is the conditions under which a society could possess a socially eligible set, and so create a public moral constitution all can live with (whether or not it is optimal).

3.3 Abandoning the Optimizing Stance

Recall that our interest in a socially eligible set is that, even if all the perspectives in our contract cannot all converge on a single best rule for regulating some area of social life, they might converge on a set of injunctive rules, which all rank as better than no moral injunctive rule at all on this matter. For such an eligible set to obtain it must be the case that our contractors do not insist on what might be called the "optimizing stance"—that the only rule that is acceptable is one's top-ranked rule. Here is where we must break with a great deal of moral and political philosophy, which identifies moral thinking with an optimizing perspective: thinking through the issue from his own perspective on justice Alf decides what is the best injunctive rule, or best principle, and so he concludes *that, and that alone*, is what morality requires. As Kurt Baier says, "Where interests conflict, there are many possible regulations dealing with the conflict. The directive embodying the regulation would not be properly moral (as opposed to being legal or conventional) unless it *purported* to be the *best possible* way of regulating such a conflict."[139] If Alf and Betty, who do not share a normalized perspective on justice, insist on the optimal choice as given by his or her perspective—each can see only as part of an acceptable moral constitution what he or she sees as the best rule—they will almost surely fail to endorse a set of eligible moral rules. Diverse perspectives will disagree about what is best because they disagree about justice. If we accept the optimizing stance, the idea of a contractarian theory of justice is either an illusion (because the contract, which was supposed to justify a conception of justice in the face of diversity,

---

[139] Baier, "Moral Obligation," p. 226. Emphasis in original.

really presupposes a fully normalized perspective on justice) or a dead end (because no agreement will be achieved). But perhaps this simply shows the folly of a contractarian approach. Why shouldn't a person insist on following his or her personal optimizing commitments? What good reasons could one have for not doing so?

The fundamental reason is that the optimizing stance precludes a great good—one which that very perspective on justice almost surely endorses—of a social life of widespread moral accountability (§IV.2.1.2). Suppose that Alf, occupying his perspective, insists that only his optimal rule is acceptable as a basis for the moral regulation of some important interaction (say, about the rights of bodily integrity), while Betty insists that only her (incompatible) optimal rule could qualify as the basis of a practice of moral accountability. When they meet each other Alf will not be able to suppose that a goodwilled Betty, who reasons about justice as well as he can expect of another, will see that she ought to conform to his preferred rule. Employing her capacity for rational moral reflection and agency, she has constructed a reasonable perspective on justice; given it, she simply cannot come to the conclusion that his proposal is the best rule (as we have seen, her perspective categorizes and evaluates the world differently). But if Alf recognizes all this, he cannot infer ill will on her part, for he too embraces the optimizing stance, and he sees her perspective on justice as a reasonable one. Thus their reactive attitudes at the heart of the practice of moral accountability are undermined—and thus also the practice itself.

The orthodox moral philosopher will insist that this is just too bad, but true justice is true justice, and Alf cannot renounce the conclusions of his perspective that his rule best tracks true justice.[140] The Open Society, however, does not ask him to do so; indeed, if his perspective is to be part of a system that is morally improving (§IV.4), it is critical that he *not* renounce the conclusions of his perspective. Moral improvement depends on Alf (and others) seeking the best answers and, hopefully, convincing others that his is a better answer. What he must renounce is his claim that the optimal rule as identified

---

[140] See, for example, Mack, "Peter Pan Strikes Back"; Arneson, "Rejecting *The Order of Public Reason.*"

by his perspective on justice is the sole acceptable basis of a system of moral accountability—that it *must* be part of our moral constitution. As we have seen, it is this insistence that undermines the practice of accountability—a practice that his own perspective on justice surely values.

Some moral philosophers are, as they say, willing to "bite this bullet" and accept that their optimizing stance precludes relations of moral responsibility.[141] Strawsonians will be deeply skeptical that they really can leave behind their participant perspective in favor of the theory of morality endorsed from what they see as the objective perspective. Their insistence on the correct, objective point of view and their formal pronouncements are forgotten when they reenter the participant perspective of an agent among others and react to the slights, lack of respect, and ill will that they attribute to others when they conclude that their moral rights have been neglected. But even from the objective perspective of the moral philosopher examining a system of relations from the outside, a system of rules to which goodwilled rational moral agents cannot hold each other accountable must be a terribly flawed system, for we have good formal and empirical evidence that without accountability and punishment, systems of moral rules are invaded by defectors, undermining the very basis of moralized, stable, social cooperation.[142]

The optimizing stance is also self-defeating, once we take a more inclusive view of optimization. Our analysis in chapter II concluded that an individual perspective on justice will almost surely be unable to find its ideal; being confined to a neighborhood, the identification of its own ideal will be elusive. However, as we saw in chapter III, other perspectives can uncover parts of the landscape beyond one's ken; revealing features of the social world that are not salient on one's own view, they can help bring one's own ideal into closer view. But this requires, we saw, a network of interconnected communities of inquiry—what we termed "republican communities of moral inquiry." It is precisely the framework for such interactions that the moral constitution of the Open Society provides. Adopting the optimizing stance

---

[141] See, e.g., Wall, "On Justificatory Liberalism," pp. 143–44.

[142] On these matters see *The Order of Public Reason*, chaps. 3 and 4.

toward the moral constitution precludes one's perspective participating in this framework for inquiry; relations of accountability, and shared empirical and normative expectations between one's own perspectives and those from whom one could learn, will be undermined. To participate in shared moral inquiry with other perspectives on justice one must provide the foundations for moral relations of accountability in one's interactions with them. To wish to learn from other views, while insisting that only one's own view is correct and that all must live by it, is hardly a basis for a community of shared inquiry. By seeking to optimize in this way one forgoes optimizing in the sense of better understanding one's own commitments regarding justice.

It might be wondered why, if one cannot insist that one's ideal be institutionalized in the face of disagreement by other perspectives, one should care about improving one's understanding of ideal justice. It would seem that the Open Society allows one to better know one's ideal, but simultaneously instructs one not to pursue it. Why, then, care about the ideal? Those who believe that inquiry into ideal justice is more like theoretical than practical inquiry[143] will not see this as a pressing worry, but those who accept that recommendations are critical to justice (§I.1.5), will indeed wonder what is the point of such moral "inquiry." We shall return to the idea of moral improvement (§IV.4), but this much is manifest: the Open Society invites all to share their ideals, and show other perspectives how our common life can be made more just. Especially given the polycentric nature of the Open Society, ideals of a more just society can spread from one network to another, often deeply changing the public moral constitution. Sometimes this consists in the elimination of unjust categories such as racial or gender classifications, sometimes in the development of new rules of personal privacy and bodily integrity. That the public moral constitution denies the claim of any perspective to implement its controversial ideal of justice by no means implies that deeper understandings of different visions of the ideal do not help shape our common life together. The benefits of exchange of ideas among different communities of moral inquiry can be widespread even if none of the ideas is accepted as a blueprint for our shared moral life.

---

[143] See here Estlund, "Utopophobia," pp. 132ff.

We can generalize this idea beyond inquiry into justice to more diffuse benefits. In a recent analysis of the conditions of tolerance and the gains from interacting with those with different ideological perspectives, Ryan Muldoon, Michael Borgida, and Michael Cuffaro develop a model based on Ricardo's account of trade, which indicates that

> as tolerance is a measure of how willing to engage with others with different ideological commitments one is, tolerance increases one's chances of discovering a satisfactory tradeoff between material gains and ideological purity. This suggests, then, that if one has an interest in material gain, then one has a corresponding reason to become more tolerant. On this model, increased tolerance results in increased reward, even when the potential discomfort of engaging with someone with different ideological preferences is taken into account. From this model, we see that rational actors ought to choose to become as tolerant as they can, with the expectation that this tolerance will be amply rewarded. Tolerance, then, can be thought of not just as a liberal duty to others, but as a rational duty to oneself: to promote one's own self-interest best, one ought to be more tolerant of others. Rationality thus motivates individuals to see others who are different as potential partners in exchange, rather than as merely potential sources of ideological conflict.[144]

Those with different perspectives—on justice, but on other matters too—provide opportunities for productive exchange based on comparative advantage; the more one fruitfully interacts with diverse others (even granting that this might offend some of one's sensibilities about justice), the more opportunities for advantageous trades (or, more broadly, productive interactions). Again it is important that the Open Society arose in the great trading cities, in which not only different skills but different cultures and moral perspectives interacted. Thus satisfaction of a variety of goals typically strongly inclines against the optimizing stance. When people insist on their optimum choice as the only acceptable common rule, they preclude widespread acceptance of a practice of accountability that provides a framework

---

[144] Muldoon, Borgida, and Cuffaro, "The Conditions of Tolerance," p. 330.

for a wide-ranging system of cooperation among diverse agents, which provides innumerable opportunities for mutual benefit.

3.4 The Social Space of the Open Society

Rawls tells us that the aim of his account of public reason is to arrive at a public moral constitution "that all can live with."[145] In the terms of our analysis, the fundamental claim is that in a society with a number of perspectives on justice N, versions of the institutions of the Open Society (§IV.2) will be in the socially eligible set for a group of perspectives coming near to N. This is not to say that all, or indeed many, perspectives will rank rules consonant with the elements of the Open Society as the best rules by which to live, but they will be rules that a maximally large subset of perspectives can live with. Yet, as Rawls also observes:

> No society can include within itself all ways of life. We may indeed lament the limited space, as it were, of social worlds, and of ours in particular; and we may regret some of the inevitable effects of our culture and social structure. As Isaiah Berlin long maintained (it was one of his fundamental themes), there is no social world without loss: that is, no social world that does not exclude some ways of life that realize in special ways certain fundamental values. The nature of its culture and institutions proves too uncongenial.[146]

Some perspectives will conclude that no moral rules at all are better than the moral constitution of the Open Society: they place little importance on a cooperative social life supported by a practice of accountability, little weight on the improvement of their own perspective's ability to better locate its ideals, and little importance on a framework of mutual exchange. All this is possible—and no doubt occurs. But to conclude that the space of the Open Society is inadequate in the face of perspectival diversity is to retreat into the social world of one's own perspective, forgoing the great benefits of a practice of

---

[145] Rawls, "Kantian Constructivism in Moral Theory," p. 306.
[146] Rawls, *Justice as Fairness*, p. 154. The passage also occurs in *Political Liberalism*, p. 197.

accountability and productive interchange with diverse communities of moral inquiry.[147]

Many worry that, in a diverse society, any attempt to show that almost all perspectives must endorse a moral rule is doomed to failure: we are almost surely to be left with no socially eligible set.[148] One response to this worry is, of course, to reflect again on the basic elements of the Open Society, and the great benefits that they provide almost all perspectives. But two other points should be kept in mind. (*i*) The polycentric (§IV.2.2) nature of the Open Society does not require that all perspectives must share all features of the moral constitution. While no doubt the most fundamental aspects must be shared by all (say, basic understandings of the contours of jurisdictions), we should not suppose that all rules must hold over the entire range of perspectives. Networks crystallize to solve commonly recognized problems— those seeking solutions to shared problems adopt rules to accomplish their aims. Those who worry that diverse societies have "empty eligible sets" take an overly abstract view of moral life and why we participate in it. (*ii*) However, it is by no means necessarily unfortunate that many moral rules will fail to be justified—we should not seek a maximally large eligible set or a comprehensive moral constitution. As Hayek stressed, the Open Society's extension of the range and diversity of individuals to whom its moral rules apply inherently brings about a limitation of the content of those rules.[149] If we compare the smothering moralization of the Victorian period with our contemporary moral constitution, we are struck by just how much less social morality regulates. It is a thinner, and a far less stultifying, moral constitution. Recent studies of social norms such as female genital cutting, racial discrimination, condemnation of homosexuality, and public gender inequality have made it manifest how many deeply oppressive social rules characterize various societies. That many perspectives conclude that such rules are worse than no moral rules at all on these matters is a great advance, not a handicap, in the development of the Open Society.

[147] Rawls, *Justice as Fairness*, p. 128.
[148] See, e.g., D'Agostino, "The Orders of Public Reason."
[149] Hayek, *Law, Legislation, and Liberty*, vol. 2, *The Mirage of Social Justice*, p. 146.

Nevertheless, Rawls and Berlin are certainly correct that, in the end, some perspectives will conclude that even the most fundamental elements of the Open Society are worse than no moral constitution at all. Some perspectives are, in the end, unable to share a framework of moral accountability with diverse others. Even the Open Society must be prepared to normalize to some, hopefully to a very small extent. Such "Excluded Perspectives," which cannot find sufficient space in the Open Society, will almost surely be those that are committed to the optimizing stance, or some near approximation to it. Faced with different rules to live by, the Excluded Perspectives can live only by those that they think best, and so they cannot endorse the characteristic institutions of the Open Society, which seek to provide as much space for all as is possible. Such perspectives may live along with, but are not part of, the Open Society, treating its rules as at best mere descriptive norms rather than moral injunctions. Here, we still can do deals with such perspectives on a purely instrumental basis focusing on mutual benefit[150]—insofar as effective deals can be done without a supporting moral framework that undergirds trust among strangers.[151] Philosophers are apt to worry whether, in the absence of accountability relations, we can still act to defend ourselves against such strangers in our midst, and coerce them if need be. Nothing I have said here denies that the Open Society may exercise such defense, including through the law.[152] There is no reason we should leave ourselves at the mercy of those who refuse to live on terms that others can endorse. Yet such Excluded Perspectives are apt to be a source of social conflict and instability. Alienated from the public social world, Excluded Perspectives take refuge in the social world of their comprehensive conception, while viewing the moral constitution of the Open Society as alien

[150] The idea is wonderfully explained by Moehler, "The Scope of Instrumental Morality."

[151] There is reason to doubt this. Unless Betty is committed to injunctive norms, she is apt to keep the bargain only if threatened with punishment. She will be tempted to play "snatch" rather than "exchange." See Schwab and Ostrom, "The Vital Role of Norms and Rules in Maintaining Open Public and Private Economies."

[152] This distinguishes the present analysis from that of some followers of Rawls, who seem to be committed to the impossible project of always justifying coercion. For an excellent analysis, see Van Schoelandt's "Justification, Coercion, and the Place of Public Reason."

oppression. It is a great loss to all when any perspective is, as it were, normalized out of the social contract, though no doubt such loss can be only minimized, not entirely avoided.

4 Imperfect Coordination on the Moral Constitution

4.1 Coordination as Diversity Reducing

Thus far the most that could be claimed is that versions of the rules characteristic of the Open Society (§IV.2) will be in the socially eligible set of a very wide range of perspectives, and no effective basis of social cooperation could achieve a more widespread endorsement. Even granting that, I have said nothing about how any rule, specific enough to be part of a practice of responsibility, might be selected. We can, for instance, think of a range of rights of privacy; different perspectives will rank them differently given their understandings of justice. That a contract yields a socially eligible set with no optimal element does not tell us how to choose from this set, *only that we have reason to make a choice* (§IV.3.1).

On Peter Vanderschraaf's insightful analysis, this means that the parties to our "contract" are in the true "circumstances of justice." On his non-Humean account of the circumstances of justice, they can be modeled as a "conflictual coordination game... with multiple strict equilibrium points such that the parties engaged in the game differ over their most favored equilibria. In a conflictual coordination game, the parties have open to them a variety of ways to coordinate, but their interests conflict over which way to coordinate."[153] In our case, they disagree in their rankings of the rules of justice over some matter in the socially eligible set, but they recognize that a moral constitution obtains only when they successfully coordinate on one of them. Figure

---

[153] Vanderschraaf, "The Circumstances of Justice," p. 330. Vanderschraaf's overall analysis differs from that presented here; on his view justice appears to exclude settling on a Nash equilibrium in pure strategies, leading instead to a correlated equilibrium in which everyone gives up something. I have argued elsewhere that such a "compromise requirement" is not appropriate in the context of rule selection, especially once dynamic considerations are taken into account. *The Order of Public Reason*, pp. 403ff.

Betty

	Rule R_A	Rule R_B
Rule R_A (Alf)	2nd / 1st	3rd / 3rd
Rule R_B (Alf)	3rd / 3rd	1st / 2nd

Figure 4-5. An Impure Coordination game

4-5 provides a toy game example of the basic problem of our perspectival contractors in the circumstances of justice.

Unless they coordinate on one member of the socially eligible set, they do not have a mutually acknowledged rule, which provides the basis of a practice of responsibility in which they share the same normative expectations (§IV.2.1.2). Either Rule R_A or R_B is better than lack of coordination (no shared rule at all, the "z" option), and thus both are Nash equilibriums: if they coordinate on R_A or R_B neither can achieve a better outcome by unilateral defection, acting on the alternative rule. If Alf acts on R_A, Betty's best response is to also act on R_A; if Betty acts on R_B, Alf's best response is also to act on R_B. If Alf justifies his action because it is called for by R_A it must be the case that not only is R_A in the socially eligible set, but it is the rule on which they have coordinated, and so both have empirical and normative expectations that they will act on it. A justified appeal to R_A presupposes that it is the rule from the socially eligible set on which they have coordinated (even though Betty believes it is not the best, given her understanding of justice). As we saw earlier, the functional nature of the moral constitution implies an existence requirement (§IV.2.1.3). This points to a fundamental revision in theorizing about public reason and justice, which has not been appreciated (indeed, it has not been glimpsed) by most of those who are content with justifying a "family" of liberal conceptions. The justification of a rule of justice depends not simply on the reasons of the parties for specific rules, but on their coordination on some single eligible element. The justification of an appeal to a rule of justice R as a basis of a practice of moral accountability in a group requires (*i*) it is in the socially eligible set of that group *and* (*ii*) they have been able to coordinate on it.

Note that the very need for the group to coordinate on a rule is inherently diversity reducing: the value of coordination simultaneously decreases diversity within a group (by inducing them to select within the socially eligible set), leading members to converge, while increasing the diversity (of moral constitutions) between groups.[154] Different societies are apt to coordinate on different constitutions, even if they share the same socially eligible set. Thus we can expect significant diversity among the moral constitutions of open societies even when each has the same range of perspectives represented.

This choice from the eligible set can be made in a wide variety of ways. Sometimes we can envisage a procedure that all would accept, say, some form of democratic vote. But here too we are likely to find disagreements about the best procedure—one thing democratic theory after Arrow must realize is that there is no flawless way of voting over three or more options.[155] "When sincere and good people differ," Nozick observed, "we are prone to think they must accept some procedure to decide their differences, some procedure they... agree is reliable and fair.... [But] this disagreement may extend all the way up the ladder of procedures."[156] However, the core lesson from Sen's work is not that we must justify a meta–choice procedure to determine what, from some metaperspective, is the best in the eligible set, but that rational agents will see the need *that a choice is made*. In our case, they will see the need to coordinate on some member of the socially eligible set as the rule that they will employ in their moral constitution. Experimental evidence in many-generational-iterated impure coordination games indicates that, indeed, people settle on a tradition of playing one or the other (pure) equilibriums, despite their disagreement on which is the best way to coordinate. In deciding what equilibrium to

---

[154] For a general analysis, see Page, *Diversity and Complexity*, pp. 109–10, 138–40.

[155] Some, such as Donald Saari, have recently argued the Borda count is manifestly the best. For a critical analysis, see Risse, "Why the Count de Borda Cannot Beat the Marquis de Condorcet." For Saari's reply, see "Which Is Better: The Condorcet or Borda Winner?"

[156] Nozick, *Anarchy, State and Utopia*, p. 98.

play, the current generation draws on both the history of play and, more importantly, a socialization process in which the present generation teaches and passes on current conventions to the next generation.[157] In another work I have shown how social evolution can secure a similar result.[158]

Philosophers generally assume that this variety of reasonable ways to practically overcome the indeterminacy of justification is regrettable. Surely, they reason, it would be best if there were some aggregation method that unequivocally and uncontroversially determined what the rational choice to be made from a set of eligible options is. Without such a determinate and uniquely best decision procedure (Condorcet voting, a rational bargain, etc.), even if a society manages to solve the coordination game in figure 4-5 (say by a social process that has produced a constitution with R_A), Betty will continue to push for her favored R_B. The matter, after all, was not definitely, rationally settled. Thus the never-ending pursuit of the philosopher's Holy Grail of THE DETERMINATE SOLUTION. I believe this is a fundamental mistake. It is the very absence of an unequivocal and determined best solution to the problem of equilibrium selection that is the engine of moral improvement in the Open Society.

4.2 The Changing Moral Constitution

To see this, consider first a sort of indeterminacy that I have thus far been ignoring. I have been supposing that the relevant perspectives concur on the classifications that constitute the public rules, and thus when they coordinate on R_i they coordinate on what they see as the very same rule (§IV.3.1). To be a bit more formal, we have supposed that they agree on R_i in the following sense: in circumstances C, R_i prohibits (requires) ϕ-type actions. We also have supposed that they agree in their interpretation of the classification of circumstances (states of affairs) that constitute C, and the classification of actions as ϕ-type. However, given that perspectives see the social world very differently, we might expect that they will disagree in how they under-

[157] Schotter and Sopher, "Social Learning and Coordination Conventions in Intergenerational Games," p. 507.
[158] See my *The Order of Public Reason*, chap. 7.

stand the relevant circumstances and classifications. Even supposing that they concur on the core or paradigm cases, they might differ on "how to go on" in less obvious cases. To a great extent, the judgments of the large majority are apt to dictate what the proper interpretation is; if we wish to coordinate, then we will typically follow the large majority's belief on what that involves. Because participants in a practice of responsibility have empirical and normative expectations as to how others should act, when these expectations are not met, they will call each other out. So long as (*i*) it can be observed what action Alf (occupying perspective Σ_A), thinks R calls for, and (*ii*) the majority concludes that this action clearly disappoints their expectations about R-compliant behavior, they will be able to call Alf out and reestablish coordination. Thus the specification of a rule is by no means a one-time act, but an ongoing process. Again, note how important it is that the rule be part of a practice of moral accountability, rather than simply a descriptive norm (§IV.3.2).

In some circumstances C, though, it may not be manifest to the large majority what the relevant rule is, and so Alf may be able to exploit this ambiguity by choosing the rule that allows him to act as he prefers (ranks best), and yet still meet the normative expectations of others. In an important series of experiments, Bicchieri and her co-investigators have found that exploitation of such norm ambiguity is easily induced. In a notable experiment with Alex Chavez, subjects played Ultimatum Games (§IV.2.5). In the Bicchieri-Chavez study 106 college students played Ultimatum Games with limited options and different amounts of information provided to the Responders. In what they called the "full information" condition, Proposers had three choices on how to split $10: (5, 5), (8, 2) (the 8 going to the Proposer), or a flip of a coin between the (5, 5) and (8, 2) options. Responders knew that these were the Proposer's options, and which option the Proposer chose. Assuming that the Responders think the coin toss is fair and will accept its outcome, the expected payoff of the coin flip for Proposers is .5(5) + .5(8), or 6.5, higher than the expected 5 from the equal-split option (recall that simple [8, 2] offers are very likely to be rejected, leaving the Proposers with nothing). Participants were quizzed on their normative expectations, and it was found that coin toss was widely seen as fair by Responders, and most Proposers correctly believed that Responders thought so. Thus in the full information condition we would expect that Proposers would tend to select "coin," as it gave them a higher expected payoff than equal splits (it is important that they correctly expected Responders to accept the outcome of the toss). This would be a case of Proposers exploiting rule ambiguity: since both equal splits and equal chances seem like fair ways to divide money (both were thought by Responders to be rules that apply to this circumstance), Proposers could take a more selfish choice (with the expected payoff of 6.5 rather than 5) and yet still meet the normative expectations of Responders. In the "limited" information condition, Responders knew that the three options were available to the Proposers, but they did not know which was actually chosen; all they knew was whether the offer was (5, 5) or (8, 2), but they did not know how the (8, 2) offer came about (whether it was the result of a coin or a selfish offer). In this condition Bicchieri and Chavez expected that more Proposers would select (8, 2). Because the Responders did not know how the outcome was selected, and so it *could* have been selected by a toss of the coin in which (8, 2) was selected, Responders could not judge whether or not the choice was selfish or in conformity with the equal chances norm. Consequently the Proposers would expect that Responders may well accept (8, 2), and so be tempted to make the low offer. In the "private information" condition, the Responders did not know that coin toss was available to Proposers, and Proposers were aware that Responders thought that direct (5, 5) and (8, 2) splits were the only options. In this final condition Bicchieri and Chavez did not expect Proposers to choose coin; even if it was truly the coin that selected (8, 2), Responders would take this as simply a selfish choice on the part of Proposers, and so be highly apt to reject. The predictions were well borne out. Subjects did seek to exploit norm ambiguity, systematically selecting the action most advantageous to them when doing so satisfied—or at least did not clearly flout—normative expectations.[159]

---

[159] Bicchieri and Chavez, "Behaving as Expected." See also Bicchieri and Chavez, "Norm Manipulation, Norm Evasion." In an attempt to replicate the first experiment's results with children it was found that young Responders, though they reported the coin toss to be fair, rejected the outcome when they ended up with a low offer. See Castelli et al., "Fairness Norms and Theory of Mind in an Ultimatum Game."

When there is normative ambiguity individuals can choose what rules to follow, and so can act on their preferred rule which, in this situation, is competing with another. Bicchieri and her coworkers' studies were designed to highlight the choice of norms in light of self-interest, but we should not forget that interest often tracks broader normative commitments: those who seek normative change often do so because they do not think their interests are sufficiently catered for. More generally, normative convictions given one's perspective on justice may also figure into rule choice in ambiguous situations. This is significant. Because it is important to coordinate on a rule from the socially eligible set, and each coordination outcome is a Nash equilibrium, and because, further, the rules of the moral constitution are part of a practice of responsibility and so one is apt to be called out for violation, it would seem that once we coordinate on a rule we are locked into it. Rule ambiguity loosens this. Individuals can explore and promote alternative rules, not simply by flouting the current rule and so risk being held accountable and perhaps punished, but by exploiting the ambiguity of normative situations to act on what one's perspective deems to be superior rules (in the socially eligible set) while still satisfying the normative expectations of others. Indeed, in one study Bicchieri and Hugo Mercier found that when exploiting normative ambiguity, a person is apt to be concerned with providing a "public justification" that shows that the action is reasonable.[160] Norm innovation and improvement are consistent with acting within the scope of a public moral constitution; the very ambiguity that results from the inevitable lack of complete agreement on what the moral constitution requires provides the opportunity for improvement of the moral constitution of the Open Society. As Hayek observed, "it is, in fact, desirable that the rules should be observed only in most instances and that the individual should be able to transgress them when it seems to him worthwhile to incur the odium this will cause…. It is this flexibility of voluntary rules which in the field of morals makes gradual evolution and spontaneous growth possible, which allows further modifications and improvements."[161] In cases of rule ambiguity one may do so with-

[160] Bicchieri and Mercier, "Self-Serving Biases and Public Justifications in Trust Games."

[161] Hayek, *The Constitution of Liberty*, p. 63.

out risking the "odium" normally associated with breaking the rules of a practice of accountability.

4.3 How Diversity Maintains the Open Society

Diversity, I have been arguing, is the source of improvements in the moral constitution of the Open Society. Diverse perspectives can apply their different understandings of justice to explore new rules. In situations of rule ambiguity, those with a revisionary perspective can take advantage of the space of ambiguity to act on what they see as the best rule that will not run head-on into existing normative and empirical expectations. If other perspectives concur on the advantages of the revisionary rule, the moral constitution can develop in ways that a wide range of perspectives will see as a clear improvement. It is important that this process does not require unanimity; as long as the revised rule is within the socially eligible set of the relevant network, there can be movement throughout the socially eligible set (which, of course, itself can expand) without all concurring with this movement. We can expect constant tension between those perspectives seeking to explore modifications of the moral constitution and those seeking to uphold the current one. These tussles, conflicts, and disagreements about the rules are inherent in the Open Society of diverse moral perspectives, each seeking ways of interacting that move us toward its view of greater justice. So long as this movement is within the socially eligible set of rules, changes do not amount to one perspective imposing its view of justice on the others, which would undermine the relations of accountability on which the moral constitution of the Open Society depends.

It would appear, however, that this constant disagreement about the rules and attempts to change that are resisted show that the Open Society cannot achieve the sort of stable coordination on rules of justice that Rawls sought. Although traditional moral and political philosophy may intelligibly insist that stability is not itself a desideratum of morality or a theory of justice,[162] when we take up the search for a

---

[162] This is, alas, a fairly widespread view today. See, for example, Cohen, *Rescuing Justice and Equality*, part 2; Estlund, "Human Nature and the Limits (If Any) of Politi-

moral constitution something like stability is of critical importance.[163] Stability is the tendency of a moral constitution to return to a justified equilibrium (in which acting on a moral constitution is the best reply to others doing so) in the face of both internal and external shocks that induce deviation from it.[164] If we are seeking to evaluate a moral framework, we need to know whether it provides the basis for a stable justified moral constitution in a narrow or a wide range of conditions; if the former, we may well doubt that the constitution can perform its expected function given the vicissitudes of human life. Now Rawls, and almost all political philosophers who have considered the matter, have supposed that stability is induced by homogeneity and endangered by diversity. A society that shares the same basic outlook on justice, it is thought, can weather storms better than one in which people have diverse perspectives on justice. Rawls's proposed solution to the problem of stability in *A Theory of Justice* was to argue for a surprising degree of homogeneity not only concerning justice but in our understanding of the good, which would lead us to remain faithful to justice as fairness, even in the face of injustice by others. His later work, acknowledging greater diversity not only about the good but about justice itself, struggled to show how such a deeply divided society could nevertheless be stably just.[165]

The idea of a society that is apt to maintain just social relations in the face of endogenous and exogenous disruptions can be understood in two ways: stability and robustness. Let us call "stability" the tendency of a system to return to the same equilibrium, and "robustness" the tendency of a system to maintain an equilibrium (on a justified moral constitution)—a robust system returns to *an* equilibrium, but not necessarily the same one.[166] To better see the contrast compare two

---

cal Philosophy." For a sustained, characteristically intemperate, critique of stability, see Barry, "John Rawls and the Search for Stability."

[163] "Other things equal, persons in the original position will adopt the most stable scheme of principles." Although the "criterion of stability is not decisive," if the parties find that a conception is unworkable, this would force a reconsideration of their initial choice. Rawls, *A Theory of Justice*, pp. 398–99, 472, 505.

[164] Ibid., p. 401; Weithman, *Why Political Liberalism?*, p. 45. On the idea of a justice equilibrium, see also my "A Tale of Two Sets."

[165] I make this argument in some detail in "The Turn to a Political Liberalism."

[166] I am following Page, *Diversity and Complexity*, pp. 149–50.

societies, *A* and *B*. Society *A* is a highly normalized society. All the admissible perspectives share the same view of justice; not only do they agree on what the best rule of justice is, but they agree in their overall rankings. Thinking the same way, they arrive at the same conclusions. They agree on the best choice; if there is anything else in the eligible set, it is Pareto dominated by the single best element. In such a society there is very little pressure to abandon the optimizing stance (§IV.3.3) as everyone can have their optimal choice. There will be no good reasons for people in *A* to accept that one should live with less than the best rule. As Baier says, the sole moral rule will be identified with the best rule. And so it may well be that the socially eligible set reduces to a singleton. Everyone accepts, and knows that others accept, *one correct view, which many will see as the only correct view* (it is in this sense that *A* is homogeneous). Society *B*, in contrast, has not achieved moral agreement on one and only one constitution as the best; for all rules in the constitution there is a large eligible set with deep disagreement about the best element. Although for any rule in the constitution there is a working coordination on it as the rule they will live by, normative ambiguity and more explicit movements to move within the socially eligible set are a cause of ongoing efforts by many perspectives to change the moral constitution in what they see as a more just direction.

To fix ideas, take just one rule in the moral constitution of each society, *R*, say, a rule that marriage is a long-term monogamous commitment between two adults. Suppose further that the current rule in both *A* and *B* about this matter is *R*, but in society *A* rule *R* is the not only the universally agreed-on best rule, but the only rule in the socially eligible set, and all have settled on it; in contradistinction, in *B* rule *R* is in the eligible set but some perspectives are actively seeking to replace it with R^*, another rule in the socially eligible set. Now consider what occurs if, say, under a wave of religiosity (such as has occurred periodically in America) or immigration, a perspective arises that strongly believes that polygamy is the best form of marriage, and certainly is an acceptable form of marriage. Should this perspective grow, society *A*'s moral constitution will be under stress; it has been premised on the assumption that all acceptable perspectives must agree on what is the best option. It thus must either simply deny that the new perspective is "reasonable" or begin searching for a new consensus on the best marriage arrangement. Its stability now looks illusory—it was based on an assumption that the constitution is a stable response to a certain array of views, but is unable to adjust to the inclusion of a new one. In this sense it is a liberal, but not an open, society (§IV.1.4). In contrast, society B has a number of marriage rules in the socially eligible set, which the perspectives order differently. It thus witnesses debate and contestation; perhaps our polygamous perspective seeks to exploit rule ambiguity, advocating lifelong polygamous cohabitation with claims to common law rights. Society B thus has the resources to adjust to the new perspective, and give it social space to press its case for change. Society B is *robust* as it can maintain its justification by either maintaining the R equilibrium or moving to a new, R^*, equilibrium. The moral constitution is more fragile in A; it has fewer moral resources to adapt to changing perspectives (given that it was based on normalization, this should not be surprising). A society that has significant moral disagreement *within a socially eligible set* has greater resources to maintain a basic charter for its social world that all can live with. Such a society will often exhibit a sort of punctuated equilibrium, converging on an equilibrium for a sustained period and then, after disruption, gravitating to a new one, but always within the set of the type of rules all can live with.

The worry arises, however, whether this robustness actually invites instability. Consider representative persons Alf and Betty in, respectively, societies A and B, again both of which have justified constitutions with rule R. Suppose at some point in society A people are overwhelmingly acting according to this R-including constitution; Alf, a member of A, will act on it so long as his commitment to maintain a practice of accountability (and the coordination benefits it helps secure) plus his expectation of being punished outweigh his temptation to defect in order to better pursue his perspective's ideals. Radically simplifying, then, for Alf to continue acting justly it must be the case that (letting p indicate the relevant probability):

(EQ. 1) p[benefits (practice of responsibility)] $\geq p$[benefits (defection)] $- p$[costs (punishment)]

The probable benefits of continued moral relations based on the R-including constitution only need outweigh the probable benefits of defection discounted by probable punishment. Contrast this to Betty, in society B. She has an additional incentive to defect on the moral constitution—the expected payoff that her defection might drive B to, say, her favored R^*-including constitution. So for her to have reason to conform to the current R-including constitution, it must be the case that:

(EQ. 2) p[benefits (practice of responsibility under R-constitution)] $\geq p$[benefits (defection)] + p[benefits (practice of responsibility having achieved R^*-constitution)] – p[costs (punishment)]

The probable benefits of moving society to what she sees as a better moral constitution can provide her with a moral reason to violate the present moral constitution. And even if probability of [benefits (of getting R^*-constitution)] is very low, she would still have incentive to pursue it when, given rule ambiguity, others would accept both R and R^* as meeting their normative expectations. (Again, rule ambiguity is highly conducive to rule innovation.) In contrast, when it is clear that only action in conformity with R will meet normative expectations, and so Betty can expect to be held accountable and perhaps punished for R^*-based action, her incentive to act on R^* will be much less (as eq. 2 indicates). To be sure, if Betty thinks there are enough like-minded others so that they could actually move to the R^*-constitution and this action will be important in doing so, then she may still act on R^*. Other things equal, Betty in society B will thus have more incentive than a comparable Alf in A to defect on the R-including moral constitution. We face the prospect that the very possibility of change to another eligible constitution, which is required for robustness, will tend to destabilize the current moral constitution, inducing people to defect in order to achieve a moral constitution they consider superior. Here then, is our problem: how do we achieve sufficient stability while also allowing us to exploit the moral resources that promote robustness and moral change?

As equation 2 shows, increasing punishment certainly can induce stability on a specific equilibrium by discouraging those who would seek to move to another moral constitution in the eligible set. Although recent analysis shows that punishment is indispensible in maintaining equilibrium on norms and moral rules (§IV.2.1.2), the problem with punishment is that it can potentially stabilize *any* equilibrium, in or out of the eligible set.[167] And, of course, liberals rightly recoil at the prospect of a social order that can be sustained only by high levels of force.

A moral constitution requires significant *stability* if it is to perform its coordinating task, helping to settle expectations about future interactions while, at the same time, it should possess sufficient *flexibility* to be capable of responding to disruptions by switching to a new equilibrium, and encouraging the search for a better constitution. Now we can imagine ideal members of a moral order that have precisely the correct trade-off rate between valuing stability and inducing change, but, of course, we do not know at any particular time what this trade-off rate is. In environments with a low rate of change, stability is generally appropriate; in times of storm and stress, flexibility is apt to be more valuable. And, in any event, we should no more expect homogeneity on this value than on any other. But that is not such a great worry, for we do not really need individuals to agree on the optimal trade-off rate. Recent studies in cultural evolution, the philosophy of science, organizational theory, and democratic theory converge in showing that diverse populations—those that are divided between more reformist/innovative agents and those that incline toward conservative or conformist values or behavior—often arrive at better collective outcomes than those characterized by a single type.[168]

Consider a society such as B_{DIV}, divided between those who are critical of the existing constitution, searching for ways to improve it, and those who place high value on stability and so are very reluctant to move to a new equilibrium. Contrast this to society B_{CON}, an orderly society whose members all value stability, and society B_{REF}, a society of reformists whose members all place high value on achieving what they see as the best constitution (though, of course, the various re-

---

[167] See Boyd and Richerson, *The Origin and Evolution of Cultures*, chap. 9.
[168] See, for example, ibid., chaps. 1 and 2; Weisberg and Muldoon, "Epistemic Landscapes and the Division of Cognitive Labor."

formists will not concur on what that is). There is strong reason to think that under a range of environmental conditions, B_{DIV} will outperform B_{CON} and B_{REF} in the sense of better maintaining a justified moral constitution over a sustained period. As Page demonstrates, there are two lines of analysis that support this: averaging and decreasing returns to type.[169] (*i*) Homogenous B_{CON} populations will perform very well (*a*) in environments with minimal disruptions and (*b*) assuming that it has initially achieved a justified equilibrium. B_{CON} will perform badly when (*c*) there are severe and regular disruptions that render the current equilibrium difficult to maintain and (*d*) the current equilibrium is not in the socially eligible set. On the other hand, B_{REF} does well under (*c*) and/or (*d*), but worse than B_{CON} under conditions (*a*) and (*b*). In a range of environments homogenous B_{CON} and B_{REF} groups will experience wide variation in their ability to maintain a justified constitution; in contrast the diverse B_{DIV} is almost certain to have less variation in its performance, and it can be shown that systems such as B_{DIV}, with less variation, generally outperform less diverse systems such as B_{CON} and B_{REF}.[170]

(*ii*) A similar result can be shown by appealing to decreasing returns to type.[171] Suppose we start out with B_{CON} and replace n conservative members with reformist members, where n constitutes a small proportion of the society. This new group, $B_{CON}{}^{*}$, will almost certainly outperform B_{CON}; given that there is still a large proportion of conservative members, the small n of conservatives lost will not much reduce the impact of the prostability perspective, but the small n of reformist citizens will make contributions that otherwise would not exist, alerting the other citizens to new possibilities and problems (for example, that the current equilibrium is flawed in ways not previously appreciated). If we think in terms of one's marginal value to achieving a long-term justified moral constitution, the new n reformist members have a higher marginal value than the conservative members they replaced.[172]

[169] Page, *Diversity and Complexity*, chaps. 6 and 7.

[170] This result relies on several theorems, which show the benefits of averaging performance over a wide variety of circumstances. See ibid., chap. 6. Recall how averaging across diverse perspectives increases predictive performance (appendix B).

[171] Page, *Diversity and Complexity*, chap. 7.

[172] Various caveats are necessary here, of course. If reformist and conservative citi-

Both lines of reasoning support the conclusion that, while a diverse society may depart from its current equilibrium, it possesses underlying features that enhance its ability to maintain itself in the face of external and internal changes.

4.4 The Perspectives of Reform and Order

The moral and political constitutions of the Open Society require both stability to maintain an equilibrium, and dynamic exploration of better rules. Jonathan Haidt, drawing on moral psychology rather than diverse system dynamics, has recently come to much the same conclusion: different types of perspectives focus more heavily on one or the other of these tasks and thus complement each other. Haidt's research provides support for the idea that those devoted to a reformist ideology (which he associates with liberals) and conservatives do indeed have different basic moral outlooks, and that these different moral outlooks yield different orientations to alterations in the current moral constitution. Haidt's hypothesis that moral reasoning is grounded in six "foundations" or "dimensions" is given in figure 4-6. Haidt finds that liberal subjects display responses and justifications that more strongly focus on liberty/oppression and care/harm dimensions. We must be careful; this is not to say that they are without "intuitions" based on the other foundations, but that their reactions are more inclined to those two foundations (or dimensions) as are, especially, their justifications. Thus on their view, morality is essentially about treating all as free and equal, avoiding harm, and ensuring that needs are met.[173] In contrast, Haidt argues, those associated with conservative political views have a stronger tendency to rely on all foundations, both in their reactions and justifications.[174]

---

zens tend to come into conflict and so destabilize the constitution, then the benefits of diversity may be swamped. See Page, *Diversity and Complexity*, pp. 194ff. My aim here is not to show that diversity never poses problems for the Open Society, but that diversity of perspectives on justice has critical, and almost always overlooked, benefits.

[173] Haidt, *The Righteous Mind*, chap. 5.

[174] Ibid., p. 161. "Very conservative" respondents rely more on authority and loyalty. In the discussion referred to here, Haidt was relying on an earlier version of this the-

Name	Features
Liberty/oppression	Antibullying; anti–constraining others; antityrant; related to egalitarianism
Fairness/anticheating	Emphasis on playing by the rules, and doing one's part in cooperative schemes; rewards according to desert
Care/harm	Emphasis on not harming others; disapproval of cruelty; sympathetic concern with the needs of others
Loyalty/betrayal	Loyalty to groups in which we participate; sensitivity to those who betray our group
Authority/subversion	Respect for rank and status relations; sensitivity to inappropriate behavior given status
Sanctity/degradation	Attribution of intrinsic value and sacredness to objects and symbols; disapproval of that which disrespects these values; disgust

Figure 4-6. Haidt's moral foundations. Source: Haidt, *The Righteous Mind*, pp. 153–54, 181–85.

The range of foundations on which Haidt's conservatives draw bears out the long-held view that conservatives tend to be guardians of the current moral constitution. Conservative subjects are far more apt to be loyal to current moral rules and respect their authority even to the point of seeing them as sacred (they are not understood as *mere* social rules).[175] And they are ready to expend resources in policing them, ensuring that others do not cheat. As Haidt concludes, their moral outlook supports the importance of protecting our current "moral capital," our practices that ensure a cooperative and peaceful social life. "Moral communities are fragile things, hard to build and easy to destroy.... If you don't value moral capital, then you won't foster values, norms, practices and identities, and technologies that increase it."[176] He continues:

ory, which specified only five foundations; some of the foundations are differently characterized in this earlier version.

[175] Ibid., p. 290.
[176] Ibid., p. 293.

If you are trying to change an organization or society and you do not consider the effects of your changes on moral capital, you're asking for trouble. This, I believe, is *the fundamental blind spot of the left*.... It tends to overreach, change too many things too quickly, and reduce the stock of moral capital inadvertently. Conversely, while conservatives do a better job of preserving moral capital, they often fail to notice certain classes of victims, fail to limit the predation of powerful interests, and fail to see the need to change or update institutions as times change.[177]

Haidt is led to the nineteenth-century idea of the parties of order and of change: "Here's the most basic of all ideological questions: Preserve the present order, or change it? At the French Assembly of 1798, the delegates who favored preservation sat on the right side of the chamber, while those who favored change sat on the left. The terms *right* and *left* have stood for conservatism and liberalism ever since."[178]

Haidt's work in moral psychology leads him to a conclusion that I have reached by another route: that a moral and political order composed of diverse perspectives performs better—*from the moral point of view of the Open Society*—than a homogeneous order of either alone. As Mill stressed,

A party of order or stability, and a party of progress or reform, are both necessary elements of a healthy state of political life; until the one or the other shall have so enlarged its mental grasp as to be a party equally of order and of progress, knowing and distinguishing what is fit to be preserved from what ought to be swept away. Each of these modes of thinking derives its utility from the deficiencies of the other; but it is in a great measure the opposition of the other that keeps each within the limits of reason and sanity.[179]

The philosophical quest for THE DETERMINATE SOLUTION, like ideal theory itself, expresses the desire for the intellectual comfort of convincing oneself that issues have been definitely settled (in one's own

---

[177] Ibid., p. 294. Emphasis in original.
[178] Ibid., p. 277. Emphasis in original.
[179] Mill, *On Liberty*, p. 253.

mind) that are never definitely settled. We do not know what the possibilities are, or the real nature of our proposed solutions. Today's solution is tomorrow's problem. If we all agreed on what is settled our moral constitution would ossify—serving not as the framework of a dynamic open society but as a monument to our past aspirations.

CHAPTER V

Advancing from the Citadel

It is as if I had performed a strategic retreat into an inner citadel—my reason, my soul.... I have withdrawn into myself; there, and there alone, I am secure.

—ISAIAH BERLIN

1 RECOUNTING THE JOURNEY

OUR INQUIRY INTO IDEAL THEORY BEGAN WITH IDENTIFYING UNDER what conditions ideal theory is inherently distinct from a theory of moral improvement. Few doubt that a political philosophy can rank social orders in terms of their justice but, as Sen pointed out, that does not require specification of the ideally just social world. Without claiming to have identified necessary and sufficient conditions for a theory to be sensibly described as "ideal" (a hopeless task), I argued for a sufficient and, I think, enlightening condition: a theory of justice makes ineliminable reference to an ideally just condition if it specifies two distinct dimensions along which judgments of justice are made: how inherently just a social world is (the Social Realizations Condition), and how similar that social world is to the ideally just social world (the Orientation Condition). Here we have an interesting class of theories in which understanding of the ideal is absolutely necessary for our judgments as to whether one social state is more just than another. It may be less inherently just, but closer to the ideal, or more inherently just, but further from the ideal.

Chapter II developed a more rigorous analysis that sought to better understand these conditions and how they relate to each other. Critical to this analysis was the idea of a perspective on ideal justice. A perspective is, as it were, a formally complete specification of an ideal theory. It takes a set of evaluative considerations (e.g., liberty, equality, desert) and evaluates a variety of social worlds—the features of those worlds that are relevant to justice—determining how just that world is. Because the ideal is necessary, a perspective also judges the similarity of the basic features of social worlds to the ideal and how far they are from the ideal. One of the real benefits of thinking more formally about the ideal—developing a model of ideal theory—is that we can appreciate that such ideal theory is a useful and distinctive enterprise only when the problem of securing justice is "moderately rugged." If similarity of features and inherent justice are perfectly correlated, reference to the ideal is unnecessary; if they are perfectly uncorrelated the problem becomes chaotic. These moderately rugged landscapes are characterized by neighborhoods, in which the justice of near social words is correlated but, outside some area, the justice of other social worlds is not correlated with our present world. Critical to my analysis was the Neighborhood Constraint: we know far more about the inherent justice of social worlds within our neighborhood than of far-flung worlds outside of it. I stressed that what is in our neighborhood and what is feasible to institute—in the sense of bringing about what we expect to bring about[1]—are by no means identical notions, but we should expect them to be reasonably well correlated. Assuming that the ideal is not in our current neighborhood, we are liable to mistake what, and where, it is. As we approach an ideal, we have good reason to suspect that it will not be what we expected, and we now can see a better social state.

The very essence of ideal theory is that it confronts us with The Choice. In our neighborhood we have better grasp of the justice of possible social worlds, and so we can locally optimize—seek the best world in our neighborhood. If local optimization always put us on a path to the ideal, the ideal would not be necessary. Sen's constant improvement model would suffice. If the ideal is necessary, sometimes it must tell us that the Mount Everest of justice lies in a different direction than local optimization. And thus The Choice. Do we make our world more like the ideal, and so making it less like the most just social state in our neighborhood? But we do not know the ideal well, as it lies outside our neighborhood. When should we choose modifications

---

[1] As opposed to making random jumps around the space and seeing what happens.

moving toward the ideal and not make our world more similar to a more just world we can know reasonably well?

Ideal theory always confronts The Choice. However, if an ideal theory could expand its knowledge of the landscape of justice, it could come to better know its ideal. It would still have to make The Choice, but at least it would have a more certain ideal target. Chapter III was devoted to exploring ways to do this. As recent research in other fields has shown, a diversity of perspectives can be an amazingly effective way to solve the sort of rugged optimization problem posed by ideal theory. While we identified ways in which diversity can increase knowledge of the ideal, we saw that as diversity increases, and so diverse teams can better explore the entire landscape, the perspective breaks up into competing theories of the ideal. Thus rather than exploring different perspectives *on* an ideal, we end up with competing theories *of* the ideal. These theories can still benefit from each other's searches in important ways, but it will often be well-nigh impossible for them to share their insights. Sometimes one can learn from some aspects of one perspective's search, other times from another, and sometimes perspectives will combine and sometimes fission. The result will be a complex problem of partially overlapping, and shifting, "republican" communities of moral inquiry.

The Open Society, I have argued, provides a framework in which these different perspectives can search, share, debate, and, yes, dismiss each other's insights, while engaging in other cooperative social relations. What constitutes learning and insight is internal to a perspective, but I do believe chapters II and III demonstrate that being cocooned in its own view of the problem condemns a perspective to never really understanding its own ideal and the nature of justice and its optimization landscape. The Open Society, I argued, provides a liberal framework in which different republican communities of inquiry can make up their own minds (dictated by their perspectives) as to whom they will learn from, whose ideas they will borrow and adapt, and whose predictive models they will consider.

The critical question of chapter IV was whether diverse perspectives could endorse a common moral constitution with its attendant practice of moral accountability. As in so many places, Rawls shows us the way forward—we must construct an artificial, public social world that all can share, given our various perspectives on justice. Critical to securing such a public social world is that perspectives abandon the *optimization stance*: only the public world that my perspective on justice judges optimal is acceptable. In the fifteenth and sixteenth centuries, most religious citizens over much of Europe abandoned the optimization stance. They accepted that the social world they constructed with their fellow citizens could not reproduce their sectarian perspective on a Godly world. They learned to do what so many contemporary political philosophers insist—in their work if not in their lives—cannot be done: to hold themselves accountable according to rules of justice they do not deem optimal.

A task of a liberal theory of public reason, I have argued, is to show how a public social world might be constructed that is open to the widest possible range of perspectives on justice. Each perspective on justice has a stake in securing such a social world, for in unexpected ways, diverse perspectives can break through the myopia to which even sophisticated perspectives are subject. Yet, of course, a perspective cannot embrace a public social world that does not adequately express its fundamental commitments. There are limits on the public worlds in which a perspective can participate. I have argued that a highly plausible proposal is that the characteristic institutions of the Open Society are maximally friendly to diversity as such while securing the endorsement of the constituent perspectives. I have followed Berlin and Rawls in acknowledging that the social space of the Open Society has limits. Some perspectives will be convinced that they have nothing to learn from others and take their current perspective on justice as the best that could be attained. The Open Society will have no attractions for them, and so they are apt to take up an uncompromising optimization stance, withdrawing into the illusory certainties of their perspectives of the right, the good, and the holy.

An Open Society, I have argued, must balance the parties of stability and change. Only a relatively stable public social world is truly open to diversity. If the basic framework of social relations is constantly shifting as new perspectives enter and leave our public world, its inhabitants will be deeply uncertain about the consequences of openness. If current members of the public order do not have the firm expectations about the basis of their future relations, they are apt to see the immigration of peoples and ideas as potentially threatening their plans—the social space they have counted on to live their lives. But the Open Society is not static, caught in the current coordination equilibrium, never able to move to better arrangements. There is no point to encouraging discovery if the terms of our lives together are fixed once and for all. The very indeterminacy of justification of our public social world allows the space within it to push and pull for new equilibriums in the eligible set that move us in directions that are acceptable to all, and are seen as an improvement by many. In this way, perspectives' convictions about greater justice can spur new moral constitutions.

2 ADIEU TO THE WELL-ORDERED SOCIETY

This thesis of this book implies a break with contemporary social and political thought, which has been deeply influenced by Rawls's ideal of a well-ordered society: a society that "not only is designed to advance the good of its members but... also is effectively regulated by a public conception of justice. That is, it is a society in which (1) everyone accepts and knows that the others accept the same principles of justice, and (2) the basic social institutions generally satisfy and are generally known to satisfy these principles."[2] Drawing on a normalized, homogenized perspective, in *A Theory of Justice* Rawls's original position yielded a conception that all think is best (since everyone reasons in the exact same way, this is not too surprising). When it is public knowledge that the relevant principles are accepted by all, are satisfied, and known to be satisfied, a well-ordered society obtains. Such a society has the allure of the ideal: our fundamentally divergent views of justice are left behind, and we all can pursue our aims confident that all are devoted to the same principles of justice and we all know our institutions manifest them. And even if, now, mired in our actual societies with deep moral and political disagreements, divided between Red states and Blue states, religiously informed disagreements about justice, and an array of competing ideologies, the ideal of such a society can guide us, and help reconcile us to this conflict-ridden and often manifestly unjust social world.

[2] Rawls, *A Theory of Justice*, p. 4.

I have tried to show that such an ideal is ultimately a mirage, yet one that tyrannizes over our thinking and encourages us to turn our backs on pressing problems of justice in our own neighborhood. It is a mirage because even if we actually had full confidence and complete agreement about the principles of justice, we would disagree about what social states best satisfied them. And even within some perspective, as it approaches the social state in which the basic social institutions generally satisfy these principles, it will discover its estimates of its functioning were wrong, and their realizations are flawed. As we approach what we thought was the end of our journey we find that our destination was not what we envisaged, and yet another ideal arises on the horizon. Yet, to get there we had to make The Choice, forsaking some local improvements to keep our eye on the ideal, the well-ordered society.

The well-ordered society is a dangerous illusion. The very aim that the ideal theorist cherished, to know justice and just social states as well as possible, requires an open, diverse society, in which innumerable perspectives simultaneously cooperate and compete, share and conflict. In this society there will be a crisscrossing network of communities exploring and refining moral ideals and gaining insights into their own ideals by their interactions with others. In order to be successful and robust, the Open Society, I have tried to show, must be based on a moral constitution that provides the basis of a practice of responsibility and accountability among a maximally wide array of perspectives, allowing us to reap the fruits of the cooperation and competition that diversity allows. This is the truth retained from the idea of a well-ordered society: we must indeed have a common public moral framework by which to resolve our disputes and hold each other accountable. But this is a working convergence on a common framework from multiple, deeply different perspectives, which are based on very different ideals of justice, not a normalized perspective on justice.

None of this is to say that life in the Open Society is comforting, or provides a totally satisfying conception of life with others. Indeed, empirical evidence indicates that diverse groups are better at solving problems, yet participants find them less satisfying than homogeneous groups.[3] The Open Society makes an offer that we are tempted to refuse: in it, one will find out more about justice as understood on one's own perspective, but one is not free to simply enact this ideal for the entire society. Hopefully, perspectives can employ this knowledge to improve the moral constitution of the Open Society and seek to convince others that its view of justice is as truly powerful as its adherents find it. But others are apt to be unimpressed with much of the view and are instead devising their own ideals. And they are disappointed that others seem to have so little uptake of *their* insights. While the Open Society frustrates the utopian aspiration, it does far better in responding to palpable problems of justice: the oppression, horrendous deprivations, and cruelties that surround all of us. Here diverse perspectives on justice can converge on local improvements, improving the basic rules of justice and in so doing enhancing our practice of responsibility. If we look back on the incredible moral changes in the past century, we have seen the steady elimination of rules that marginalized perspectives never endorsed, but to which they were subjected by power—and very often the power of a dominant normalized perspective, insisting that it was the sole arbiter of justice. It is remarkable—indeed astounding—that after the train of moral and human disasters of the twentieth century, many of which were based on a deep and sincere conviction by rulers that they had uncovered the one correct perspective on justice and could chart a course to "Paradise Island," so many political philosophers still succumb to the allure of the ideal, and insist that our society should choose to set out for it. The Open Society is not even tempted to make The Choice to pursue the mirage of the ideal rather than to work toward a better public moral constitution, eliminating palpable oppression and seeking ways to improve its rules.

Life in the Open Society is often frustrating. Convinced that we are at the end of history, and finally know once and for all what is just, we are confronted by disagreement, skepticism, and recalcitrance—about truths we see *so clearly*. Most of us do not feel at home in the public

---

[3] Ellison and Mullin, "Diversity, Social Goods Provision, and Performance in the Firm."

social world, which by near unanimity is judged imperfect. Yet, because we are not at the end of history, because like other "knowledge," that of justice is changeable and improvable, the pursuit of justice outside the Open Society is a recipe for dead ends, failures, and even political tyranny. As Popper realized over three-quarters of a century ago, the spell of Platonic perfection and the mirage of the final ideal are powerful influences on the philosophical mind. Yet to pursue such an ideal ultimately is to turn our back on the dynamism and uncertainty of collective inquiry and so the moral improvements for which we all strive.

3 The Citadel of the Ideal

Finally, many political philosophers will insist that nothing I have said in this work shows that ideals of justice can possibly be improved by life in the Open Society. What I have called the "Social Realizations Condition," they will say, is only about social "rules of regulation."[4] To be sure, these philosophers will respond, we might learn better ways to *institute* JUSTICE, but we could never learn more about JUSTICE. The truths of JUSTICE are in our hearts, our deepest "intuitions," and no mere facts about their realizations could ever cause us to doubt them.[5] Should all our attempts to live according to these principles lead to disaster, such experience would never lead us to revise our convictions about JUSTICE. Humans may simply not be up to JUSTICE.

This thought apparently deeply worried Rawls. He closes his second preface to *Political Liberalism* with the anguished doubt: "The wars of this century with their extreme violence and increasing destructiveness, culminating in the manic evil of the Holocaust, raise in an acute way the question whether political relations must be governed by power and coercion alone. If a reasonably just society that subordinates power to its aims is not possible and people are largely amoral, if not incurably cynical and self-centered, one might ask with

---

[4] See Cohen, *Rescuing Justice and Equality*, esp. pp. 308, 323ff.

[5] Many political philosophers appear to adopt Mrs. Bunter's view of facts. "My old mother always used to say, my lord, that facts are like cows. If you stare them in the face hard enough, they generally run away." Sayers, *Clouds of Witness*.

Kant whether it is worthwhile for human beings to live on the earth."[6] Paul Weithman thus describes Rawls's project as one of a "naturalistic theodicy"[7] showing that we are, after all, fit for JUSTICE. There is certainly something akin to the religious about a conception of justice that may be outside the plausible horizons of humanity. As does the theologian, many philosophers see justice as somehow existing apart from humanity, coming down to judge us with its stern standards that, like wayward children, we simply might be too naughty or weak to follow. As Frans de Waal observes, "According to most philosophers, we reason ourselves to moral truths. Even if they don't invoke God, they're still proposing a top-down process in which we formulate the principles and then impose them on human conduct."[8] The fundamental convictions at the root of much religion and moral and political philosophy are that "humans don't know how to behave and that someone must tell them."[9]

This can be a most comforting view to the philosopher. Nothing the children do could ever lead the philosopher to doubt her claims about these standards. That would be as absurd as sin showing that God does not exist, or that His commandments were erroneous. Having retreated to the certainty of her intuitions, she observes humanity and judges whether it is up to her findings. Thus, as perhaps did Plato, the philosopher paints an ideal that she would never want humans to try to implement, because they are not up to the ideal. Indeed, as we have seen, some go so far as to embrace the view that their inquiries into the ideal may well be useless to humans (§I.1.4).

The alternative view to us not being up to justice is that justice is up to us. Justice is the way that our species has found to live well together, to prosper, and to discover. When one thinks one has hit upon a standard of justice, and finds again and again that attempts to construct "rules of regulation" to implement it have repeatedly led to disaster, the proper response is not to shake one's head sadly that the children are not yet up to JUSTICE. Rather, the embarrassing fact for

[6] Rawls, *Political Liberalism*, p. lx. Note the lack of recognition of the role that ideals of justice played in the human disasters of the twentieth century.

[7] Weithman, *Why Political Liberalism?*, pp. 8ff.

[8] de Waal, *The Bonobo and the Atheist*, p. 17.

[9] Ibid., p. 23.

the philosopher is he is the one who has erred. He got justice wrong. Only a philosopher or a theologian would think it obvious that, if their ideals lead to ruin, the flaw is not theirs, but in the creatures for whom the ideals were set.

Of course we all have our convictions and beliefs, and some of these may be based on faith or sentiment that simply cannot be overturned by evidence. But how large groups of humans should live together is not one of these matters. About that we can learn from others, their experiences, their data, their different ways of seeing what to us looks to us so clear. Our ideals of justice are ideals about how our rather unusual species can live in ways that are good or beneficial to all, and about that we have been learning for tens of thousands, nay hundreds of thousands, of years. Political philosophers will have far more to contribute if they abandon their citadels of certain principles and ideals, and acknowledge that they are participants in a process of collective discovery. Perhaps not surprisingly, it was Hayek—an economist, not a philosopher—who truly, deeply appreciated this.

> If we are to advance, we must leave room for a continuous revision of our present conceptions and ideals which will be necessitated by further experience. We are as little able to conceive what civilization will be, or can be, five hundred or even fifty years hence as our medieval forefathers or even our grandparents were able to foresee our manner of life today.[10]

---

[10] Hayek, *The Constitution of Liberty*, pp. 23–24.

Appendix A

On Measuring Similarity

(i) Building Up from Intuitive Pairwise Judgments

SIMILARITY COMPARISONS OF POSSIBLE SOCIAL WORLDS ARE FUNDA-mental to satisfying the Orientation Condition. As noted in the text, I employ a standard idea of similarity judgments of the form of a pairwise comparison of pairs: "world a is more similar to world b than world a is to world c," denoted as $(a{\sim}b){>}(a{\sim}c)$. To yield a complete transitive ordering of the domain $\{X\}$ additional axioms are required:

(1) Symmetry: $[(a{\sim}b){>}(a{\sim}c)]{\rightarrow}[(b{\sim}a){>}(c{\sim}a)]$;

(2) Asymmetry: $[(a{\sim}b){>}(a{\sim}c)]{\rightarrow} \neg[(a{\sim}c){>}(a{\sim}b)]$;

(3) Reflexivity: $\forall i,j \in \{X\}$, where $i \neq j$: $[(i{\sim}i){>}(i{\sim}j)]$;

(4) Transitivity: $[(a{\sim}b){>}(a{\sim}c)]$ & $[(b{\sim}c){>}(b{\sim}d)]{\rightarrow}[(a{\sim}c){>}(a{\sim}d)]$.

To see how a perspective could generate a similarity ordering from pairwise comparison of pairs, start with three social worlds, a, b, and c. From this set we can begin by asking: what ordered triplets of the set $\{a, b, c\}$ are consistent with the intuitive judgment (a datum) that $(a{\sim}b){>}(a{\sim}c)$? On reflection we can see that $(a{\sim}b){>}(a{\sim}c)$ is consistent with $\{a, b, c\}$, $\{c, b, a\}$, $\{c, a, b\}$, OR $\{b, a, c\}$. We can thus exclude $\{b, c, a\}$ and $\{a, c, b\}$, as those orderings are not consistent with our assumed similarity judgment.

Note that in an important sense $\{a, b, c\}$ is equivalent to $\{c, b, a\}$ insofar as, at least initially, we do not care whether our similarity ordering runs from right to left or from left to right. As long as we stick with a direction once one is imposed there is no worry about which way the dimension runs. (In an analogous way $\{c, a, b\}$ is equivalent in this sense to $\{b, a, c\}$.) Suppose, then, that we choose the directionality imposed by $\{a, b, c\}$. We can thus set aside the $\{c, b, a\}$ ordering and turn our attention to the second equivalent pair, $\{c, a, b\}$

and $\{b, a, c\}$, that is consistent with our initial intuitive judgment. Here we can choose $\{c, a, b\}$, dropping the opposite "direction" of $\{b, a, c\}$, and, having done this, we will have imposed a direction on our dimension, leaving us with the judgment that $(a\mathord{\sim}b)\mathord{>}(a\mathord{\sim}c)$ is consistent with $\{a, b, c\}$ OR $\{c, a, b\}$.

Now suppose a second intuitive similarity judgment is made by a perspective: $(c\mathord{\sim}b)\mathord{>}(c\mathord{\sim}a)$. This is not consistent with $\{c, a, b\}$. (Nor would it be consistent with $\{b, a, c\}$, the "other direction" of the $\{c, a, b\}$ ordering.) So we are left with $\{a, b, c\}$. Notice that we have taken multiple similarity judgments and derived an ordered triplet that arrays the options along a dimension. We thus have generated "*in-betweenness*" (b is in between a and c) from "more similar than" relations. We can then build out from the ordered triplet to yield an entire dimension in terms of similarity (or, in terms of our model, an ordered set of all social worlds in $\{X\}$). Note that this is more enriched metric information than a simple ordinal ranking. If we have $\{a, b, c\}$ we can find out whether b is more similar to a or c, giving us more than in-betweenness, as we also get "in between but closer to."

That we tend to array domains along a single dimension is well documented in empirical research. Subjects from around the world gravitate to single-dimensional classification systems when they are forced to think formally about classifications. When asked to sort elements in a domain $\{X\}$, participants repeatedly select some single common dimension and sort according to it, avoiding the problem of aggregating different dimensions of similarity.[1] Indeed, studies indicate that people have difficulty learning categories that depend on even two dimensions of similarity (e.g., the length and the orientation of a line).[2] However, in their informal classifications people seem to employ family resemblances, which allow them to sort on multiple dimensions. Moreover, Philip Tetlock's studies indicate that given opti-

[1] The classic study is Medin, Wattenmaker, and Hampson, "Family Resemblance, Conceptual Cohesiveness, and Category Construction." See also Ahn and Medin, "A Two-Stage Model of Category Construction"; Canini et al., "Revealing Human Inductive Biases for Category Learning by Simulating Cultural Transmission." This does not seem to be simply a feature of Western reasoners; for a cross-cultural study, see Norenzayan et al., "Cultural Preferences for Formal versus Intuitive Reasoning."

[2] Ashby and Maddox, "Human Category Learning"; Ashby, Queller, and Berretty, "On the Dominance of Unidimensional Rules in Unsupervised Categorization."

mal conditions virtually everyone can make decisions commensurating different dimensions of evaluation, which lends support to our intuitive procedure.[3]

(II) KEYNES'S WORRY AND MULTIDIMENSIONAL WEIGHTING SYSTEMS

John Maynard Keynes argues that it is implausible to expect a complete ordering by aggregating individual pairwise similarity judgments, along the lines of the procedure in (I). As do I, Keynes presents a pairwise comparisons of pairs analysis of similarity:

> When we say of three objects A, B, and C that B is more like A than C is, we mean, not that there is any respect in which B is in itself quantitatively greater than C, but that, if the three objects are placed in an order of similarity, B is nearer to A than C is. There are also, as in the case of probability, different orders of similarity. For instance, a book bound in blue morocco $[f_1, h_1]$ is more like a book bound in red morocco $[f_2, h_1]$ than if it were bound in blue calf $[f_1, h_2]$ and a book bound in red calf $[f_2, h_2]$ is more like the book in red morocco $[f_2, h_1]$ than if it were in blue calf $[f_1, h_2]$.[4]

It is easy to misread Keynes here because of the rather confusing "than if it were bound" locution, as the reference to "it" is not pellucid. However, we should read Keynes as saying that blue morocco $[f_1, h_1]$ is more similar to red morocco $[f_2, h_1]$ than "it" (the blue morocco book $[f_1, h_1]$) would be if it were a blue calf $[f_1, h_2]$ book; thus the claim is that a book bound in red morocco is more similar to one bound in blue morocco than a red morocco book is to a blue calf book. So $[(f_2, h_1)\sim(f_1, h_1)] > [(f_2, h_1)\sim(f_1, h_2)]$. And that seems quite right. Keynes also holds that it makes perfect sense to say that "a book bound in red calf $[f_2, h_2]$ is more like the book in red morocco $[f_2, h_1]$ than if it [the red calf book] were in blue calf $[f_1, h_2]$," so $[(f_2, h_1)\sim(f_2, h_2)] > [(f_2, h_1)\sim(f_1, h_2)]$.

---

[3] Tetlock, "Coping with Trade-Offs: Psychological Constraints and Political Implications." See Fred D'Agostino's discussion in *Incommensurability and Commensuration*, pp. 68ff.

[4] Keynes, *A Treatise on Probability*, p. 36, where f_1 = blue; f_2 = red; h_1 = morocco; h_2 = calf.

However, Keynes goes on to argue that these comparisons might not be completable. Continuing the above example, he remarks that "there may be no comparison between the degree of similarity which exists between books bound in red morocco $[f_2, h_1]$, and blue morocco $[f_1, h_1]$, and that which exists between books bound in red morocco $[f_2, h_1]$ and red calf $[f_2, h_2]$."[5] To say whether (f_2, h_1) is more similar to (f_1, h_1), or to (f_2, h_2), would require judging whether morocco (h_1) is more similar to calf (h_2) than blue (f_1) is to red (f_2). Keynes's claim here is that red-blue and morocco-calf constitute "*different* orders of similarity."[6] To make a similarity judgment over these pairs would require comparing the similarity of two colors to the similarity of two leathers, but these involve similarities of different types.

In this example, the comparison of which he is skeptical does not seem overly perplexing—if we include the idea of a perspective, which inherently categorizes and stresses some features of the world over others. Suppose I am a leather fancier when it comes to bindings; what really is salient to me is leather. If so, I will have no difficulty at all saying that a book in red morocco is more similar to a book in blue morocco than it is to a book in red calf. On my perspective, leather is the salient similarity, and the organization of my books in my library will show this.

However, a more fundamental worry remains. Suppose that the leathers become more and more dissimilar so that one book is bound in rat (h_3). So now I have to ask is the red morocco book more similar to the blue rat book or to the red calf book? At some point as we compare more and more dissimilar leathers it could seem that I will eventually think similar color determines overall similarity, so that I might well conclude that the red morocco book is more similar to the red calf book than it is to the blue rat book. Thus, in arriving at overall similarity I am using the leather order of similarity until some point where I jump to the color order of similarity, because I am saying that at this point that the difference in leather is so great that the similarity in color is determinative of the overall similarity judgment. It is this judgment about which Keynes is skeptical.[7]

---

[5] Ibid.
[6] Ibid. Emphasis in original.
[7] As is Morreau, "It Simply Does Not Add Up," esp. pp. 480–81.

I think, in turn, we should be skeptical of this skepticism. For one thing, similarity of "leather" is itself a multidimensional criterion: suppleness, sheen, durability are all qualities of leather; to make similarity judgments of the "order of similarity" of leather implies that one *has* made similarity judgments along several dimensions and managed to commensurate them, so that one can say "the difference in suppleness is greater than the difference in sheen." So to really stay true to the incommensurability of all different orders of similarity claim, we would have to resort to truly unidimensional orders, perhaps only atomic properties, with no comparisons except along one and only one dimension. That we do something is good evidence that it can be done.

However if we remain worried by Keynes's argument, and so if we still need to assuage it to ensure that those comparisons are completable, we can go beyond the simple pairwise comparison procedure in (1). Following the lead of Martin Weitzman,[8] we can suppose that the features of members of a domain (social worlds, buildings, ecosystems) can be measured on multiple dimensions. For example, classifications of similarity in architecture might focus on classification systems involving "the period of the building, its style, distinguishing features, location, and so forth."[9] For each of these classifications, a specific building can be classified into a number of subcategories (recognized periods, styles, sizes, etc.). One procedure would be to determine similarity in terms of shared characteristics; those that share many subcategory classifications are very similar, those that have few common subclassifications less similar. Of course a perspective can get more fine grained with richer similarity/diversity measures.[10] More sophisticated perspectives develop richer conceptions of the various dimensions by which objects are sorted—say not only counting shared features (as in our architectural example) but generating cardinal measures of the extent to which two objects, a and b, share a given feature f. Whereas in our original architectural case we may say that buildings a and b are similar because they share, say, five out of six classifications (same style, same period, etc.), we could develop a richer scalar/cardinal system where buildings rate, say, 0–100 on whether they are

---

[8] Weitzman, "On Diversity." See also Page, *Diversity and Complexity*, pp. 58ff.
[9] Weitzman, "On Diversity," pp. 365ff.
[10] For details on how this can be done, see ibid.

Dissimilarity of pairs	f	g	h
a-b	5	15	4
b-c	7	5	2
a-c	12	10	6
Weights	.6	.3	.1

Figure A-1. A similarity weighting system

classical, whether they have Gothic influences, and so on, such that 100 represents the maximal possible difference within a subcategory while 1 represents the minimum.[11]

If a given perspective develops such a rich conception of the relevant dimensions, there is no special problem in the perspective aggregating these subscores into an overall score, *given the way it views the relative importance of these dimensions.* We must remember that the understanding of similarity and its underlying attributes is specific to a particular perspective on justice. There is no claim that the underlying taxonomy or classification system for generating a complete ordering of the domain {X} is shared by all plausible perspectives or is uncontroversial. To better see how a perspective might commensurate different dimensions consider a very simple aggregation system. Suppose that a, b, and c are three social worlds, and suppose that perspective Σ identifies three types of features, f, g, and h, that are relevant to justice and that Σ has diversity measures for each feature along the lines we have been discussing. Thus we might have judgments as in figure A-1.

So, assuming that we simply sum up the weights of differences, we would have the similarity of $(a, b) = .6(5) + .3(15) + .1(4) = 3.85$; $(b, c) = .6(7) + .3(5) + .1(2) = 4.85$; $(a, c) + .6(12) + .3(10) + .1(6) = 10.8$, so $[(a \sim b) > (a \sim c)]$, $[(b \sim a) > (b \sim c)]$. This, of course, is just a toy example; there is no need for such a simple additive weighting system, nor need we suppose such precise measures. (Note that since the overall result is similarity judgments in the form of pairwise comparison of overlapping pairs, the overly precise scoring system is not reproduced in the

---

[11] Weitzman shows how such richer information can be developed from the basic idea of pairwise similarity judgments. Ibid.

final judgments.) In any event, the aim is simply to show how such comparisons might be accomplished.

Michael Morreau has presented an Arrow-inspired impossibility proof, showing that it is impossible to arrive at these sort of aggregative, overall similarity judgments by aggregating various dimensions of similarity and meet versions of the standard Arrovian conditions.[12] It is essential to realize that such Arrow-inspired impossibility proofs depend on restricting the various "dimensional" information to pairwise ordinal information. Perhaps the most fundamental insight of axiomatic social choice theory is that the possibility of producing a complete, transitive, overall ordering of a domain of options (such as the overall similarity of social worlds) fundamentally depends on the richness of dimensional information that can be drawn on in generating the ordering of that domain.[13] In standard cases involving social choice/welfare functionals, the "dimensional" information is each individual's cardinal rankings of the options (each individual's cardinal ranking is "a dimension") from which a social, overall ordering can be generated. In our case of similarity judgments, the dimensional information is the different scalar measures of each dimension of similarity (e.g., features of social worlds), and then a perspective employs this to generate an overall similarity ordering of the domain $\{X\}$. As Sen has demonstrated, we can certainly generate complete, transitive orderings of a set of options by aggregating multiple dimensions of evaluation when the dimensional information is rich (say, cardinal) rather than mere ordering information, and we can at least approximately commensurate this richer dimensional information.[14] Arrow-like results, showing deep problems with aggregating information over a number of dimensions, are powerful, but much of their power derives from the severe limitations on the sorts of information they allow: information is restricted to purely pairwise, ordinal judgments on all

---

[12] Morreau, "It Simply Does Not Add Up," pp. 483ff.

[13] It must be stressed that though this second procedure employs cardinal/scalar information concerning the various dimensions of similarity, with regard to the SO element of the model, we are still seeking only to derive an ordering of the similarity of social worlds. This is formally similar to Sen's "Social Welfare Functionals," which generate an overall *ordering* from richer, *more-than-ordering*, dimensional information. "On Weights and Measures."

[14] On this critical point, see ibid.

dimensions, thus only noncomparative ordinal information can be used to generate overall similarity judgments. While in some contexts this severe information restriction supposed by Arrow-type theorems is reasonable, in the case of a single perspective on justice seeking to understand the structure of domain {X} of possible social worlds, it is extraordinarily constraining. A perspective seeks to organize and evaluate a set of possible social worlds: we have no reason to posit severe restrictions on the sorts of information such that, when sorting worlds on some feature (say, income distribution or freedom), it can use only pairwise ranking judgments rather than richer, scaling information.

In this regard it is worth noting that the basic similarity orderings using the procedure in (1) above, yield superordinal information: if we have a triplet {a, b, c} we can find out not only whether b is "in-between" a and c (basic ordinal information) but also whether b is closer to ("more similar to") a than to c; this superordinal information would be ignored in translating judgments of "more similar to" into simple pure ordinal judgments for an Arrow-type theorem. An Arrow-inspired proof must reduce this information to strictly ordinal, which measures only "in-betweeness. This highlights the way in which Arrow-like theorems are restrictive in the information they allow.

(III) N-Dimensional Space

Instead of an ordering approach, we could have developed a more complex multidimensional model, in which a perspective Σ would locate worlds a, b, and c in an N-dimensional similarity space, and then employ an N-dimensional metric, which would measure the N-dimensional distance between a and b and a and c to yield an overall conclusion whether a is closer to b or to c. The more formally minded may find this a more satisfying analysis, though much more would depend on the distance metric (DM) than in the simple ordering model, where the similarity ordering (SO) is much more important, as I think it should be. In a more complex model the topology of the N-dimensional space would be a critical element of a perspective: distance would be critical, and that could be measured differently. For

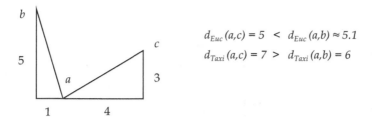

Figure A-2. Comparison of Euclidean and taxi-cab metrics

example, arguably the two most familiar metrics are the Euclidean metric and the taxi-cab metric (sometimes referred to as the Manhattan norm or box metric).[15] The Euclidean metric defines distance according to the familiar formula for the shortest linear distance between two points:

$$d_{Euc}(x, y) = \sqrt{\sum_{i=1}^{n}(x_i - y_i)^2}$$

(which in two dimensions simplifies to the formula for the length of the hypotenuse of a right triangle). The taxi-cab metric, on the other hand, defines distance in two-dimensional space according to the shortest distance between two points from the perspective of taxi navigating a rectangular street grid (hence the name), which in higher dimensional space can be represented as:

$$d_{Taxi}(x, y) = \sum_{i=1}^{n}|x_i|.$$

As figure A-2 indicates the Euclidean and taxi-cab metrics will sometimes disagree about which of two points is closer to a third.

N-dimensional similarity space thus raises a number of interesting complexities and possibilities for increased diversity. However, I believe that the simple basic ordering model is sufficient to make my general points; a more complex topology of similarity would not make a great deal of difference to the core philosophical points, and would be much more complex.

[15] I am drawing here on Gaus and Hankins, "Searching for the Ideal."

Appendix B

On Predictive Diversity

THE KEY TO THE DIVERSITY PREDICTION THEOREM IS TO DETERMINE (*i*) the average error of individual predictive models and (*ii*) the collective error of the models taken together, and see how (*i*) compares with (*ii*).[1] First, a measure of (*i*), average individual error, is required. Taking a cue from Francis Galton's famous weight-judging competition (and somewhat simplifying the numbers), suppose we are trying to guess (*A*) the weight of an ox which actually weighs 1,000 pounds[2] (let us simply use thousands of pounds, so call this "1K"), and then (*B*) the weight of a bull, which actually weighs 2,000 pounds (2K). Suppose an individual employs his or her predictive model for both competitions; assume it predicts the same weight for the ox and for the bull, 1,500 pounds (1.5K). We cannot compute its average error by simply taking each error and averaging. That would give us an error of .5 + (−.5) = 0. But obviously the model is manifestly error prone. We avoid this by

---

[1] I am following the presentations of Page, *The Difference*, pp. 205–12, and Wagner, Zhao, Schneider, and Chen, "The Wisdom of Reluctant Crowds."

[2] "A little more than a year ago, I happened to be at Plymouth, and was interested in a Cattle exhibition, where a visitor could purchase a stamped and numbered ticket for sixpence, which qualified him to become a candidate in a weight-judging competition. An ox was selected, and each of about eight hundred candidates wrote his name and address on his ticket, together with his estimate of what the beast would weigh when killed and "dressed" by the butcher. The most successful of them gained prizes. The result of these estimates was analogous, under reservation, to the votes given by a democracy, and it seemed likely to be instructive to learn how votes were distributed on this occasion, and the value of the result. So I procured a loan of the cards after the ceremony was past, and worked them out.... It appeared that in this instance the *vox populi* was correct to within 1 per cent, of the real value; it was 1207 pounds instead of 1198 pounds, and the individual estimates were distributed in such a way that it was an equal chance whether one of them selected at random fell within or without the limits of −3.7 per cent, or +2.4 per cent, of the middlemost value of the whole." Francis Galton, *Memories of My Life*, pp. 280–81.

	Ox (A) (correct = 1)	Bull (B) (correct = 2)	Error $(A-1)^2 + (B-2)^2$
α	.5	1	1.25
β	2	3	2
γ	1.75	2.75	1.13
collective prediction	1.42	2.25	.24

Figure B-1. An example of predictive diversity

first squaring the errors, $[(.5^2) + (-.5^2)] = .25 + .25 = .5$, giving us the average error of this model. Figure B-1 gives the individual errors for three predictive models, α, β, and γ, applied to our two weight-judging contests.

The average individual error here is $(1.25+2+1.13)/3$, or 1.46. More generally, average individual

$$\text{error} = \frac{1}{n}\sum_{i=1}^{n}(x_i - x_{correct})^2.$$

The collective prediction (*cp*) is the average of the individual predictions; the models collectively predict that the ox weighs 1.42K and the bull 2.25K. We thus can now compute (*ii*), their collective error: $(1.42-1)^2 + (2.25-2)^2 = (.42)^2 + (.25)^2 = .18 + .06 = .24$. The collective error (.24) is less than the average individual error (1.46).

The reason for this is the *predictive diversity* of the group, which is defined as

$$\frac{1}{n}\sum_{i=1}^{n}(x_i - x_{cp})^2,$$

where x_i is the individual's prediction and x_{cp} is the collective prediction. To calculate the predictive diversity for our example:

α's squared distance from *cp*: $(.5-1.42)^2 + (1-2.25)^2 = 2.4$

β's squared distance from *cp*: $(2-1.42)^2 + (3-2.25)^2 = .9$

γ's squared distance from *cp*: $(1.75-1.42)^2 + (2.75-2.25)^2 = .36$

This yields a prediction diversity (average of the squared distances) of $2.4 + .9 + .36 / 3$, or 1.22.

We thus arrive at Page's *Diversity Prediction Theorem* that

Collective Error = Average Individual – Predictive Diversity.

In our example the collective error of .24 equals the average individual error of 1.46 minus predictive diversity of 1.22. Although in our example the collective prediction is better than any individual prediction, that does not generally hold: an excellent individual predictor can beat the collective prediction. But the collective prediction will always beat the average of individual predictions. This is an important result: even if our predictive models are not very good, a diverse perspective or society can draw on diverse predictive models (understood as predictive diversity as defined above), and so significantly enhance its confidence in its estimates of the justice of alternative social worlds.

An especially interesting mechanism of collective intelligence is information markets. Perhaps the best known is the Iowa Election Markets, which is essentially a market for future political events. As I write (August 23, 2014) there is a market for predicting the 2014 congressional elections; there are basically four possibilities in the overall congressional prediction market: (1) Democrats control both the House and Senate; (2) Democrats control the House and the Republicans the Senate; (3) Republicans control the House and the Democrats the Senate; (4) the Republicans control both. For each "share" one buys, one gets $1 if correct, and nothing if one is not. At this moment the price for option 4 is roughly 64¢; if one buys an option at 64¢, and the Republicans control both houses on November 4, 2014 (as they did), one receives $1. Option (3) is selling at 25¢, and option (1) at 3/10 of a cent. An important feature of such markets is that predictors' bets give information about the accuracy of their prediction—by putting their money where their predictions are, those predictors who have high confidence in their predictions have inordinate influence. If high confidence is correlated with possessing better models, information markets thus not only draw on predictive diversity but give extra influence to the best models. Moreover, not only does the market have a current price, but traders can issue bids and asks; it turns out that the traders who do this, rather than just take the current price, are those with most information, and have the greatest impact on the market.[3]

[3] Sunstein, *Infotopia*, chap. 4.

Works Cited

Ahn, W. K., and D. L. Medin. "A Two-Stage Model of Category Construction." *Cognitive Science*, vol. 16 (1992): 81–121.

Aligica, Paul Dragos. *Institutional Diversity and Political Economy: The Ostroms and Beyond.* Oxford: Oxford University Press, 2014.

Aligica, Paul Dragos, and Peter J. Boettke. *Challenging Institutional Development: The Bloomington School.* London: Routledge, 2009.

Arneson, Richard. "Rejecting *The Order of Public Reason.*" *Philosophical Studies*, vol. 170 (September 2014): 537–44.

Ashby, F. G., and W. T. Maddox. "Human Category Learning." *Annual Review of Psychology*, vol. 56 (2005): 149–78.

Ashby, S. Queller, and P. M. Berretty. "On The Dominance of Unidimensional Rules in Unsupervised Categorization." *Perception and Psychophysics*, vol. 61 (1999): 1178–99.

Auyang, Sunny Y. *Foundations of Complex-Systems Theories in Economics, Evolutionary Biology and Statistical Physics.* Cambridge: Cambridge University Press, 1998.

Bacon, Francis. *New Atlantis*, edited by Alfred B. Gough. Oxford: Clarendon Press, 1915 [1627].

Baier, Kurt. "Moral Obligation." *American Philosophical Quarterly*, vol. 3 (July 1966): 210–26.

Barry, Brian. "John Rawls and the Search for Stability." *Ethics*, vol. 105 (July 1995): 874–915.

Barry, Christian, and Laura Valentini. "Egalitarian Challenges to Global Egalitarianism: A Critique." *Review of International Studies*, vol. 35 (2009): 485–512.

Bellamy, Edward. *Looking Backward.* New York: Dover, 1996 [1880].

Benn, Stanley. *A Theory of Freedom.* Cambridge: Cambridge University Press, 1988.

Berlin, Isaiah. *The Roots of Romanticism.* Princeton, NJ: Princeton University Press, 1997.

Berneri, Marie Louise. *Journey through Utopia.* London: Routledge and Kegan Paul, 1950.

Bicchieri, Cristina. *The Grammar of Society: The Nature and Dynamics of Norms.* Cambridge: Cambridge University Press, 2006.

———. *Norms in the Wild: How to Diagnose, Measure and Change Social Norms.* New York: Oxford University Press, 2016.

Bicchieri, Cristina, and Alex Chavez. "Behaving as Expected: Public Information and Fairness Norms." *Journal of Behavioral Decision Making*, vol. 23 (2010): 161–78.

———. "Norm Manipulation, Norm Evasion: Experimental Evidence." *Economics and Philosophy*, vol. 29 (special issue 2, July 2013): 175–98.

Bicchieri, Cristina, and Hugo Mercier. "Norms and Beliefs: How Change Occurs." In *The Complexity of Social Norms*, edited by Maria Xenitidou and Bruce Edmonds. New York: Springer, 2014: 37–54.

Bicchieri, Cristina, and Hugo Mercier. "Self-Serving Biases and Public Justifications in Trust Games." *Synthese*, vol. 190 (2013): 909–22.

Binmore, Ken. *Natural Justice*. Oxford: Oxford University Press, 2005.

Bowles, Samuel, and Herbert Gintis. *A Cooperative Species: Human Reciprocity and Its Evolution*. Princeton, NJ: Princeton University Press, 2011.

Boyd, Robert, and Peter J. Richerson. *The Origin and Evolution of Cultures*. Oxford: Oxford University Press, 2005.

Brennan, Geoffrey. "Feasibility in Optimizing Ethics," *Social Philosophy and Policy*, vol. 30 (January 2013): 314–29.

Brennan, Geoffrey, Lina Eriksson, Robert E. Goodin, and Nicholas Southwood. *Explaining Norms*. Oxford: Oxford University Press, 2013.

Brennan, Geoffrey, and Philip Pettit. "The Feasibility Issue." In *The Oxford Handbook of Contemporary Philosophy*. Oxford: Oxford University Press, 2005: 258–79.

Bringhurst, Piper L., and Gerald Gaus. "Positive Freedom and the General Will." In *The Oxford Handbook of Freedom*, edited by David Schmidtz. Oxford: Oxford University Press, forthcoming.

Broome, John. *Ethics Out of Economics*. Cambridge: Cambridge University Press, 1999.

Buchanan, James M., and Gordon Tullock. *The Calculus of Consent: Logical Foundations of Constitutional Democracy*. Ann Arbor: University of Michigan Press, 1962.

Buck-Morss, Susan. *Dreamworld and Catastrophe: The Passing of Mass Utopia in East and West*. Cambridge, MA: MIT Press, 2000.

Canini, K. R., T. L. Griffiths, W. Vanpaemel, and M. L. Kalish. "Revealing Human Inductive Biases for Category Learning by Simulating Cultural Transmission." *Psychonomic Bulletin and Review*, vol. 21 (2014): 785–93.

Carey, Brian. "Towards a 'Non-ideal' Non-ideal Theory." *Journal of Applied Philosophy*, vol. 32 (May 2015): 148–62.

Castelli, Ilaria, Davide Massaro, Cristina Bicchieri, Alex Chavez, and Antonella Marchetti. "Fairness Norms and Theory of Mind in an Ultimatum Game: Judgments, Offers, and Decisions in School-Aged Children." *Plos One*, vol. 9, no. 8 (August 2014). www.plosone.org.

Chapman, John W. "Justice, Freedom and Property." In *Nomos XXII: Property*, edited by J. Roland Pennock and John W. Chapman. New York: New York University Press, 1980: 289–324.

Chwe, Michael Suk-Young. *Rational Ritual: Culture, Coordination and Common Knowledge*. Princeton, NJ: Princeton University Press, 2001.

Cialdini, Robert B., Carl A. Kallgren, and Raymond B. Reno. "A Focus Theory of Normative Conduct: A Theoretical Refinement and Reevaluation of the Role of Norms in Human Behavior." *Advances in Experimental Social Psychology*, vol. 24 (1990): 201–34.

Cohen, G. A. *Rescuing Justice and Equality*. Cambridge, MA: Harvard University Press, 2008.

———. *Why Not Socialism?* Princeton, NJ: Princeton University Press, 2009.

Cummins, Denise Dellarosa. "Evidence for the Innateness of Deontic Reasoning." *Mind and Language*, vol. 11 (June 1996): 160–90.

———. "Evidence of Deontic Reasoning in 3- and 4-Year-Olds." *Memory and Cognition*, vol. 24 (1996): 823–29.

D'Agostino, Fred. "From the Organization to the Division of Cognitive Labor." *Politics, Philosophy and Economics*, vol. 8 (2009): 101–29.

———. *Incommensurability and Commensuration: The Common Denominator*. Burlington, VT: Ashgate, 2003.

———. *Naturalizing Epistemology: Thomas Kuhn and the Essential Tension*. London: Palgrave, 2010.

———. "The Orders of Public Reason." *Analytic Philosophy*, vol. 54 (March 2013): 129–55.

de Waal, Frans. *The Bonobo and the Atheist: In Search for Humanism among the Primates*. New York: W. W, Norton, 2013.

Dewey, John. *Individualism, Old and New*. London: George Allen and Unwin, 1931.

Dworkin, Ronald. "Liberalism." In *Public and Private Morality*, edited by Stuart Hampshire. Cambridge: Cambridge University Press, 1978: 113–43.

Economic Freedom in the World 2013 Annual Report. Fraser Institute. www.fraserinstitute.org.

Ellison, Sara Fisher, and Wallace P. Mullin. "Diversity, Social Goods Provision, and Performance in the Firm." *Journal of Economics and Management Strategy*, vol. 23 (Summer 2014): 465–81.

Elster, Jon, *Logic and Society: Contradictions and Possible Worlds*. New York: John Wiley and Sons. 1978.

Engels, Friedrich. "Socialism: Utopian and Scientific." In *The Marx-Engels Reader*, 2nd ed., edited by Robert C. Tucker. New York: W. W. Norton, 1978: 681–717.

Enoch, David. "The Disorder of Public Reason." *Ethics*, vol. 124 (October 2013): 141–76.

Estlund, David. *Democratic Authority: A Philosophical Framework*. Princeton, NJ: Princeton University Press, 2008.

———. "Human Nature and the Limits (If Any) of Political Philosophy." *Philosophy and Public Affairs*, vol. 39 (2011): 207–35.

———. "Prime Justice." In *Political Utopias: Contemporary Debates*, edited by Michael Weber and Kevin Vallier. Oxford: Oxford University Press, forthcoming.

———. "Utopophobia." *Philosophy and Public Affairs*, vol. 42 (2014): 114–34.

Farrelly, Colin. "Justice in Ideal Theory: A Refutation." *Political Studies*, vol. 55 (2007): 844–64.

Fehr, Ernst, and Urs Fischbacher. "Third Party Punishment and Social Norms." *Evolution and Human Behavior*, vol. 25 (2004): 63–87.

Feinberg, Joel. *Harm to Others*. New York: Oxford University Press, 1984.

Forst, Ranier. "Political Liberty: Integrating Five Conceptions of Autonomy." In *Autonomy and Challenges to Liberalism: New Essays*, edited by John Christman and Joel Anderson. Cambridge: Cambridge University Press, 2006: 226–42.

Foucault, Michel. *Discipline and Punish: The Birth of the Prison*, 2nd ed., translated by A. Sheridan. New York: Vintage Books, 1995.

Freedom House Freedom in the World 2014 Report. http://www.freedomhouse.org/report-types/freedom-world#.U-QOVIBdW2A.

Freeman, Samuel. *Justice and the Social Contract*. New York: Oxford University Press, 2007.

Friedman, David. *The Machinery of Freedom*. New York: Harper and Row, 1973.

Friedman, Milton. "The Methodology of Positive Economics." In *The Philosophy of Economics: An Anthology*, 3rd ed., edited by Daniel Hausman. Cambridge: Cambridge University Press, 2008: 145–78.

Galton, Francis. *Memories of My Life*. New York: Dutton, 1909.

Gaus, Gerald. "Constructivist and Ecological Modeling of Group Rationality." *Episteme*, vol. 9 (September 2012): 245–54.

——. "The Egalitarian Species." *Social Philosophy and Policy*, vol. 31 (Spring 2015): 1–27.

——. *Justificatory Liberalism: An Essay on Epistemology and Political Theory*. Oxford: Oxford University Press, 1996.

——. "The Limits of *Homo Economicus*." In *Essays on Philosophy, Politics and Economics: Integration and Common Research Projects*, edited by Christi Favor, Gerald Gaus, and Julian Lamont. Stanford, CA: Stanford University Press, 2010: 14–37.

——. "Locke's Liberal Theory of Public Reason." In *Public Reason in the History of Political Philosophy*, edited by Piers Norris Turner and Gerald Gaus. New York: Routledge, forthcoming.

——. "Mill's Normative Economics." In *The Blackwell Companion to Mill*, edited by Christopher Macleod and Dale Miller. New York: Wiley-Blackwell, forthcoming.

——. "Moral Constitutions." *Harvard Review of Philosophy*, vol. 19 (2013): 4–22.

——. "On Dissing Public Reason: A Reply to Enoch." *Ethics*, vol. 125 (July 2015): 1078–95.

——. *On Philosophy, Politics, and Economics*. Belmont, CA: Wadsworth-Thomson, 2008.

——. *The Order of Public Reason*. Cambridge: Cambridge University Press, 2011.

——. "Retributive Justice and Social Cooperation." In *Retributivism: Essays on Theory and Practice*, edited by Mark D. White. Oxford: Oxford University Press, 2011: 73–90.

——. "Sectarianism without Perfection? Quong's Political Liberalism." *Philosophy and Public Issues*, vol. 2 (Fall 2012): 7–15.

——. "Social Complexity and Evolved Moral Principles." In *Liberalism, Conservatism, and Hayek's Idea of Spontaneous Order*, edited by Peter McNamara. London: Palgrave Macmillan, 2007: 149–76.

——. "Social Contract and Social Choice." *Rutgers Law Journal*, vol. 43 (Spring/Summer 2012): 243–76.

——. *Social Philosophy*. Armonk, NY: M. E. Sharpe, 1999.

——. "A Tale of Two Sets: Public Reason in Equilibrium." *Public Affairs Quarterly*, vol. 25 (October 2011): 305–25.

——. "The Turn to a Political Liberalism." In *The Blackwell Companion to Rawls*, edited by David Reidy and Jon Mandle. New York: Wiley-Blackwell, 2014: 235–50.

Gaus, Gerald, and Keith Hankins. "Searching for the Ideal." In *Political Utopias: Contemporary Debates*, edited by Michael Weber and Kevin Vallier. Oxford: Oxford University Press, forthcoming.

Gaus, Gerald, and Shaun Nichols. "Moral Learning in the Open Society: The Theory and Practice of Natural Liberty." *Social Philosophy and Policy*, forthcoming.

Gaus, Gerald, and John Thrasher. "Rational Choice and the Original Position: The (Many) Models of Rawls and Harsanyi." In *The Original Position*, edited by Timothy Hinton. Cambridge: Cambridge University Press, 2016: 39–58.

Gauthier, David. *Morals by Agreement.* Oxford: Clarendon Press, 1986.

———. "Twenty-Five On." *Ethics,* vol. 123 (July 2013): 601–24.

Gavrilets, Sergey. "High-Dimensional Fitness Landscapes and Speciation." In *Evolution—the Extended Synthesis,* edited by Massimo Pigliucci and Gerd B. Müller. Cambridge, MA: MIT Press, 2010: 45–80.

Gilabert, Pablo. "Comparative Assessments of Justice, Political Feasibility, and Ideal Theory." *Ethical Theory and Practice,* vol. 15 (2012): 39–56.

Gilabert, Pablo, and Holly Lawford-Smith. "Political Feasibility: A Conceptual Exploration." *Political Studies,* vol. 60 (2012): 809–25.

Godwin, William. *An Enquiry concerning Political Justice, and Its Influence on General Virtue and Happiness,* 2 vols. London: G.G.J. and J. Robinson, 1793.

———. *Of Population: An Enquiry concerning the Power of Increase in the Numbers of Mankind, Being an Answer to Mr. Malthus's Essay on that Subject.* London: Longman, Hurst, Rees, Orme, and Brown, 1820.

Goldwater, Barry. *The Conscience of a Conservative.* Bottom of the Hill Publishing, 2010.

———. "Extremism in the Defense of Liberty." In *Conservatism in America Since 1930,* edited by Gregory L. Schneider. New York: New York University Press, 2003: 238–46.

Goodwin, Barbara, and Keith Taylor. *The Politics of Utopia: A Study in Theory and Practice.* London: Hutchinson, 1982.

Gray, John. *Post-Enlightenment Liberalism.* London: Routledge, 1993.

Güth, Werner, and Reinhard Tietz. "Ultimatum Bargaining Behavior: A Survey and Comparison of Experimental Results." *Journal of Economic Psychology,* vol. 11 (1990): 417–49.

Habermas, Jürgen. "Reconciliation through Public Reason: Remarks on John Rawls's Liberalism." *Journal of Philosophy,* vol. 92 (March 1995): 109–31.

Hadfield, Gillian K., and Stephen Macedo. "Rational Reasonableness: Toward a Positive Theory of Public Reason." *Law and Ethics of Human Rights,* vol. 6 (2012): 7–46.

Hadfield, Gillian K., and Barry R. Weingast. "What Is Law? A Coordination Account of the Characteristics of Legal Order." *Journal of Legal Analysis,* vol. 4 (2012): 471–514.

Haidt, Jonathan. *The Righteous Mind: Why Good People Are Divided by Politics and Religion.* New York: Pantheon, 2012.

Hamlin, Alan. "Feasibility Four Ways." *Social Philosophy and Policy,* forthcoming.

Hamlin, Alan, and Zofia Stemplowska. "Theory, Ideal Theory and the Theory of Ideals." *Political Studies Review,* vol. 10 (2012): 48–62.

Harman, Gilbert. *Reasoning, Meaning and Mind.* Oxford: Clarendon, 1999.

Haworth, A. "Planning and Philosophy: The Case of Owenism and the Owenite Communities." *Urban Studies,* vol. 13 (1976): 147–53.

Hayek, F. A. *The Constitution of Liberty.* London: Routledge and Kegan Paul, 1960.

———. *Law, Legislation, and Liberty,* vol. 1: *Rules and Order.* Chicago: University of Chicago Press, 1973.

———. *Law, Legislation, and Liberty,* vol. 2: *The Mirage of Social Justice.* Chicago: University of Chicago Press, 1976.

———. "The Use of Knowledge in Society." *American Economic Review,* vol. 35 (September 1945): 519–30.

Hazelhurst, Brian, and Edwin Hutchins. "The Emergence of Propositions from the Co-ordination of Talk and Action in a Shared World." *Language and Cognitive Processes*, vol. 13 (1998): 373–424.

Henrich, Joseph, and Natalie Smith. "Comparative Evidence from Machiguenga, Mapuche, and American Populations." In *Foundations of Human Sociality: Economic Experiments and Ethnographic Evidence from Fifteen Small-Scale Societies*, edited by J. Henrich, R. Boyd, S. Bowles, et al. Oxford: Oxford University Press, 2004: 125–67.

Hillinger, Claude, and Victoria Lapham. "The Impossibility of a Paretian Liberal: Comment by Two Who Are Unreconstructed." *Journal of Political Economy*, vol. 79 (November–December, 1971): 1403–5.

Hobbes, Thomas. *Leviathan*, edited by Edwin Curley. Indianapolis: Hackett, 1994 [1651].

Hobhouse, L. T. *Liberalism*. Oxford: Oxford University Press, 1964 [1911].

Hong, Lu, and Scott E. Page. "Problem Solving by Heterogeneous Agents." *Journal of Economic Theory*, vol. 97 (2001): 123–63.

———. "Groups of Diverse Problem Solvers Can Outperform Groups of High-Ability Problem Solvers." *Proceedings of the National Academy of Sciences of the United States of America*, vol. 101, no. 46 (November 16, 2004): 16385–89.

Jubb, Robert. "Tragedies of Non-ideal Theory." *European Journal of Political Theory*, vol. 11 (2012): 229–46.

Kauffman, Stuart A. *The Origins of Order*. New York: Oxford University Press, 1993.

Kautsky, Karl. *Thomas More and His Utopia*. London: Lawrence and Wisehart, 1979 [1888].

Kenyon, Timothy. "Utopia in Reality: 'Ideal' Societies in Social and Political Theory." *History of Political Thought*, vol. 3 (January 1982): 123–55.

Keynes, John Maynard. *A Treatise on Probability*. London: Macmillan, 1921.

King, Martin Luther, Jr. "I Have a Dream...." Speech at the March on Washington, 1963. http://www.archives.gov/press/exhibits/dream-speech.pdf.

Kirk, Russell. *The Conservative Mind*. BN Publishing, 2008.

Kohlberg, Lawrence. *The Philosophy of Moral Development*. New York: Harper and Row, 1981.

Kuhn, Thomas. *The Essential Tension*. Chicago: University of Chicago Press, 1977.

Kumar, Krishan. *Utopia and Anti-Utopia in Modern Times*. Oxford: Basil Blackwell, 1987.

———. "Utopian Thought and Communal Practice: Robert Owen and the Owenite Communities." *Theory and Society*, vol. 19 (1990): 1–35.

Lagerspatz, Eerik, Heikki Ihäheimo, and Jussi Kotkavirta, eds. *On the Nature of Social and Institutional Reality*. Jyväskylä, Finland: University of Jyväskylä Printing House, 2001.

Landemore, Hélène. *Democratic Reason*. Princeton, NJ: Princeton University Press, 2013.

———. "Yes, We Can (Make It Up on Volume): Answers to Critics." *Critical Review: A Journal of Politics and Society*, vol. 26 (2014): 184–237.

Landemore, Hélène, and Scott E. Page. "Deliberation and Disagreement: Problem Solving, Prediction, and Positive Dissensus." *Politics, Philosophy and Economics*, 1–26 (2014). doi: 10.1177/1470594X14544284.

Lawford-Smith, Holly. "Ideal Theory—a Reply to Valentini." *Journal of Political Philosophy*, vol. 18 (2010): 357–68.

———. "Non-ideal Accessibility." *Ethical Theory and Moral Practice*, vol. 16 (2013): 653–69.

———. "Understanding Political Feasibility." *Journal of Political Philosophy*, vol. 21 (2013): 243–59.

Lenin, V. I. *What Is to Be Done?* In *Selected Works in Two Volumes*, with introductory essays by J. V. Stalin. Moscow: Foreign Languages University Press, 1952: vol. 1, 203–410.

Lipsey, R. G., and K. J. Lancaster. "The General Theory of Second Best." *Review of Economic Studies*, vol. 24 (1956): 11–33.

List, Christian, and Philip Pettit. *Group Agency: The Possibility, Design, and Status of Corporate Agents.* Oxford: Oxford University Press, 2011.

Locke, John. *A Letter concerning Toleration.* In *"Two Treatises of Government" and "A Letter concerning Toleration,"* edited by Ian Shapiro. New Haven, CT: Yale University Press, 2003: 215–54.

Lorenz, Edward N. *The Essence of Chaos.* Seattle: University of Washington Press, 1998.

Macedo, Stephen. "Why Public Reason? Citizens' Reasons and the Constitution of the Public Sphere." http://ssrn.com/abstract=1664085.

MacIntyre, Alasdair. *Whose Justice? Which Rationality?* Notre Dame, IN: Notre Dame University Press, 1988.

Mack, Eric. "Peter Pan Strikes Back." http://www.cato-unbound.org/issues/october -2011/new-liberalism.

Mack, Eric, and Gerald Gaus. "Classical Liberalism and Libertarianism: The Liberty Tradition." In the *Handbook of Political Theory*, edited by Gerald Gaus and Chandran Kukathas. London: Sage, 2004: 115–30.

Mackie, Gerry. "Effective Rule of Law Requires Construction of a Social Norm of Legal Obedience." In *Cultural Agency Reloaded: The Legacy of Antanas Mockus*, edited by Carlo Tognato. Cambridge, MA: Cultural Agents Initiative of Harvard University, forthcoming.

Majone, Giandomenico. "On the Notion of Political Feasibility." *European Journal of Political Research*, vol. 3 (1975) 259–14.

Malthus, Thomas Robert. *Malthus—Population: The First Essay (An Essay on the Principle of Population, as It Affects the Future Improvement of Society, with Remarks on the Speculations of Mr. Godwin, M. Condorcet, and Other Writers).* Ann Arbor, MI: Ann Arbor Paperback, 1959 [1798].

Marx, Karl. *Capital,* translated by Eden and Cedar Paul, introduction by C.D.H. Cole. 2 vols. London: Dent, 1930 [1867].

May, Kenneth O. "A Set of Independent Necessary and Sufficient Conditions for Simple Majority Decision." *Econometrica*, vol. 20 (October, 1952): 680–84.

McKelvey, Bill. "Avoiding Complexity Catastrophe in Coevolutionary Pockets: Strategies for Rugged Landscapes." In "Application of Complexity Theory to Organization Science," special issue of *Organization Science*, vol. 10 (May–June 1999): 294–321.

Meade, J. E. *The Just Economy.* London: Allen and Unwin, 1976.

Medin, D. L., W. D. Wattenmaker, and S. E. Hampson. "Family Resemblance, Conceptual Cohesiveness, and Category Construction." *Cognitive Psychology*, vol. 19 (1987): 242–79.

Meyer, Frank S. "Freedom, Tradition, and Conservatism." In *"In Defense of Freedom" and Related Essays*, edited by William C. Dennis. Indianapolis: Liberty Fund, 1996: 14–29.

———. *In Defense of Freedom: A Conservative Credo*. In *"In Defense of Freedom" and Related Essays*, edited by William C. Dennis. Indianapolis: Liberty Fund, 1996: 33–151.

———. "In Defense of John Stuart Mill." In *"In Defense of Freedom" and Related Essays*, edited by William C. Dennis. Indianapolis: Liberty Fund, 1996: 164–69.

Mikhail, John. *The Elements of Moral Cognition: Rawls' Linguistic Analogy and the Cognitive Science of Moral and Legal Judgment*. Cambridge: Cambridge University Press, 2010.

Mill, John Stuart. *Chapters on Socialism*. In *The Collected Works of John Stuart Mill*, edited by J. M. Robson, vol. 5. Toronto: University of Toronto Press, 1967: 703–57.

———. *On Liberty*. In *The Collected Works of John Stuart Mill*, edited by J. M. Robson, vol. 18. Toronto: University of Toronto Press, 1965: 213–310.

———. *The Principles of Political Economy with Some of Their Applications to Social Philosophy*. In *The Collected Works of John Stuart Mill*, edited by J. M. Robson, vols. 2 and 3. Toronto: University of Toronto Press, 1965.

———. *The Subjection of Women*. In *The Collected Works of John Stuart Mill*, edited by J. M. Robson, vol. 21. Toronto: University of Toronto Press, 1965: 249–340.

Miller, David. *Justice for Earthlings: Essays in Political Philosophy*. Cambridge: Cambridge University Press, 2013.

Mockus, Antanas. "Building Citizenship Culture in Bogotá." *Journal of International Affairs*, vol. 65 (Spring/Summer 2012): 143–46.

———. "Bogotá's Capacity for Self-Transformation and Citizenship Building." In *Cultural Agency Reloaded: The Legacy of Antanas Mockus*, edited by Carlo Tognato. Cambridge, MA: Cultural Agents Initiative of Harvard University, forthcoming.

Moehler, Michael. "The Scope of Instrumental Morality." *Philosophical Studies*, vol. 167 (2014): 431–51.

———. "The (Stabilized) Nash Bargaining Solution as a Principle of Distributive Justice." *Utilitas*, vol. 22 (2010): 447–73.

More, Thomas. *Utopia*, edited by Henry Morley. London: Cassell, 1901 [1516].

Morreau, Michael. "It Simply Does Not Add Up: Trouble with Overall Similarity." *Journal of Philosophy*, vol. 107 (2010): 469–90.

Mueller, Dennis C. *Public Choice III*. Cambridge: Cambridge University Press, 2003.

Muldoon, Ryan. *Beyond Tolerance: Re-imagining Social Contract Theory for a Diverse World*. New York: Routledge, forthcoming.

———. "Diversity and the Social Contract." Ph.D. diss., University of Pennsylvania, 2009.

———. "Expanding the Justificatory Framework of Mill's Experiments in Living." *Utilitas*, forthcoming.

———. "Justice without Agreement." http://papers.ssrn.com/s013/papers.cfm?abstract_id=2653832.

———. "Perspective-Dependent Harm." http://papers.ssrn.com/s013/papers.cfm?abstract_id=2653852.

Muldoon, Ryan, Michael Borgida, and Michael Cuffaro. "The Conditions of Tolerance." *Politics, Philosophy and Economics*, vol. 11 (2011): 322–44.

Muldoon, Ryan, Chiara Lisciandra, Mark Colyvan, Jan Sprenger, Carlo Martini, and Giacomo Sillari. "Disagreement behind the Veil of Ignorance." *Philosophical Studies*, vol. 170 (September 2014): 377–94.

Norenzayan, A., E. E. Smith, J. B. Kim, and R. E. Nisbett. "Cultural Preferences for Formal versus Intuitive Reasoning." *Cognitive Science*, vol. 26 (2002): 653–84.

Nozick, Robert. *Anarchy, State and Utopia*. New York: Basic Books, 1974.

O'Neill, Martin, and Thad Williamson, eds. *Property-Owning Democracy: Rawls and Beyond*. New York: Wiley-Blackwell, 2014.

O'Neill, Onora. "Abstraction, Idealization and Ideology in Ethics." *Royal Institute of Philosophy Lecture Series*, vol. 22 (1987): 55–69.

———. "Justice, Gender and International Boundaries." In *The Bounds of Justice*, by O'Neill. Cambridge: Cambridge University Press, 2000: 143–67.

———. *Towards Justice and Virtue: A Constructive Account of Practical Reasoning*. Cambridge: Cambridge University Press, 1996.

Orwell, George. *1984*. New York: Signet Classic, 1961.

Ostrom, Elinor. "Collective Action and the Evolution of Social Norms." *Journal of Economic Perspectives*, vol. 14 (2000): 137–58.

———. *Governing the Commons: The Evolution of Institutions for Collective Action*. Cambridge: Cambridge University Press, 1990.

Owen, Robert. *A New View of Society, and Other Writings*. London: Dent, 1972 [1813].

Owen, William. *Diary of William Owen from November 10, 1824 to April 20, 1825*. Indianapolis: Bobbs-Merill, 1906.

Page, Scott E. *The Difference*. Princeton, NJ: Princeton University Press, 2007.

———. *Diversity and Complexity*. Princeton, NJ: Princeton University Press, 2011.

Passmore, John. *The Perfectability of Man*. London: Duckworth, 1971.

Plato. *The Republic*, translated by Francis MacDonald Cornford. Oxford: Oxford University Press, 1941.

Platteau, J.-P. *Institutions, Social Norms and Economic Development*. London: Harwood Academic Publisher.

Popper, Karl R. *The Open Society and Its Enemies*, 4th ed., 2 vols. London: Routledge and Kegan Paul, 1962.

———. *The Poverty of Historicism*, 2nd ed. London: Routledge and Kegan Paul, 1961.

Quong, Jonathan. *Liberalism without Perfection*. Oxford: Oxford University Press, 2011.

———. "Three Disputes about Public Reason: Commentary on Gaus and Vallier." www.publicreason.net/wp-content/PPPS/Fa112008/JQuong1.pdf.

Räikkä, Juha. "The Feasibility Condition in Political Theory." *Journal of Political Philosophy*, vol. 6 (1998): 27–40.

Rand, Ayn. *Anthem*. New York: Signet, 1961.

Rawls, John. "Distributive Justice." In *John Rawls: Collected Papers*, edited by Samuel Freeman. Cambridge, MA: Harvard University Press, 1999: 130–53.

———. "The Idea of Public Reason Revisited." In *John Rawls: Collected Papers*, edited by Samuel Freeman. Cambridge, MA: Harvard University Press, 1999: 573–615.

———. "The Independence of Moral Theory." In *John Rawls: Collected Papers*, edited by Samuel Freeman. Cambridge, MA: Harvard University Press, 1999: 286–302.

———. "Justice as Fairness." In *John Rawls: Collected Papers*, edited by Samuel Freeman. Cambridge, MA: Harvard University Press, 1999: 47–72.

Rawls, John. *Justice as Fairness: A Restatement.* Cambridge, MA: Harvard University Press 2001.

——. "Kantian Constructivism in Moral Theory." In *John Rawls: Collected Papers*, edited by Samuel Freeman. Cambridge, MA: Harvard University Press, 1999: 303–58.

——. *The Law of Peoples.* Cambridge, MA: Harvard University Press, 1999.

——. *Lectures on the History of Political Philosophy*, edited by Samuel Freeman. Cambridge, MA: Harvard University Press, 2007.

——. *Political Liberalism*, expanded ed. New York: Columbia University Press, 2005.

——. "Reply to Alexander and Musgrave." In *John Rawls: Collected Papers*, edited by Samuel Freeman. Cambridge, MA: Harvard University Press, 1999: 232–53.

——. "Themes in Kant's Moral Philosophy." In *John Rawls: Collected Papers*, edited by Samuel Freeman. Cambridge, MA: Harvard University Press, 1999: 497–528.

——. *A Theory of Justice.* Cambridge, MA: Harvard University Press, 1971.

——. *A Theory of Justice*, rev. ed. Cambridge, MA: Harvard University Press, 1999.

Risse, Mathias. "Why the Count de Borda Cannot Beat the Marquis de Condorcet." *Social Choice and Welfare*, vol. 25 (2005): 95–113.

Robbins, Lionel. *The Theory of Economic Policy in English Classical Political Economy.* London: Macmillan, 1952.

Robeyns, Ingrid. "Ideal Theory in Theory and Practice." *Social Theory and Practice*, vol. 34 (July 2008): 314–62.

Royal Society of Chemistry and American Chemical Society. *The Discovery and Development of Penicillin, 1928–1945.* London: Alexander Fleming Laboratory Museum, 1999.

Rubinstein, Ariel. *Economic Fables.* Open Book Publishers, 2012. http://www.open bookpublishers.com/product/136.

Saari, Donald. "Which Is Better: The Condorcet or Borda Winner? *Social Choice and Welfare*, vol. 26 (2006): 107–29.

Santos-Lang, Christopher. "Our Responsibility to Manage Evaluative Diversity." *SIGCAS Computers and Society*, vol. 44 (July 2014): 16–19.

Satz, Debra. "Amartya Sen's *The Idea of Justice*: What Approach, Which Capabilities?" *Rutgers Law Journal*, vol. 43 (Spring/Summer 2012): 277–93.

——. *Why Some Things Should Not Be for Sale: The Moral Limits of Markets.* Oxford: Oxford University Press, 2012.

Sayers, Dorothy L. *Clouds of Witness.* New York: Harper Collins, 1986.

Scanlon, T. M. *What We Owe Each Other.* Cambridge, MA: Harvard University Press, 1998.

Schmidtz, David. "Nonideal Theory: What It Is and What It Needs to Be." *Ethics*, vol. 121 (July 2011): 772–96.

Schneider, Gregory L. *The Conservative Century: From Reaction to Revolution.* Lanham, MD: Rowman and Littlefield, 2009.

Schotter, Andrew, and Barry Sopher. "Social Learning and Coordination Conventions in Intergenerational Games: An Experimental Study." *Journal of Political Economy*, vol. 111 (June 2003): 498–529.

Schwab, David, and Elinor Ostrom. "The Vital Role of Norms and Rules in Maintaining Open Public and Private Economies." In *Moral Markets: The Critical Role of Values in the Economy*, edited by Paul Zak. Princeton, NJ: Princeton University Press, 2008: 204–27.

Schwartz, Pedro. *The New Political Economy of J. S. Mill.* London: Weidenfeld and Nicolson, 1968.

Sen, Amartya. "Choice Functions and Revealed Preference." In *Choice, Welfare and Measurement*, by Sen. Cambridge, MA: Harvard University Press, 1982: 41–53.

———. *Collective Choice and Social Welfare.* San Francisco: Holden-Day, 1970.

———. *The Idea of Justice.* Cambridge, MA: Harvard University Press, 2009.

———. "Liberty, Unanimity and Rights." *Economica*, n.s., vol. 43 (August, 1976): 217–45.

———. "Maximization and the Act of Choice." In *Rationality and Freedom*, by Sen. Cambridge, MA: Harvard University Press, 2002: 159–205.

———. *On Ethics and Economics.* Oxford: Blackwell, 1986.

———. "On Weights and Measures: Informational Constraints in Social Welfare Analysis." *Econometrica*, vol. 45 (October 1977): 1539–72.

———. "The Possibility of Social Choice." In *Rationality and Freedom*, by Sen. Cambridge, MA: Harvard University Press, 2002: 65–118.

———. "A Reply." *Rutgers Law Journal*, vol. 43 (Spring/Summer 2012): 317–35.

Shikher, Serge. "Predicting the Effects of NAFTA: Now We Can Do It Better!" *Journal of International and Global Economic Studies*, vol. 5 (December 2012): 32–59.

Sidgwick, Henry. *The Methods of Ethics*, 7th ed. Chicago: University of Chicago Press, 1962 [1907].

Simmons, A. John. "Ideal and Nonideal Theory." *Philosophy and Public Affairs*, vol. 38 (January 2010): 5–36.

Smith, Adam. *Theory of Moral Sentiments*, edited by D. D. Raphael and A. L. Macfie. Indianapolis: Liberty Fund, 1984.

Smith, Peter. *Explaining Chaos.* Cambridge: Cambridge University Press, 1998.

Stemplowska, Zofia. "What's Ideal about Ideal Theory?" *Social Theory and Practice*, vol. 34 (July 2008): 319–40.

Stemplowska, Zofia, and Adam Swift. "Ideal and Nonideal Theory." In *The Oxford Handbook of Political Philosophy*, edited by David Estlund. Oxford: Oxford University Press, 2012: 373–89.

Strawson, Peter. "Freedom and Resentment," *Proceedings of the British Academy*, vol. 48 (1962): 188–211.

Stuntz, W. "Self-Defeating Crimes." *Virginia Law Review*, vol. 86 (2000): 1871–82.

Sugden, Robert. "Spontaneous Order." *Journal of Economic Perspectives*, vol. 3 (Autumn 1989): 85–97.

Sunstein, Cass. *Infotopia: How Many Minds Produce Knowledge.* Oxford: Oxford University Press, 2006.

Surowiecki, James. *The Wisdom of Crowds.* New York: Anchor Books, 2005.

Swift, Adam. "The Value of Philosophy in Nonideal Circumstances." *Social Theory and Practice*, vol. 34 (July 2008): 363–87.

Tanner, Edward. *Why Things Bite Back.* London: Fourth Estate, 1996.

Temkin, Larry S. *Rethinking the Good: Moral Ideals and the Nature of Practical Reasoning.* Oxford: Oxford University Press, 2011.

Tetlock, Philip. "Coping with Trade-Offs: Psychological Constraints and Political Implications." In *Elements of Reason: Cognition, Choice and the Bounds of Rationality*, edited by Arthur Lupia, Matthew D. McCubbins, and Samuel L. Popkin. Cambridge: Cambridge University Press, 2000: 239–63.

Thompson, Abigail. "Does Diversity Trump Ability? An Example of the Misuse of Mathematics in Social Sciences." *Notices of the American Mathematical Society*, vol. 61 (2014): 1024–30.

Thrasher, John. "Uniqueness and Symmetry in Bargaining Theories of Justice." *Philosophical Studies*, vol. 167 (2014): 683–99.

Thrasher, John, and Gerald Gaus. "The Calculus of Consent." In *The Oxford Handbook of Classics in Contemporary Political Theory*, edited by Jacob Levy. Oxford: Oxford University Press, forthcoming.

Tomasi, John. *Free Market Fairness*. Princeton, NJ: Princeton University Press, 2012.

Valentini, Laura. "Ideal vs. Non-ideal Theory: A Conceptual Map." *Philosophy Compass*, vol. 7 (2012): 654–64.

———. "On the Apparent Paradox of Ideal Theory." *Journal of Political Philosophy*, vol. 17 (2009): 332–55.

Vallier, Kevin. "A Moral and Economic Critique of the New Property-Owning Democrats: On Behalf of a Rawlsian Welfare State." *Philosophical Studies*, vol. 172 (2015): 283–304.

van Damme, Eric, Kenneth G. Binmore, Alvin E. Roth, Larry Samuelson, Eyal Winter, Gary E. Bolton, Axel Ockenfels, Martin Dufwenberg, Georg Kirchsteiger, Uri Gneezy, Martin G. Kocher, Matthias Sutter, Alan G. Sanfey, Hartmut Kliemt, Reinhard Selten, Rosemarie Nagel, and Ofer H. Azara. "How Werner Güth's Ultimatum Game Shaped Our Understanding of Social Behavior." *Journal of Economic Behavior and Organization*, vol. 108 (2014): 292–318.

Vanderschraaf, Peter. "The Circumstances of Justice." *Politics, Philosophy and Economics*, vol. 5 (2006): 321–51.

Van Schoelandt, Chad. "Justification, Coercion, and the Place of Public Reason." *Philosophical Studies*. doi: 10.1007/s11098-014-0336-6.

———. "Rawlsian Functionalism and the Problem of Coordination." Paper delivered to the 2015 meeting of the Pacific Division of the American Philosophical Association, April, Vancouver, British Columbia.

Van Schoelandt, Chad, and Gerald Gaus. "Political and Distributive Justice." In *The Oxford Handbook of Distributive Justice*, edited by Serena Olsaretti. Oxford: Oxford University Press, forthcoming.

Wagner, Christian, Sesia Zhao, Christopher Schneider, and Huaping Chen. "The Wisdom of Reluctant Crowds," Proceedings of the 43rd Hawaii International Conference on System Sciences, 2010, IEEE Computer Society. www.computer.org/csdl/proceedings/hicss/2010/3869/00/01-12-06.pdf.

Waldrop, M. Mitchell. *Complexity: The Emerging Science as the Edge of Order and Chaos*. New York: Simon and Shuster, 1992.

Waldron, Jeremy. *God, Locke and Equality: The Christian Foundations in Locke's Political Thought*. Cambridge: Cambridge University Press, 2002.

Wall, Steven. "On Justificatory Liberalism." *Philosophy, Politics, and Economics*, vol. 9 (May 2010): 123–50.

Ward, Benjamin. *The Ideal World of Economics: Liberal, Radical and Conservative Economic World Views*. New York: Basic Books, 1979.

Watts, D. J., and S. H. Strogatz. "Collective Dynamics of 'Small-World' Networks." *Nature*, vol. 393 (June 1998): 440–42. doi: 10.1038/30918.

Weber, Roberto A., and Colin F. Camerer. "Cultural Conflict and Merger Failure: An Experimental Approach." In "Managing Knowledge in Organizations: Creating, Retaining, and Transferring Knowledge," special issue of *Management Science*, vol. 49 (April 2003): 400–415.

Weisberg, Michael, and Ryan Muldoon. "Epistemic Landscapes and the Division of Cognitive Labor." *Philosophy of Science*, vol. 76 (April 2009): 225–52.

Weithman, Paul. *Why Political Liberalism? On John Rawls's Political Turn*. New York: Oxford University Press, 2010.

Weitzman, Martin L. "On Diversity." *Quarterly Journal of Economics*, vol. 107 (May 1992): 363–405.

Wiens, David. "Against Ideal Guidance." *Journal of Politics*, vol. 77 (April 2015): 433–46.

———. "Demands of Justice, Feasible Alternatives, and the Need for Causal Analysis." *Ethical Theory and Moral Practice*, vol. 16 (2013): 325–38.

———. "Political Ideals and the Feasibility Frontier." *Economics and Philosophy*, June 2015: 1–31, published online May 28, 2015. doi: 10.1017/S0266267115000164.

———. "Prescribing Institutions without Ideal Theory." *Journal of Political Philosophy*, vol. 20 (2012): 45–70.

———. "Will the Real Principles of Justice Please Stand Up?" In *Political Utopias: Contemporary Debates*, edited by Michael Weber and Kevin Vallier. Oxford: Oxford University Press, forthcoming.

Wilde, Oscar. *The Soul of Man under Socialism*. Portland, ME: Thomas B. Mosher, 1905.

Wiles, P.J.D. *Economic Institutions Compared*. New York: Wiley, 1977.

Wolff, Robert Paul. *The Poverty of Liberalism*. Boston: Beacon, 1968.

———. *Understanding Rawls: A Reconstruction and Critique of a Theory of Justice*. Princeton, NJ: Princeton University Press, 1977.

Young, Iris Marion. *Responsibility for Justice*. Oxford: Oxford University Press, 2011.

Zhou, Xueguang. "Organizational Decision Making as Rule Following." In *Organizational Decision Making*, edited by Zur Sahpira. Cambridge: Cambridge University Press, 2002: 257–81.

Index